2/97

ESSENTIAL ENGLISH COMPOSITION

FOR COLLEGE-BOUND STUDENTS

by Dr. Leo Lieberman
and Prof. Jeffrey Spielberger

Department of English
Bronx Community College
City University of New York

Prentice Hall
New York • London • Toronto • Sydney • Tokyo • Singapore

Third Edition

Prentice Hall General Reference
15 Columbus Circle
New York, NY 10023

An Arco Book

Arco, Prentice Hall, and colophons are
registered trademarks of Simon & Schuster, Inc.

Library of Congress Cataloging-in-Publication Data

Lieberman, Leo.
    Essential English composition for college-bound students / by Leo
  Lieberman and Jeffrey Spielberger. -- 3rd ed.
      p.   cm.
    "An Arco book."
    ISBN 0-671-86401-7
    1. English language--Composition and exercises. 2. English
  composition test--Study guides.   I. Spielberger, Jeffrey.
  II. Title.
  PE1408.L5574 1993
  808'.042'076--dc20   93-2054
                                                               CIP

Manufactured in the United States of America

1 2 3 4 5 6 7 8 9 10

Contents

Part Two **TESTS OF ENGLISH COMPOSITION**

Introduction

Every college seeks to help students to write well, to express themselves clearly and intelligently. Writing is both a skill and an art. As a skill, it can be taught and perfected through practice.

A good athlete knows that before he begins to swim or play ball or run he must do warm-up exercises. A good singer understands that before singing an aria, he might want to practice some vocal exercises. A writer too might wish to sharpen his mind with writing exercises before composing an essay. This book will provide the conscientious student with many warm-up drills and exercises. However, exercises are not enough. An athlete is judged on the playing field, and a writer is judged by his essays. Therefore, this book has a section on writing the essay which will provide many useful clues and specific examples to improve writing.

This book has a second function. All of us, sometimes in our lives, have to take tests. Those people who go on to college know that sitting for examinations is part of a monthly (or even weekly) routine. Thus, wise students must discover how to prepare effectively for examinations, how to take examinations, and how to evaluate the results of the examinations. This book will serve this function as well by providing a step-by-step analysis of some of the special examinations that the average secondary school and college student may have to confront.

Test taking is not a pleasant experience, but it need not be a dismal one. For the reader of this work who follows all the suggestions and obeys all the signposts, it can be a rewarding one.

We hope that the reader of this book will benefit in two ways. First, the reader will become a wiser test taker, more at ease with the testing process. Second, and perhaps more important, the reader will learn to communicate effectively by being a good writer.

GUIDE TO GOOD WRITING

CHAPTER 1

Basic Rules of Grammar

Agreement and Reference _____

BASIC RULE 1: Many grammatical errors result from failing to make different parts of a sentence agree in number, person, or gender. The parts of a sentence must agree in the following ways:

(1) The verb must agree with the subject in number and in person. If the subject is singular, the verb form must also be singular; if the subject is in the third person—*he, she, it*—the verb must also be in the third person.

The chief problem is identifying the true subject of the sentence and determining whether it is singular or plural.

(2) The pronoun must agree with its antecedent (the word to which it refers—sometimes called its *referent*) in number, in person, and in gender. Of the three, gender causes the writer the least difficulty.

The chief problem is identifying the antecedent and determining its number, person, and gender.

Subject Problems

The first step in making the parts of a sentence agree is to identify the subject. Certain subjects present special problems.

1. Collective Words

A **collective** names a group of people or things. Although usually singular in form, it is treated as either singular or plural according to the sense of the sentence:

Singular when members of the group act, or are considered as a *unit*:

> The junior **class is sponsoring** the fund drive.

Plural when the members act, or are considered, individually:

> The jury **are** unable to agree on a verdict.

Common collectives include:

> assembly, association, audience, board, cabinet, class, commission, committee, company, corporation, council, counsel, couple, crowd, department, family, firm, group, jury, majority, minority, number, pair, press, public, staff, United States

The following short words—though seldom listed as collectives—are governed by the rule for collectives. They are singular or plural according to the intended meaning of the sentence.

> all, any, more, most, none, some, who, which

1

When a prepositional phrase follows the word, the number of the noun in the phrase controls the number of the verb. When no such phrase follows, the writer signals his intended meaning by his choice of the singular or the plural verb.

> Some of the **work has been done.**
> Some of the **papers have been graded.**

2. Units of Measure

When a number is used with a plural noun to indicate a unit of measurement (money, time, fractions, portions, distance, weight, quantity, etc.), a singular verb is used. When the term is thought of as individual parts, a plural verb is used.

> **Ten years seems** like a long time.
> **Ten years have gone** by since I last saw him.

When fractions and expressions such as *the rest of, the remainder of, a part of, percent of,* etc., are followed by a prepositional phrase, the noun or pronoun in that phrase governs the number of the verb.

> **Four-fifths** of the job **was** finished on time.
> **Four-fifths** of the letters **were** finished on time.
> The **rest** (or **remainder**) of the work **is** due Friday.
> The **rest** (or **remainder**) of the papers **are** due Friday.

3. Confusing Singular and Plural Forms

It is sometimes hard to tell by its form whether a word is singular or plural. Some words that end in *-s* may be singular, and some seemingly singular words may be plural.

These words are singular, though they are plural in form:

> apparatus, news, summons, whereabouts
>
> The **news is** disturbing.
> His **whereabouts has** not yet been determined.

These words are plural, though they are singular (or collective) in meaning:

> assets, earnings, means (income), odds, premises, proceeds, quarters, savings, wages, winnings
>
> Her **wages are** earmarked for college expenses.
> The **odds are** against our finishing on time.

These words may be either singular or plural, depending on their meaning, even though they are plural in form:

> ethics, goods, gross, headquarters, mechanics, politics, series, species, statistics, tactics
>
> **Statistics is** the only course I failed in school.
> The **statistics prove** that I am right.

These nouns are plural, though they may appear to be singular because they have foreign or unusual plural forms.

The **analyses have** been completed. (*Analyses* is the plural of *analysis*.)

His conclusion seems sound, but his **criteria are** not valid. (*Criteria* is the plural of *criterion*.)

4. Indefinite Pronouns

These indefinite pronouns are singular. When they are used as subjects, they require singular verbs; when used as antecedents, they require singular pronouns.

anybody, anyone, any one (any one of a group), anything, each, either, every, everybody, everyone, every one (every one of a group), everything, neither, nobody, no one, nothing, one, somebody, someone, some one (some one of a group), something

Anyone is welcome, as long as **he** (not **they**) behaves **himself.**
Each of us **is** obliged to sign **his** own name.
Either of the alternatives **is** suitable.
Everyone must buy **his** book for the course.

Even when two indefinite pronouns are joined by *and*, they remain singular in meaning.

Anyone and **everyone is** invited.
Nothing and **no one escapes** her attention.

Many a (unlike *many*) is singular in meaning and takes a singular verb and pronoun.

Many a new **student feels** insecure during **his** first few weeks at school.
But: **Many students feel** insecure during **their** first few weeks at school.

More than one, though its meaning is plural, is used in the singular.

More than one vacation plan **was** changed because of the new requirement.

These words are plural:

both, few, many, several, others

Both of us **have received** new assignments.
Few will be able to finish **their** work on time.
Many plan to work all weekend.

5. Relative Pronouns

The verb in a relative clause must agree in number and in person with the relative pronoun *(who, which, that, what)* serving as the subject of the clause. The relative pronoun, in turn, must agree with its antecedent. Therefore, before we can make the verb agree with the relative pronoun, we must find the antecedent and determine its person and number.

Have you talked with the man **who was** waiting to see you? (*Man* is the antecedent of the relative pronoun *who,* and the verb *was* must agree with this antecedent in person and number.)

Where are the books **that were** left on the table? (The verb in the relative clause—*were*—must agree with the relative pronoun—*that*—which must agree with its antecedent—*books.*)

In sentences that contain the phrases *one of the* or *one of those,* the antecedent of the relative pronoun is not one, but the plural words that follow.

One of the letters **that were** on my desk has disappeared.
Here is one of those students **who are** applying for the position.

6. Subjects Joined by *And*

When two or more subjects are joined by *and,* whether the subjects are singular or plural, they form a compound subject, which is considered plural.

The **date and the time** of the meeting **have** not been decided.

Phrases or clauses serving as subjects follow the same rule: When two or more phrases or clauses serving as the subject of a sentence are joined by *and,* the resulting compound subject is considered plural.

Rising early in the morning and **taking a walk before breakfast make** a person feel invigorated all day.

Exception: When the subjects joined by *and* refer to the same person or object or represent a single idea, the whole subject is considered singular.

Ham and eggs is the traditional American breakfast.
The **growth and development** of our country **is** described in this book.

The article or personal pronoun used before each member of the compound subject indicates whether we see the subject as a single idea or as different ideas.

My teacher and friend helps me with my problems. (one person)
My teacher and my friend help me with my problems. (two people)

7. Subjects Joined by *Or* or *Nor*

When singular subjects are joined by *or* or *nor,* the subject is considered singular.

Neither the **principal nor** the **assistant principal knows** that **he** is scheduled to attend the meeting.
One or the **other** of us **has** to go.

When one singular and plural subject are joined by *or* or *nor,* the subject closer to the verb determines the number of the verb.

Neither the student nor the **teachers were able** to attend.
Neither the teachers nor the **student was** able to attend.

Caution!   Avoid shifts in number or person.

Once you establish a word as either singular or plural, keep it the same throughout the sentence. Be sure that all verbs and all pronouns referring to that word agree with it in number.

> *Not:* A **person needs** someone to turn to when **they are** in trouble.
> *But:* A **person needs** someone to turn to when **he is** in trouble.

Be consistent. If you decide that a collective is singular, keep it singular throughout the sentence—use a singular verb to agree with it and a singular pronoun to refer to it.

If you establish the collective as plural, see that both the verb and the pronoun are plural.

> The committee **has** announced **its** decision.
> The committee **have** adjourned and gone to **their** homes.

Most indefinite pronouns are singular and require singular verbs and pronouns.

> *Not:* **Has anyone** turned in **their** report? (The indefinite pronoun *anyone* takes both a singular verb and a singular pronoun.)
> *But:* **Has anyone** turned in **his** report?

Do not apply a verb form from one part of the sentence to another (elliptically) unless the same form is grammatically correct in both parts.

> *Not:* The **statistics were** checked and the report filed.
> *But:* The **statistics were** checked and the **report was** filed.

Avoid shifting the person of pronouns referring to the same antecedent.

> *Not:* **As the ship** entered **her** berth, **its** huge gray shadow seemed to swallow us.
> *But:* As the **ship** entered **its** berth, **its** huge gray shadow seemed to swallow us.
> *or:* As the **ship** entered **her** berth, **her** huge gray shadow seemed to swallow us.

Structure Problems

Usually it is easy for us to identify the subject or antecedent and determine its number and person. But occasionally a puzzling sentence comes along. The subject is there, but something in the structure of the sentence tries to make us believe that another word is the subject.

Verb Precedes Subject

When the verb precedes the subject in the sentence (either in a question or in a declarative sentence), locate the true subject and make the verb agree with it.

> **Are** the **file cabinet and the bookcase** in this room?
> Clearly visible on the desk **were** the **papers** he had asked us to file.
> From these books **come some** of our best **ideas.**

Where, here, and *there,* when introducing a sentence, do not influence the number or person of the verb. In such sentences, find the real subject and make the verb agree with it.

> Where **are** the individual **sessions** to be held?
> Where **is** the meeting **room**?
> There **are** two **books** on the table.
> There **is** a **book** on the table.

What, who, which, the interrogative pronouns, do not affect the number of the verb. Again, find the subject of the sentence and make the verb agree with it.

> What **is** the **status** of the scholarship fund drive?
> What **are** your **recommendations** on this problem?
> Who **is** going to accompany you to the meeting?
> Who, in this group, **are members** of your committee?
> Which **is** the **memo** that he means?
> Which **are** the **standards** that we are to apply?

The expletive *it* or *there* introduces the verb and stands for the real subject, which comes later in the clause. The expletive *it* requires a singular verb, even when the real subject is plural. Following the expletive *there,* the verb is singular or plural according to the subject which follows it.

> It **is solutions** we are looking for, not problems.
> It **is** doubtful that he will start today.
> There **are** enclosed five copies of the pamphlet you requested.

Words Intervene between Subject and Verb

The presence of explanatory or parenthetical phrases, or other modifiers, between the subject and verb does not change the number or person of the subject. Locate the real subject of the sentence and make the verb agree with it.

> The **amount** shown, plus interest, **is** due within 30 days.
> The **letter** with its several attachments **was** received this morning.
> Our **letters**, like our speech, **are** indications of our knowledge of English.
> **No one** but those present **knows** of this information.

Subject and Predicate Differ in Number

After forms of the verb *to be* we often find a construction (called the *predicate nominative*) which means the same thing as the subject. When the predicate nominative differs in number from the subject, the verb must agree with the element that precedes it (the subject).

> Our main **problem is** keeping up with the reading and handing in our reports on time.
> Keeping up with the reading and handing in our reports on time **are** our main problem.

Construction Shift and Parallelism

Use the same grammatical construction for each of the words or ideas in a sentence if these words or ideas require balance, according to the meaning which the sentence is carrying.

> *Not:* **Singing** and **to dance** are not permitted here.
> *But:* **Singing** and **dancing** (or **To sing** and **to dance**) are not permitted here.

> *Not:* This term, the children are learning the value of **courtesy** and **being kind.**
> *But:* This term, the children are learning the value of **courtesy** and **kindness.**

Special Problems of Pronoun Reference

Ambiguous Antecedents

Do not use forms of the same pronoun to refer to different antecedents.

> *Not:* The teacher told John that **he** thought **his** work was improving. (Does the teacher think that his own work is improving, or that John's work is improving?)
> *But:* John was told by **his** teacher that **his** work was improving.

Place the pronoun as close as possible to its antecedent to avoid ambiguity or confusion.

> *Not:* The letter is on the desk **that** we received yesterday.
> *But:* The **letter that** we received yesterday is on the desk.

Indefinite Antecedents

Be sure that the reference to an antecedent is quite specific.

> *Not:* When you have finished the book and written your summary, please return **it** to the library. (What are you returning? The book or the summary?)
> *But:* When you have finished the book and written your summary, please return **the book** to the library.

Implied Antecedents

As a general rule, the antecedent of a pronoun must appear in the sentence—not merely be implied. And the antecedent should be a specific word, not an idea expressed in a phrase or clause. *It, which, this,* and *that* are the pronouns that most often lead our meaning astray. Any of these pronouns may refer to an idea expressed in a preceding passage if the idea and the reference are *unmistakably* clear. But too often the idea that is unmistakably clear to the speaker or writer is nowhere to be found when the listener or reader looks for it.

> *Not:* Although the doctor operated at once, **it** was not a success and the patient died.
> *But:* Although the doctor performed the **operation** at once, **it** was not a success and the patient died.
> *or:* Although the doctor operated at once, the **operation** was not a success and the patient died.

Vague Reference

The usage illustrated below—the impersonal use of *it, they,* and *you*—is not incorrect. But using these impersonal pronouns tends to produce vague, wordy sentences.

Not: In the Manual **it** says to make three copies.
But: The Manual says to make three copies.

Not: In the letter **it** says he will be here on Thursday.
But: The letter says he will be here on Thursday.
or: He says, in his letter, that he will be here on Thursday.

Not: **They** say we are in for a cold, wet winter.
But: The almanac predicts a cold, wet winter.

Agreement Exercises *(Answers are on pages 39 to 40.)*

EXERCISE I In each of the following sentences, underline the subject(s) before you choose the correct verb(s).

1. (speak, speaks) All the students in the class _____ clearly when they answer questions.

2. (play, plays) Miss Olipo _____ the piano whenever she has spare time.

3. (need, needs) If you _____ money, don't ask your sister; she _____ money, too.

4. (go, goes) If Jane _____ to the theatre, I will go with her.

5. (seem, seems) The pills in the jar _____ to be the correct ones.

6. (run, runs) The bus to Manhattan _____ every twenty minutes.

7. (eat, eats) The cat _____ its food two times a day.

8. (study, studies) Roger _____ his vocabulary words every evening.

9. (know, knows) You and I _____ what really happened.

10. (try, tries) My professor says that he _____ to be as fair as possible when he grades the examinations; I _____ to study as hard as possible when I take the examinations.

EXERCISE II To see if you understand the basic principles of agreement, try the following drill. Choose the correct word.

1. (is, are) There _____ many events in the month of November.

2. (was, were) Where _____ you last Friday?

3. (have, has) Neither Mr. Smith nor his parents _____ the necessary papers.

   4. (do, does) Each of us ＿＿＿＿＿＿＿ his best to accomplish the assigned tasks.

   5. (want, wants) John and Mary ＿＿＿＿＿＿＿ to do well but do not always succeed.

   6. (is, are, am) Either you or I ＿＿＿＿＿＿＿ going to be chosen.

   7. (his, their) Everyone must take ＿＿＿＿＿＿＿ place before the beginning of the performance.

   8. (has, have) Neither the instructor nor the pupils ＿＿＿＿＿＿＿ selected the patient.

   9. (her, their) Every woman has ＿＿＿＿＿＿＿ own way of doing things.

   10. (was, were) She ＿＿＿＿＿＿＿ in my dance class a few years ago.

EXERCISE III   Singular or plural? Choose the correct word.

   1. (is, are) Ron and Ida ＿＿＿＿＿＿＿ meeting us for dinner next week.

   2. (draw, draws) Either Marcus or his colleagues ＿＿＿＿＿＿＿ the blueprints.

   3. (was, were) There ＿＿＿＿＿＿＿ three bonbons left in the package.

   4. (his, their) We assume that no one has left ＿＿＿＿＿＿＿ briefcase unguarded.

   5. (her, their) Each of our guests was pleased to receive ＿＿＿＿＿＿＿ party favor.

   6. (is, are) The language of Shakespeare's plays ＿＿＿＿＿＿＿ sometimes difficult to understand.

   7. (his, their) All of the players practiced ＿＿＿＿＿＿＿ foul shots.

   8. (know, knows) Neither Louise nor the other secretaries ＿＿＿＿＿＿＿ how to use that word processor.

   9. (go, goes) Either Helen or Peter ＿＿＿＿＿＿＿ out to buy a newspaper every morning.

   10. (was, were) Neither the buyers nor the builder ＿＿＿＿＿＿＿ happy about the postponement.

EXERCISE IV   In the following paragraph, ten numbered words appear in **boldface**. Look at each word and determine if it is grammatically correct. If it is, write ''C'' next to the corresponding number below. If a change is necessary, indicate the change and explain why it is needed. Do not make unnecessary changes.

Veronica, one of my favorite cousins, **are**[1] planning to be a nurse. Her mother and father **feel**[2] that nursing, of all the professions, **are**[3] one of the most worthwhile. Veronica has asked each of her friends to give **their**[4] opinion, and everyone suggested what **they**[5] thought was most helpful. Then Veronica asked me what I **think**[6] she should do. Her friends and I **am**[7] in agreement, but her parents **does**[8] not agree. They believe that the nursing profession, unlike other professions, **requires**[9] too much study and will be too exhausting. Before she makes a decision there **is**[10] several other factors Veronica must consider.

1.
2.
3.
4.
5.
6.
7.
8.
9.
10.

Case of Nouns and Pronouns

Nouns

A noun names a person, thing, idea, place, or quality. There are five classes of nouns:

1. Proper Nouns

A **proper** noun names a particular place, person, or thing. The writer's chief problem with proper nouns is recognizing them in order to capitalize them.

> Atlanta, Mr. Jones, the Commissioner of Education, Form 1040

2. Common Nouns

A **common** noun names a member of a class or group of persons, places, or things.

> hope, banana, education, form

3. Collective Nouns

A **collective** noun, singular in form, names a group or collection of individuals. The chief problem with collective nouns is determining the number of the verb to use with the collective noun. For this reason, it is discussed at length in the section on agreement of subject and verb.

> committee, jury, council, task force

4. Concrete Nouns

A **concrete** noun names a particular or specific member of a class or group.

> apple, **not** fruit; typist, **not** personnel

5. Abstract Nouns

An **abstract** noun names a quality, state, or idea.

> justice, truth, objectivity

Pronouns

Pronouns stand in place of nouns. There are six classes of pronouns:

1. Personal Pronouns

The **personal** pronoun shows which person (first, second, or third) is the subject. Personal pronouns are troublesome because of their many forms; they change form to indicate number, person, and case.

The personal pronouns are:

> I, me, mine (my), you, yours (your), he, him, his, she, her, hers, (her), it, its, **and their plurals** (we, you, they, etc.)

2. Relative Pronouns

The **relative** pronoun serves two purposes: (1) it takes the place of a noun in the clause it introduces, and (2) like a conjunction, it connects its clause with the rest of the sentence.

> who, whom, which, that, what, whoever, whomever, whichever, whatever

The relative pronoun has the same number, person, and case as its antecedent.

3. Interrogative Pronouns

The **interrogative** pronoun is the same in form as the relative pronoun, but different in function. The interrogative pronoun asks a question.

> who
> whom } refer to persons
>
> what   refers to things
> which   refers to persons or things

As adjectives, *which* and *what* may be used.

> . . . which book?   . . . what time?

4. **Indefinite Pronouns**

The **indefinite** pronouns listed here are singular, as are most indefinites:

> another, anyone, each, either, everyone, no one, nothing . . .

5. **Demonstrative Pronouns**

The **demonstrative** pronouns *(this, that, these, those)* point out or refer to a substantive which has been clearly expressed or just as clearly implied. They may be used as pronouns:

> **These** are the letters he wants.

or as adjectives:

> Bring me **those** letters.

6. **Reflexive Pronouns**

The **reflexive** pronouns are compound personal pronouns:

> myself, yourself, yourselves, himself, themselves, ourselves, herself, itself

A reflexive pronoun emphasizes or intensifies a meaning. It is not set off by commas.

> I **myself** will see that it is done.
> The director **himself** gave the order.
> I will take it to him **myself.**

A reflexive pronoun often appears as the direct object of a verb; its antecedent, as the subject of the verb.

> I taught **myself** how to type.
> He hurt **himself** when he fell.

It can, however, be the object of a preposition,

> He finished the assignment by **himself.**
> He was beside **himself** with joy.

the indirect object of a verb,

> I bought **myself** a new suit yesterday.

or a predicate nominative.

> I am just not **myself** today.

In formal usage, the reflexive pronoun is not used where the shorter personal pronoun can be substituted for it with no change in meaning.

> *Not:* Both the Director and **myself** endorse the policy.
> *But:* Both the Director and **I** endorse the policy.

Avoid the following pronoun errors:

> The use of *hisself* for *himself.*
> The use of *theirselves* for *themselves.*

> The use of *myself* instead of the personal pronoun *me* or *I* in such constructions as ''The secretary and *myself* were assigned to do this work.''

Case

Case is the property of a noun or pronoun which shows, either by inflection (change in form) or by position, the relation of the word to other parts of the sentence.

English has three cases: nominative, objective, and possessive.

All nouns and a few pronouns keep the same form in the nominative and in the objective cases.

On the other hand, some pronouns are inflected (change form) in the nominative and objective cases, as well as in the possessive. Because of this, the case of pronouns causes us more trouble than does the case of nouns, and pronouns are more frequently misused.

Nominative Case

The nominative (or subjective) case is used primarily to name the subject of a verb or the predicate complement after a linking verb (such as *seem, appear,* or any form of *be*).

> *Not:* Either **she** or **me** will be responsible.
> *But:* Either **she** or **I** will be responsible.
> (Either **she** will be . . . or **I** will be. . . .)

Note: An appositive, which is a word or group of words standing next to another word and denoting the same person or thing, is always in the same case as its antecedent (the word it stands in apposition to). Therefore, if the antecedent is in the nominative case, the appositive must also be in the nominative case. If the antecedent is in the objective case, the appositive is also in the objective case.

> *Not:* The representatives, **John and me,** are to meet on Friday.
> *But:* The representatives, **John and I,** are to meet on Friday.
> (**John and I** are to meet. . . .)

BASIC RULE 2: A noun or pronoun serving as the subject of a verb (except the subject of an infinitive) is in the nominative case.

> **I** was late for work this morning.
> **He** is planning to finish his report this week.
> Neither **he** nor **I** had heard of this before.
> The culprits, **she and I,** were reprimanded.

BASIC RULE 3: A relative pronoun *(who, whoever, which, whichever)* used as the subject of a clause is in the nominative case.

> Give the letter to **whoever** answers the door.

The clause itself may be a subject or, as in this example, an object; however, the case of the relative pronoun depends upon its use *within the clause.*

> The award will go to him **who completes the course with the highest score.**
> **Whoever is selected** must report on Monday.

The pronoun *who* used as the subject of a verb is not affected by a parenthetical expression such as *I think, he believes, they say* intervening between the subject and the verb.

> He is the person **who** I think is best qualified. (*who* is the subject of the clause)
> We asked Susan, **who** we knew **had always been** a student of English. (*who* is the subject of the clause)

BASIC RULE 4: If the word following *than* or *as* introduces a clause, even if part of the clause is understood, that word must be in the nominative case. But if the word following *than* or *as* does not introduce a clause, it must be in the objective case. To test whether the word should be in the nominative or objective case, complete the clause.

> He has been here longer than **she.** (than *she has*).
> Mary is a better stenographer than **I.** (than *I am*).
> They were as late as **we** in filing the report. (as *we were*)
> We were told as promptly as **they.** (as *they were*)

BASIC RULE 5: A noun or pronoun following a form of the verb *be* (except for the infinitive if it has its own subject) must be in the nominative case. The general rule applying to this construction is that the word following the verb *be* must be in the same case as the word before the verb. Imagine that the verb *be* has the same meaning as the equals sign ($=$) in mathematics.

> *Not:* They thought I was **him.**
> *But:* They thought I was **he.** ($I = he$)
>
> *Not:* I am expecting my sister to call. Is that **her?**
> *But:* I am expecting my sister to call. Is that **she?**

A noun or pronoun following the infinitive *to be* is in the nominative case if the infinitive has no subject.

> He was thought to be **I.**
> My brother was taken to be **I.**

Note: You may have trouble when one or both of the members of the compound subject or predicate nominative are pronouns. Try this simple test: Decide which case would be appropriate if *one* pronoun were the simple subject or predicate nominative, and then use the same case for both.

> *Example:* The new **chairmen** are **he and I.**
> *Reverse positions:* **He and I** are the new **chairmen.**
>
> *Example:* If any one of the agents is chosen, **it** should be **he.**
> *Reverse positions:* If any one of the agents is chosen, **he** should be **it.**
>
> *Example:* The **author** was thought to be **I.**
> *Reverse positions:* **I** was thought to be the **author.**

Objective Case

The objective (or accusative) case is used chiefly to name the receiver or object of the action of a verb, or to name the object of a preposition.

When one part of a compound expression (joined by a coordinate conjunction) is in the objective case, all other parts of the same expression must also be in the objective case.

BASIC RULE 6:   A noun or pronoun serving as the direct object of a verb or verbal is in the objective case.

> The driver returned **him** to his home.
> The principal called **him** and **me** to her office.

BASIC RULE 7:   A word used as the indirect object of a verb or verbal is in the objective case.

> The teacher gave **me** the report.
> The chairman assigned **him** and **me** the task of reviewing the study.

BASIC RULE 8:   A noun or pronoun serving as the object of a preposition is in the objective case.

> From **whom** did you receive the letter? (*Whom* is the object of the preposition *from*.)

Note: *But* is a preposition when *except* may be substituted for it with no change in meaning.

> Everyone is going but **me**.

A special troublemaker is the compound object *you and me* after the preposition *between*. Do not say *between you and I;* say *between you and me*.

BASIC RULE 9:   A noun or pronoun used as the subject of an infinitive is in the objective case.

> I want **her** to have this copy.
> Please let **us** know if you are coming.
> They invited **him and me** to attend this reception.
> **Whom** will we invite to speak at the convention?

BASIC RULE 10:   The verb *to be* takes the same case after it as before it. Since the subject of an infinitive is in the objective case, a word following the infinitive is also in the objective case.

> They thought him to be **me**. (Reverse, to test choice of case: They thought **me** to be **him**.)
> They did not expect the representatives to be **him and me**. (Reverse: They did not expect **him and me** to be the representatives.)

BASIC RULE 11:   The subject of a participle is in the objective case. The problem comes in determining whether a verbal is a participle or a gerund. Both may have the same form (the *ing* form of the verb), but only the subject of the *participle* is in the objective case. The subject of the *gerund* is in the possessive case.

Imagine **him flying** an airplane. (The verbal *flying* is a participle modifying *him,* and the pronoun *him* is in the objective case.)

Imagine **his flying** to Paris. (The verbal *flying* is a gerund, and the pronoun *his* is in the possessive case.)

His rushing to catch the plane was in vain. (*Rushing* is a gerund, and its subject must be in the possessive case.)

We watched **him rushing** to catch the plane. (The verbal *rushing* is a participle modifying *him;* therefore, the subject, *him,* is in the objective case.)

Possessive Case

The possessive case is used to indicate possession.

BASIC RULE 12: To form the possessive of singular words not ending in *s* (including the indefinite pronouns), add the apostrophe and *s*.

> the **agent's** report; the **Director's** office; the **secretary's** desk; **anyone's** guess; **somebody's** coat

Note: When *else* is used with an indefinite pronoun, form the possessive by adding the apostrophe and *s* to *else,* rather than to the indefinite pronoun.

> **somebody's** coat   but: **somebody else's** coat
> **anyone's** idea   but: **anyone else's** idea

BASIC RULE 13: To form the possessive of a singular word ending in *s* or an *s*-sound, add the apostrophe alone if the possessive and the regular forms of the word are pronounced alike. If the possessive form is pronounced with an additional *s*-sound, add both the apostrophe and *s*.

Singular form	Possessive form
boss	boss's (pronounced *boss-es*)
hostess	hostess' (pronounced *hostess*) or hostess's (pronounced *hostesses*)

Note: To form the possessive of a proper name ending in *s* or an *s*-sound, follow this same method. If the possessive form is pronounced with an additional *s*-sound, add both the apostrophe and *s*. If the regular and the possessive forms of the proper name are pronounced alike, add the apostrophe alone to form the possessive.

> *Either:* Charles'   *or:* Charles's
> *Either:* James'   *or:* James's
> *Either:* Mr. Simmons'   *or:* Mr. Simmons's
>   *But:* Roberts'   *not:* Roberts's

BASIC RULE 14: Do not use the apostrophe in forming the possessive of the personal and relative pronouns. The possessive forms of these pronouns are:

> *Relative:* whose
> *Personal:* her, hers (not her's), his, their, theirs, our, ours, my, mine, your, yours, its

Note: *Its* is the possessive form of the personal pronoun *it; it's* is a contraction of *it is.* Similarly, *whose* is the possessive form of the relative pronoun *who,* and *who's* is a contraction of *who is.* The examples below illustrate the correct use of these words.

Its operation is simple.
It's *(it is)* simple to operate.
Whose typewriter is that?
Who's *(who is)* going with me?

BASIC RULE 15: To form the possessive of a plural word not ending in *s,* add the apostrophe and *s.*

men's, children's, women's, people's

To form the possessive of a plural word ending in *s,* add the apostrophe only.

All of the **District Directors'** reports have been received.

Note: Avoid placing the apostrophe before the final *s* of a word if the *s* is actually a part of the singular or plural form. To test, first form the plural; then add the correct possessive sign.

Not: ladie's   *But:* ladies'

(*Ladies* is the plural form; since the word ends in *s,* add the apostrophe alone to form the possessive, *ladies'.*)

BASIC RULE 16: Use the *of* phrase in forming the possessive to avoid the "piling up" of possessives.

Not: The **taxpayer's wife's income** must be reported.
But: The **income of the taxpayer's wife** must be reported.

BASIC RULE 17: When two or more people possess the same thing jointly, form the possessive on the last word only.

She is **Mr. Roberts and Miss Henry's** secretary. (She is secretary to both people.)
These pictures are from **John and Mary's** vacation trip.

Note: When one of the words involved in the joint possession is a pronoun, each word must be in the possessive.

This is **John's, Bob's,** and **my** office.
Have you seen **Mary's** and **his** new home?

BASIC RULE 18: Be sure that a word standing parallel with a possessive is itself possessive in form.

Not: **His** work, like an **accountant,** is exacting.
But: **His** work, like an **accountant's,** is exacting.

Not: **His** task is no more difficult than his **neighbor.**
But: **His** task is no more difficult than his **neighbor's.**

BASIC RULE 19: A noun or pronoun immediately preceding a gerund is in the possessive case. A gerund is a verbal noun naming an action. A participle, which may have the same form as a gerund, functions as an adjective; its subject is in the objective case.

> **Our** being late delayed the meeting.
> **Mr. Jones'** being late delayed the meeting.
> You can always depend on **his** doing a good job.
> **Jim's** writing the letter made all the difference.

Note: There are three exceptions to this general rule:

(1) The possessive of an inanimate object is not usually formed by the apostrophe and *s*. When the subject of a gerund is a noun standing for an inanimate object, use the objective case, an *of* phrase, or a subordinate clause, whichever is most appropriate.

> *Not:* The desk's refinishing is almost complete.
> *But:* The **refinishing of the desk** is almost complete. (*of* phrase)

> *Not:* The possibility of the **meeting's ending** soon is doubtful. (objective case)
> *But:* The possibility of the **meeting ending** soon is doubtful. (objective case)

> *Not:* We missed our ride because of the **meeting's lasting so late.**
> *But:* We missed our ride because the **meeting lasted so late.** (subordinate clause)

(2) Do not use the possessive case for the subject of a gerund unless the subject immediately precedes the gerund. If subject and gerund are separated by other words, the subject must be in the objective case.

> *Not:* I can see no reason for a **man's** with his background **failing** to pass the test.
> *But:* I can see no reason for a **man** with his background **failing** to pass the test. (Without intervening words: I can see no reason for a **man's failing** to pass the test.)

> *Not:* I concede the difficulty of **his,** because of his interest, **being** completely fair.
> *But:* I concede the difficulty of **him,** because of his interest, **being** completely fair.

(3) There are no possessive forms for the demonstrative pronouns *that, this, these,* and *those.* Therefore, when these words are used as subjects of a gerund they do not change form.

> *Not:* We cannot be sure of **that's** being true.
> *But:* We cannot be sure of **that** being true.

> *Not:* What are the chances of **this'** being sold?
> *But:* What are the chances of **this** being sold?

Pronoun Exercise

(Answers to the following exercise are on page 40.)

EXERCISE I In each of the following sentences, a pronoun is in boldface. If you think that the correct pronoun is used, write "C" on the line to the left. If the pronoun is incorrect, write the correct one on the line.

_____ **1.** He indicated that **whoever** asks first will receive the book.

_____ **2.** He indicated that the book will be given to **whoever** asks first.

_____ **3.** He will give the book to **whoever** he sees first.

_____ **4.** Jo-ann and **him** will be at the reception.

_____ **5.** **Him** and Jo-ann will be at the reception.

_____ **6.** I think that the letter was intended for **they** only.

_____ **7.** He sent the package to **us** boys.

_____ **8.** He is better equipped than **she** to do the work.

_____ **9.** She is to be complimented for not criticizing **him** trying to save money.

_____ **10.** For the most part, the work was done by **we** professionals.

Verbs and Verbals

Tenses of Verbs

Tense means time. We know that, as their main function, verbs describe an action or a state of being on the part of the subject. But verbs also tell *when* the action took place or *when* the state existed. This property of verbs is called tense.

Simple and Perfect Tenses

English has six tenses: three simple tenses (**present, past,** and **future**) in which an action may be considered as simply occurring; and three compound—called **perfect**—tenses in which an action may be considered as completed. (To be *perfected* means to be *completed*.)

Present Tense: I walk, he walks
Present Perfect Tense: I have walked, he has walked

Past Tense: I walked, he walked
Past Perfect Tense: I had walked, he had walked

Future Tense: I shall walk, he will walk
Future Perfect Tense: I shall have walked, he will have walked

Progressive and Emphatic Forms

Each of the six tenses has a companion form—the progressive form. As its name indicates, the progressive says that the action named by the verb is a continued or progressive action. The progressive consists of the present participle (the *-ing* form of the verb—that is, *walking*) plus the proper form of the verb *to be*. The progressive forms of the verb *to walk* are:

Present Tense: I am walking, he is walking
Present Perfect Tense: I have been walking, he has been walking

Past Tense: I was walking, he was walking
Past Perfect Tense: I had been walking, he had been walking

Future Tense: I shall be walking, he will be walking
Future Perfect Tense: I shall have been walking, he will have been walking

The present tense and the past tense also have an emphatic form, which uses *do, does, did* as auxiliaries:

Present Tense: I do understand, she does understand
Past Tense: You did understand, they did understand

Principal Parts of Verbs

We indicate tense by changing the verb itself or by combining certain forms of the verb with auxiliary verbs. The verb tenses from which we derive every form of a verb are called the **principal parts.** The principal parts of a verb are:

The Present Tense: talk, write
The Past Tense: talked, wrote
The Present Perfect: have talked, has written

Verbs are classified as **regular** (or *weak*) and **irregular** (or *strong*), according to the way in which their principal parts are formed. Regular verbs form their past tense and present perfect tense by the addition of *-ed* to the infinitive:

Present Tense	Past Tense	Present Perfect Tense
talk	talked	has (have) talked
help	helped	has (have) helped
walk	walked	has (have) walked

The principal parts of irregular verbs are formed by changes in the verb itself:

Present Tense	Past Tense	Present Perfect Tense
see	saw	has (have) seen
say	said	has (have) said
go	went	has (have) gone

Principal Parts of Troublesome Verbs

Present Tense	Past Tense	Present Perfect Tense
abide	abode	has abode
arise	arose	has arisen
bear (carry)	bore	has borne
bear (bring forth)	bore	has borne
bid	bade	has bid, bidden

Principal Parts of Troublesome Verbs (continued)

Present Tense	Past Tense	Present Perfect Tense
bide	bode, bided	has bode, bided
bleed	bled	has bled
broadcast	broadcast, broadcast (radio and TV)	has broadcast(ed)
burst	burst	has burst
chide	chid, chidded	has chid, chidded, chidden
choose	chose	has chosen
cleave (adhere)	cleaved	has cleaved
cleave (split)	cleft, cleaved	has cleft, cleaved, cloven
cling	clung	has clung
drown	drowned	has drowned
drink	drank	has drunk
flee	fled	has fled
fling	flung	has flung
fly	flew	has flown
flow	flowed	has flowed
foresake	forsook	has forsaken
freeze	froze	has frozen
grind	ground	has ground
hang (a picture)	hung	has hung
hang (a person)	hanged	has hanged
lay (place)	laid	has laid
lead	led	has led
lend	lent	has lent
lie (rest)	lay	has lain
light	lit, lighted	has lit, lighted
raise	raised	has raised
rid	rid, ridded	has rid, ridded
ring	rang	has rung
set	set	has set
sew	sewed	has sewed, sewn
shrink	shrank, shrunk	has shrunk, shrunken
sink	sank, sunk	has sunk
sit	sat	has sat
ski	skied (rhymes with seed)	has skied
slay	slew	has slain
slide	slid	has slid, slidden
sling	slung	has slung
slink	slunk	has slunk
smite	smote	has smitten
spring	sprang, sprung	has sprung
steal	stole	has stolen
sting	stung	has stung
stink	stank, stunk	has stunk
stride	strode	has stridden
strive	strove	has striven
swim	swam	has swum
swing	swung	has swung

Principal Parts of Troublesome Verbs (continued)

Present Tense	Past Tense	Present Perfect Tense
thrust	thrust	has thrust
weave	wove	has woven
wring	wrung	has wrung

BASIC RULE 20: The past perfect tense indicates that the action or condition described was completed (perfected) earlier than some other action that also occurred in the past. Distinguish carefully between this tense and the simple past tense.

> When I **came** back from lunch, she **finished** the letter. (Both verbs are in the past tense; therefore, both actions happened at approximately the same time in the past.)
>
> When I **came** back from lunch, she **had finished** the letter. (Again, both actions occurred in the past, but the use of the past perfect *had finished* tells us that this action was completed before the other action.)
>
> We **discovered** that a detective **was following** us. (Both actions happened at the same time in the past.)
>
> We **discovered** that a detective **had been following** us. (He had been following us some time before we discovered it.)

Mood

The mood of a verb tells what kind of utterance is being made. An English verb may be **indicative, imperative,** or **subjunctive** in mood.

The Indicative Mood

The indicative mood—used to make a statement or ask a question—is used in almost all our writing and speaking.

> The test **was scheduled** for May 15.
> What **is** the correct form to be used?
> From the evidence submitted, it **seems** that he withheld information during the conference.

The Imperative Mood

The imperative mood expresses a command, a request, or a suggestion. The subject of an imperative sentence is ordinarily the pronoun *you* (not expressed, simply understood).

> **Lock** the door before you leave the house.
> **Let** us help you start this program in your school.
> Please **sign** the affidavit before returning it to us. (Note that the word *please* may be inserted with no effect on the use of the imperative, but often with a desirable effect on the listener or reader.)

The Subjunctive Mood

The subjunctive expresses a condition contrary to fact, a wish, a supposition, or an indirect command. It is going out of use in English, but the subjunctive can still be seen in the following forms:

(1) To express a wish not likely to be fulfilled or impossible to be realized.

> I wish it **were** possible for us to approve his transfer at this time. (It is *not* possible.)

(2) In a subordinate clause after a verb that expresses a command, a request, or a suggestion.

> He asked **that** the report **be** submitted in duplicate.
> It is recommended **that** this office **be** responsible for preparing the statements.
> We suggest **that** he **be** relieved of the assignment.

(3) To express a condition known or supposed to be contrary to fact.

> If I **were** in St. Louis, I should be glad to attend.
> If this **were** a simple case, we would easily agree on a solution.
> If I **were** you, I should not mind the assignment.

(4) After *as if* or *as though.* In formal writing and speech, *as if* and *as though* are followed by the subjunctive, since they introduce as supposition something not factual. In informal writing and speaking, the indicative is sometimes used.

> He talked **as if** he **were** an expert on taxation. (He's not.)
> This report looks **as though** it **were** the work of a college freshman.

Caution! **Avoid Shifts in Mood.** Once you have decided on the mood that properly expresses your message, use that mood throughout the sentence or the paragraph. A shift in mood is confusing to the listener or reader; it indicates that the speaker or writer himself has changed his way of looking at the conditions.

> *Not:* It is requested that a report of the proceedings **be** prepared and copies **should be** distributed to all members. (*Be* is subjunctive; *should be,* indicative.)
> *But:* It is requested that a report of the proceedings **be** prepared and that copies **be** distributed to all members.

Voice

Voice indicates whether the subject of the verb is performing or receiving the action described by the verb. There are two voices: **active** and **passive.**

Active Voice

If the subject is performing the action, the verb is in the active voice.

> He **hit** the ball out of the park.
> The report **summarizes** the committee recommendations.
> The admissions director **asked** the student to send his high school transcript.

Passive Voice

If the subject is being acted upon, the verb is in the passive voice. (The passive form always consists of some form of *be* plus the past participle.)

> The ball **was hit** out of the park by him.
> The committee recommendations **are summarized** in the report.
> The student **was asked** by the admissions director to send his high school transcript.

BASIC RULE 21: In general, the active voice is preferable to the passive: It is simpler and more direct. If, however, you wish to emphasize the action itself or the object of the action and not the agent, use the passive.

> Smoking is prohibited. (emphasizing the object, smoking)
> Mr. Johnson is employed by the Blank Instrument Co. (emphasizing Mr. Johnson)

Shifts in Voice

Shifts in voice—often accompanied by shifts in subject—usually occur in compound or complex sentences. Although it is not essential that all clauses in a sentence be the same in structure, any unnecessary shifts result in a disorganized sentence. Therefore, unless you have a good reason for changing, use the same subject and voice in the second clause that you used in the first.

> *Not:* As **I searched** through the drawer for the glove, the missing **key was found.** (The first subject is *I*—its verb is active; the second subject is *key*—its verb is passive.)
> *But:* As **I searched** through the drawer for the glove, **I found** the missing key. (The subject is *I* in both clauses; both verbs are active.)

Verb Form Exercises
(Answers to the following exercises are on pages 40 and 41.)

EXERCISE I　　Choose the correct form of the verb.

1. (rang, rung) The mailman _____ the bell three times.

2. (hang, hanged) The spy was _____ in the town square.

3. (lose, lost) Put the key in your pocket so you do not _____ it.

4. (fly, flew) She _____ to Washington this morning.

5. (wrote, written) They have _____ a one-act play.

6. (think, thought) Last night we _____ about your offer, but we haven't decided what to do.

7. (saw, seen) I _____ a very good movie today.

8. (frozen, freezed, froze) The ice cubes have not _____.

9. (drove, driven) Have you ever _____ across the Golden Gate Bridge?

10. (teach, teached, taught) I hope that _____ you a lesson!

EXERCISE II Fill in the correct form of the verb.

1. (to hang) The stockings were _____ near the chimney.

2. (to throw) He has _____ the ball with remarkable speed.

3. (to weave) The blankets are _____ by the Indian women and me.

4. (to slide) She _____ through the fence where it had opened.

5. (to go) Have they _____ to the meeting yet?

6. (to lose) I hope that the papers are misplaced and not _____.

7. (to drink) He _____ the medicine quickly.

8. (to lend) The money was _____ to him on low interest.

9. (to suppose) The chairman is _____ to conduct the meeting.

10. (to know) Does the gang _____ where the money is hidden?

EXERCISE III Choose the correct form of the verb.

1. (had arranged, has arranged) She was certain that he _____ for the car pool.

2. (had arranged, has arranged) She is certain that he _____ for the car pool.

3. (was, were, is) If Eisenhower _____ president today, do you think that he would be in favor of the treaty?

4. (was, were, is) The doctor told us that fish _____ important in our diet.

5. (waited, have waited) We are happy that you are finally here; we _____ a long time for your arrival.

Modifiers and Connectives _____

Classification of Modifiers

Modifiers fall generally into two categories: **adjectives** (and phrases or clauses used as adjectives) and **adverbs** (and phrases or clauses used as adverbs). Sometimes the form of the modifier clearly shows whether it is an adjective or an adverb; sometimes the form is the same for both.

Adjectives describe, limit, or make more exact the meaning of a noun or pronoun (any substantive).

Adverbs describe, limit, or make more exact the meaning of a verb, an adjective, or another adverb.

Articles

Articles are a type of adjective. The indefinite articles are *a* and *an,* and the definite article is *the.* Use *a* before words beginning with a consonant sound, *an* before those beginning with a vowel sound.

> **a** desk, **a** book
> **an** agent, **an** error, **an** unusual occurrence

The article used before each of two connected nouns or adjectives signals that the words refer to different people or things.

> We elected **a** secretary and **a** treasurer. (two persons)
> She uses **a** tan and green typewriter. (one machine, two colors)

The following words may be either adjectives or adverbs, depending on their use:

> above, bad, better, cheap, close, deep, early, fast, first, hard, late, long, loud, much, only, quick, slow, very, well

Note: In informal speech, we sometimes drop the *-ly* ending from some often-used adverbs. This practice is incorrect and, even though we occasionally let it slip by in our speech, we must not allow it in our writing.

> *Correct usage:* I am **really** glad you could come. (Not *real* glad)
> I'm feeling **considerably** better. (Not *considerable*)

Comparison of Adjectives and Adverbs

Adjectives and adverbs change form to show a greater or lesser degree of the characteristic named by the simple word. There are three degrees of comparison.

Positive Degree

The positive degree names the *quality* expressed by the adjective or adverb. It does not imply a comparison with, or a relation to, a similar quality in any other thing.

> **high** morale, a **dependable** worker, work **fast**, prepared **carefully**

Comparative Degree

The comparative degree indicates that the quality described by the modifier exists to a greater or lesser degree in one thing than in another. It is formed by adding *-er* to the positive degree or by inserting *more* or *less* before the positive form.

> Our team has **higher** morale now than ever before.
> He is a **more dependable** worker than she.
> She can work **faster** than I.

Superlative Degree

The superlative degree denotes the greatest or least amount of the quality named. It is formed by adding *-est* to the positive degree of the adjective or adverb or by inserting *most* or *least* before the positive form.

That team has the **highest** morale in the league.
He is the **most dependable** worker in the office.
This is the **most carefully** prepared report I have found.

BASIC RULE 22: The comparative degree is used to refer to only two things, the superlative to more than two.

This book is the **longer** of the two.
This book is the **longest** of the three.

There is no difference in meaning between -*er* and *more* or between -*est* and *most*. Either method may be used with some modifiers. However, most adjectives of three syllables or more and almost all adverbs are compared by the use of *more* and *most* (or *less* and *least*) rather than by the endings -*er* and -*est*. In choosing which method should be used with the modifiers that may take either method, you may base your choice on emphasis. By adding -*er* or -*est* to the root word you emphasize the *quality*, while by using *more* or *most* you stress the *degree* of comparison.

Should I have been **kinder** or **harsher** in handling that call?
That report is the **longest** of the three.
Should I have been **more firm** or **less firm** in handling that caller?
Of all the forms, this one is the **most simple** and that one is the **least simple** to fill out.

Irregular Comparisons

Some modifiers are compared by changes in the words themselves. A few of these irregular comparisons are given below; consult your dictionary whenever you are in doubt about the comparison of any adjective or adverb.

Positive	Comparative	Superlative
good	better	best
well	better	best
bad (evil, ill)	worse	worst
badly (ill)	worse	worst
far	farther, further	farthest, furthest
late	later, latter	latest, last
little	less, lesser	least
many, much	more	most

Problems with Comparison

Adjectives and Adverbs That Cannot Be Compared

Some adjectives and adverbs express qualities that do not admit freely of comparison. They represent the highest degree of a quality and, as a result, cannot be improved. Some of these words are listed below.

complete	deadly	immortally
correct	exact	infinitely
dead	horizontally	perfect

perfectly	secondly	totally
perpendicularly	square	unique
preferable	squarely	uniquely
round	supreme	universally

Comparison with *Other* or *Else*

When we use the comparative in such an expression as *This thing is better than any other,* we imply that *this thing* is separate from the group or class to which it is being compared. In these expressions we must use a word such as *other* or *else* to separate the thing being compared from the rest of the group of which it is a part.

> *Not:* Our house is cooler than any house on the block. (The mistake here is not separating the item being compared—*house*—from the group to which it is being compared.)
> *But:* Our house is cooler than any **other** house on the block. (Our house is one of the houses on the block.)

> *Not:* He has a better record than any salesman in our group.
> *But:* He has a better record than any **other** salesman in our group. (He himself is one of the salesmen in the group.)

Incomplete Comparison—Improper Ellipsis

When you make a comparison between two items, be sure that both terms of the comparison are named.

Whenever a comparison is not completed, the meaning of the sentence is obscured.

> *Obscure:* Joe's letter states the problem better than John. (We cannot tell whether it is *John* or *John's letter* that is stating the problem.)
> *Improved:* Joe's letter states the problem better than **John's.**

> *Obscure:* This text is as good, if not better than that one. (Because of the omission of the second *as* after *good,* this sentence reads ". . . as good *than.*")
> *Improved:* This text is as good **as**, if not better than, that one.
> *or:* This text is as good as that one, if not better.

> *Ambiguous:* I enjoy this kind of work more than John. (This could be interpreted as: I enjoy this kind of work more than I enjoy **John**.)
> *Improved:* I enjoy this kind of work more than John **does.**

Verbals and Verbal Phrases as Modifiers

Verbals are sometimes used as modifiers, either singly or in phrases.

> **To get the most out of the course,** you must study regularly. (infinitive phrase modifying *you*)
> **Rising,** the Director greeted his caller. (present participle modifying *Director*)

> The letter, **typed and signed by the secretary,** was mailed today. (past participles modifying *letter*)
>
> The letter, **having been corrected**, was ready for signature. (perfect participle modifying *letter*)

A dangling phrase is one which cannot logically modify the noun or pronoun to which it refers grammatically. Corrective action may be taken in either of two ways: (1) by changing the subject of the main clause to one that the phrase can refer to, or (2) by changing the phrase itself into a dependent clause, so that it has a subject of its own.

> *Dangling:* **To get the most out of this course,** careful study is necessary. (The phrase cannot logically modify *study.)*
>
> *Corrected:* **To get the most out of this course,** you must study it carefully.
>
> *or:* If you are to get the most out of this course, you must study it carefully.
>
> *Dangling:* **Rushing to meet the deadline for the project,** many errors were made. (It wasn't the errors that were rushing to meet the deadline.)
>
> *Corrected:* **Rushing to meet the deadline for the project, they** made many errors.
>
> *or:* Because they rushed to meet the deadline for the project, many errors were made.

Prepositional Phrases as Modifiers

The prepositional phrase can serve as an adjective or adverb.

> The letter was addressed to the office **of the attorney.** (adjective modifying *office*)
>
> They have gone **to the conference.** (adverb modifying *have gone*)

A prepositional phrase *dangles* when it does not, both logically and grammatically, refer to the subject of the main clause.

> *Dangling:* **With much effort,** the **report** was completed on time.
>
> *Corrected:* **With much effort, we** completed the report on time.

Dependent Clauses as Modifiers

Dependent clauses can serve as adjectives or adverbs. Parts of a dependent clause are sometimes omitted because the missing elements can be easily supplied. These incomplete clauses are known as **elliptical clauses.** An elliptical clause must be able to modify, both logically and grammatically, the subject of the main clause. If it does not, it dangles.

> *Dangling:* **Unless compiled by early June**, we cannot include the figures in this year's annual report.

Corrected: **Unless compiled by early June,** the figures cannot be included in this year's annual report.

or: Unless **the figures are** compiled by early June, we cannot include them in this year's annual report.

Placement of Modifiers

Modifiers should be placed as closely as possible to the words they modify. This is true whether the modifier is a single word, a phrase, or a clause. In English, the only way the reader can tell which word is being modified is by the location of the modifier. It's simply a matter of geography.

Many ambiguous (and unintentionally humorous) sentences result from the misplacement of modifiers.

BASIC RULE 23:   Wherever possible, avoid placing the modifier between subject and verb and between verb and object.

> *Not:* The accountant, **to explain the difference between gross income and net income,** used several illustrations.
>
> *But:* **To explain the difference between gross income and net income,** the accountant used several illustrations.

BASIC RULE 24:   Some adverbs—*only, almost, nearly, also, quite, merely, actually*—are frequent troublemakers. Be sure they are placed as closely as possible to the words they modify.

> *Example:* The problem can **only** be defined by this committee.
>
> *Could mean:* **Only** this committee can define the problem.
>
> *or:* This committee can **only define** the problem, not solve it.

Do not use *hardly, only, scarcely, barely*—so-called subtractive adverbs—together with a negative construction. If you do, you will have a double negative.

> *Not:* They **haven't only** a single blanket.
>
> *But:* They **have only** a single blanket.

BASIC RULE 25:   Phrases and clauses, like single-word modifiers, should be placed as closely as possible to the words they modify; this way there will be no danger of their attaching themselves to the wrong sentence element.

> *Not:* Mr. Dough has resigned from the presidency of the Club after having served four years **to the regret of all the members.**
>
> *But:* **To the regret of all the members,** Mr. Dough has resigned from the presidency of the Club after having served four years.

BASIC RULE 26:   Relative clauses should also be placed immediately after the word they modify, since they attach themselves to the sentence element nearest them.

> *Not:* The man has an appointment **who is waiting in my office.**
>
> *But:* The man **who is waiting in my office** has an appointment.

BASIC RULE 27:   Avoid **squinting** constructions—that is, modifiers that are so placed that one cannot tell whether they are modifying the words immediately preceding them or those immediately following them.

Obscure: The lawyer agreed **after the papers were signed** to take the case.

Could mean: The lawyer agreed to take the case **after the papers were signed.**

or: **After the papers were signed**, the lawyer agreed to take the case.

Connectives

Four kinds of words can serve as connectives: prepositions, conjunctions, relative pronouns, and relative adverbs. Each not only connects two sentence elements but also shows the relationship between them.

Prepositions

A preposition *connects* the word, phrase, or clause that follows it (its object) with some other element in the sentence *and shows the relationship* between them. A preposition can be a single word *(to, with)* or a phrase *(according to, as well as, because of, contrary to)*.

The use of many prepositions in English is purely idiomatic: There is no logical reason that one preposition is wrong and another correct in a given expression. There are no rules for choosing the correct preposition; you must simply learn the idioms.

BASIC RULE 28:   In formal writing, avoid superfluous prepositions.

> *Not:* We will divide **up** the work.
> *But:* We will divide the work.

> *Not:* He is standing near **to** the door.
> *But:* He is standing near the door.

BASIC RULE 29:   Especially in formal writing, repeat the preposition before the second of two connected elements.

> *Not:* He seemed interested **in** us and our problems.
> *But:* He seemed interested **in** us and **in** our problems.

> *Not:* He was able to complete the project **by** planning carefully and working diligently.
> *But:* He was able to complete the project **by** planning carefully and **by** working diligently.

BASIC RULE 30:   In the so-called *split* (or *suspended*) construction, in which two words are completed by different prepositions, be especially careful to use both prepositions.

> *Not:* He has an interest and an aptitude **for** his work.
> *But:* He has an interest **in** and an aptitude **for** his work. (Commas may be used in this construction: He has an interest in, and an aptitude for, his work.)

Conjunctions

Conjunctions signal the logical relationship between two thoughts.

Sentence elements are said to be *coordinate* (or *parallel*) when they are of equal rank (of equal importance) both grammatically and logically.

Determining equal grammatical importance is relatively simple: words = words; phrases = phrases; subordinate clauses = subordinate clauses; principal clauses = principal clauses.

Not parallel: His main virtues are **that he is sincere and his generosity.** (a clause linked to a word)
Improved: His main virtues are **that he is sincere and that he is generous.** (two noun clauses, now parallel; noun clause = noun clause)
or: His main virtues are his **sincerity** and his **generosity.** (two words)

BASIC RULE 31: The coordinate conjunctions, including *and, but, or, nor, for, yet, moreover,* are the connectives most frequently used to show that two ideas are equal (are parallel). Notice in the following illustrations that the two ideas connected are parallel.

> The **Director and** the **Assistant Director** will attend. (connecting a word with a word)
> He is a man **of great capability but of little experience.** (connecting a phrase with a phrase)
> He said **that he had filed a claim for a refund but that he had not heard anything further from this office.** (connecting a subordinate clause with a subordinate clause)
> **I was eager to attend the seminar; moreover, I knew that the exchange of ideas would be helpful.** (connecting an independent clause with an independent clause)

BASIC RULE 32: The correlative conjunctions—*either . . . or, neither . . . nor, not only . . . but also, both . . . and, if . . . then, since . . . therefore*—work in pairs to show that words and ideas are parallel (equal in importance).

> **Either** the **Director or** the **Assistant Director** must attend. (connecting a word with a word)
> The report is designed **not only to present a list of the problems facing us but also** to **recommend possible solutions to these problems.** (connecting a phrase with a phrase)

The significant point in the use of pairs of correlatives is that each member of the pair must be followed by the same part of speech (same grammatical construction). That is, if *not only* is followed by a verb, then *but also* must be followed by a verb; if *either* is followed by a phrase, *or* must likewise be followed by a phrase.

> *Not:* The project was a disappointment **not only** to me **but also** my assistant. (*Not only* is followed by the prepositional phrase *to me; but also* is followed by a noun.)

But: The project was a disappointment **not only** to me **but also** to my assistant. (Note that each of the correlative conjunctions is followed by a prepositional phrase.)

Not: His assignment was **both** to conduct the course **and** the evaluation of it.

But: His assignment was **both** to conduct the course **and** to evaluate it.

Modifier Exercises

(Answers are on page 41.)

EXERCISE I Read each sentence carefully and decide whether it is clear which word is being modified. If the sentence is correct as it stands, write "C" on the line to the left. If the modifier is used incorrectly, write "I" on the line and rewrite the sentence so that the meaning is clear.

_____ 1. He only gave the instructions once.

_____ 2. He rented an apartment to an elderly couple with a large living room.

_____ 3. As he walked to the subway, he noticed three teenagers coming out of the building.

_____ 4. Walking to the subway, three teenagers were coming out of the building.

_____ 5. Out of the building came three teenagers walking to the subway.

_____ 6. He saw a painting of Venus lying on a couch in the dentist's office.

_____ 7. In the museum, there are several pictures of gods and goddesses.

_____ 8. The letter is on the desk that we received yesterday.

_____ 9. It is important to respond promptly to the requests.

_____ 10. Winning the race, the crowd applauded her.

EXERCISE II Choose the correct word(s) to complete the comparison.

1. (honester, more honest) Did you expect the mayor to be _____ than the average citizen?

2. (fewer, fewest) The shortstop made the _____ errors of any infielder on the team.

3. (largest, most largest) He was just served the _____ ice cream sundae I have ever seen.

4. (worse, worst) Last month, the weather was _____ in Florida than the weather service had predicted.

5. (ordinariest, most ordinary) It is the _____ piece of clothing in the entire store.

6. (better, best) Take the _____ bicycle from the four that are not locked in the rack.

7. (more, most) She is the _____ fashionable of the two models on the runway.

8. (roundest, most rounder) Who in the ceramics class was able to make the _____ ball of clay?

9. (less, least) Their assistants performed the _____ amount of work on the project.

10. (quieter, more quieter) The librarian asked them to be _____ in the reading room.

Sentence Fragments and Run-on Sentences _____

BASIC RULE 33:   Do not use a fragment as a sentence.

A **sentence fragment** is a phrase or a dependent clause mistakenly used as a sentence. There are three basic ways to correct a sentence fragment:

(1)   Add the fragment to the sentence that precedes it.

> *Incorrect:* The flowers are on the table. In a very beautiful vase.
> *Correct:* The flowers are on the table, in a very beautiful vase.

(2)   Add the fragment to the sentence that follows it.

> *Incorrect:* Unable to gain entry into the building. The delivery-man left the package in the vestibule.
> *Correct:* Unable to gain entry into the building, the deliveryman left the package in the vestibule.

(3)   Add a subject and verb to the fragment.

> *Incorrect:* To water the plants.
> *Correct:* Dorothy needs twenty minutes to water the plants.

BASIC RULE 34:   Avoid run-on sentences.

A **run-on sentence** is two or more sentences written as one.

There are three basic ways to correct run-on sentences:

(1)   Divide the sentences by means of end-stop punctuation (a period, a question mark, or an exclamation point).

> *Run-on:* The book is fascinating she read it in one sitting.
> *Correct:* The book is fascinating. She read it in one sitting.
> *Run-on:* Are you ready we have to leave now.
> *Correct:* Are you ready? We have to leave now.
> *Run-on:* Watch out the walk is covered with ice.
> *Correct:* Watch out! The walk is covered with ice.

Note: The comma is not an end-mark. It cannot be used by itself to separate two sentences.

> *Run-on:* Today is Sunday, classes are not in session.
> *Correct:* Today is Sunday. Classes are not in session.

(2)   Use a semicolon.

> *Run-on:* The wedding was lovely we enjoyed ourselves immensely.
> *Correct:* The wedding was lovely; we enjoyed ourselves immensely.

(3)   Use a comma and a conjunction.

> *Run-on:* I like to drink coffee my sister prefers tea.
> *Correct:* I like to drink coffee, but my sister prefers tea.

> *Run-on:* The wedding was lovely we enjoyed ourselves immensely.
> *Correct:* The wedding was lovely, and we enjoyed ourselves immensely.

Some words that may cause run-ons are *however, therefore, consequently,* and *moreover.* These words are not sentence connectors. When they follow a complete thought, they should be preceded by a semicolon or a period.

> *Run-on:* Automobile showrooms are stocked with new models therefore car dealers are willing to lower prices on older models.
> *Correct:* Automobile showrooms are stocked with new models; therefore, car dealers are willing to lower prices on older models.

Without proper punctuation, even great writing becomes just an incomprehensible jumble of ideas, as illustrated by this unpunctuated version of a paragraph from *Great Expectations* by Charles Dickens:

> I give Pirrip as my father's family name on the authority of his tombstone and my sister Mrs. Joe Gargery who married the blacksmith as I never saw my father or my mother and never saw any likeness of either of them for their days were long before the days of photographs my first fancies regarding what they were like were unreasonably derived from their tombstones the shape of the letters on my father's gave me an odd idea that he was a square stout dark man with curly black hair from the character and turn of the inscription Also Georgiana Wife of the Above I drew a childish conclusion that my mother was freckled and sickly to five little stone lozenges each about a foot and a half long which were arranged in a neat row beside their grave and were sacred to the memory of five little brothers of mine who gave up trying to get a living exceedingly early in the universal struggle I am indebted for a belief I religiously entertained that they had all been born on their backs with their hands in their trousers pockets and had never taken them out in this state of existence.

To make sense out of the paragraph, we need to use end-stop and internal punctuation. Once the original punctuation is replaced, the meaning becomes clear.

> I give Pirrip as my father's family name, on the authority of his tombstone and my sister—Mrs. Joe Gargery, who married the blacksmith. As I never saw my father or my mother, and never

saw any likeness of either of them (for their days were long before the days of photographs), my first fancies regarding what they were like were unreasonably derived from their tombstones. The shape of the letters on my father's gave me an odd idea that he was a square, stout, dark man, with curly black hair. From the character and turn of the inscription, "*Also Georgiana, Wife of the Above,*" I drew a childish conclusion that my mother was freckled and sickly. To five little stone lozenges, each about a foot and a half long, which were arranged in a neat row beside their grave, and were sacred to the memory of five little brothers of mine—who gave up trying to get a living exceedingly early in that universal struggle—I am indebted for a belief I religiously entertained that they had all been born on their backs with their hands in their trousers pockets, and had never taken them out in this state of existence.

Fragment and Run-on Sentence Exercises

(Answers to the following exercises are on pages 41 and 42.)

EXERCISE I Read the following "sentences." If the sentence is complete, write "C" on the line to the left; if the sentence is incomplete (a fragment) write "I."

_____ 1. There are many problems that we must face.

_____ 2. One of which is pollution.

_____ 3. And even pollution can be divided into several areas.

_____ 4. Noise pollution, chemical pollution, air pollution.

_____ 5. I should like to address myself to the problem of air pollution.

_____ 6. In the hope of finding ways of reducing this problem.

_____ 7. A problem that will surely contaminate the world.

_____ 8. In our own life-time, if we allow it.

_____ 9. Therefore, it is vital to our interests to seek a solution.

_____ 10. This is my opinion.

EXERCISE II Write a paragraph, using the "sentences" from Exercise I in the order in which they appear. As you write, correct the sentences which are incomplete.

EXERCISE III Examine the following pairs of sentences carefully. Decide which sentence of each pair is correctly punctuated.

_____ 1. **A.** Let's try to locate the book in the library; otherwise we will have to purchase it.
　　　　B. Let's try to locate the book in the library, otherwise, we will have to purchase it.

_____ 2. **A.** First we will eat then we will talk.
　　　　B. First we will eat; then we will talk.

_____ 3. **A.** I have no hope of getting the position, however, I shall still apply.
　　　　B. I have no hope of getting the position. However, I shall still apply.

_____ **4.** **A.** It does not matter if you win or lose what matters is the effort.
         B. It does not matter if you win or lose. What matters is the effort.

_____ **5.** **A.** Do not shout. I can hear you.
         B. Do not shout, I can hear you.

EXERCISE IV Read the following sentences carefully. If the sentence is correct as written, write "C" on the line to the left of the sentence. If the sentence is incorrect and needs additional punctuation, write "I" on the line and make all the necessary corrections in punctuation.

_____ **1.** First we will complete the test then we will review the material.

_____ **2.** The weather was perfect there was a blue sky with bright sunshine and a soft breeze.

_____ **3.** If you can accomplish all the assigned tasks, it will be of great help to all of us.

_____ **4.** Several of us attended that party and the reception following dinner.

_____ **5.** We insisted on his attending the graduation exercises unfortunately he showed his displeasure to everyone.

Capitalization

The use of capital letters is a convention of language and culture. Some languages, such as many mid-Eastern and Oriental languages, do not use capital letters. But to write standard English it is necessary to learn the rules that govern the use of the capital.

Capitalize These Words

The first word of a sentence.

> *Example:* For best results, you should follow the recipe.

All proper names as well as a word used as part of a proper noun.

> *Example:* Riveira Heights is a mile from Ocean Terrace. (*but:* We have a terrace apartment.)

> The United States of America, Santa Fe Chief, American Broadcasting Company, Thomas Jefferson

Days of the week and months.

> *Examples:* We will view a film on Monday.
> The next semester begins in July.

The word *Dear* when it is the first word in the salutation of a letter.

> *Example:* Dear Ms. Smith: (*but:* My dear Ms. Smith:)

The first word of the complimentary close of a letter.

> *Example:* Truly yours, (*but:* Very truly yours,)

The first, last, and all other important words in a title.

Example: The Best of Broadway

Titles, when they refer to a particular official or family member.

Examples: The meeting was conducted by President Stevens. (*but:* Mr. Stevens, the president, conducted the meeting.)

I called Aunt Abby. (*but:* I have two aunts.)

Points of a compass, when they refer to particular regions of a country.

Example: We're going North next week. (*but:* Maine is north of New York.)

Note: Write the Far West, the Pacific Coast, the Middle East.

The first word of a direct quotation.

Example: According to Harry Emerson Fosdick, "The tragedy of war is that it uses man's best to do man's worst."

Note: When a direct quotation is interrupted, the first word of the second half of the sentence is not capitalized.

Example: "Please come," Steve said, "because we'd like to see you."

Adjectives derived from the names of religions, countries, and languages.

Examples: Jewish, Protestant, African, Egyptian, Spanish, English

Capitalization Exercises

(Answers to the following exercises are on page 42.)

EXERCISE I Rewrite the following paragraph. Capitalize wherever necessary and eliminate capital letters that are not needed.

of all the Seasons in the year, my favorite is Spring. In the Spring, the entire world seems to come to life. the Poet says that april is the cruelest Month, because he associates the pains of Birth and Life with this season. But i disagree. to Me, april is filled with Hope and is the gentlest time of the year.

EXERCISE II Proofread the following paragraph and underline all the words that need to be capitalized.

we went to the newark public library because we needed several articles for our french class. the librarian, miss brown, suggested that we look at two magazines, *holiday* and *travel*, and we did. the article i liked the best was called, "touring paris."

EXERCISE III In the following sentences, change lowercase letters to capital letters wherever needed.

1. last may we visited the northern city of buffalo.

2. roberta carradine announced that *the color purple* had won another prize.

3. We had lunch with mr. johnson on unionport road.

4. the award will be presented to dr. slone next tuesday at a meeting of the international ladies garment workers union in boston.

5. Your father is two inches taller than cousin robert.

Answers _____

AGREEMENT

I. 1. **students** speak
2. **Miss Olipo** plays
3. **you** need; **she** needs
4. **Jane** goes
5. **pills** seem
6. **bus** runs
7. **cat** eats
8. **Roger** studies
9. **you** and **I** know
10. **he** tries; **I** try

II. 1. are
2. were
3. have
4. does
5. want
6. am
7. his
8. have
9. her
10. was

III. 1. are
2. draw
3. were
4. his
5. her
6. is
7. their
8. know
9. goes
10. was

IV.
1. is—The subject, *Veronica,* is singular.
2. C—The subject, *mother and father,* is plural.
3. is—The subject, *nursing,* is singular; *professions* is not the subject.
4. his (or, if you prefer, *her*)—Since the pronoun refers to **each**, a singular, the plural *(their)* is incorrect.
5. he (or, if you prefer, *she*)—Since the pronoun refers to *everyone*, a singular, the plural *(they)* is incorrect. (In 4 and 5 the writer should be consistent and use either the masculine pronouns *(his-he)* or the feminine pronouns *(her-she).*
6. C—The subject, *I,* is singular.
7. are—The subject, *friends and I,* is plural.
8. do—The subject, *parents,* is plural.
9. C—The subject, *profession,* is singular.
10. are—The subject, *factors,* is plural.

PRONOUNS

I.
1. C (*Whoever* is the subject of the verb, *asks.*)
2. C (*whoever* is still the subject of the verb, *asks.*)
3. whomever (*whomever* is the object of the verb, *sees.*)
4. he
5. He
6. them
7. C
8. C
9. his
10. us

VERB FORM

I.
1. rang
2. hanged
3. lose
4. flew
5. written
6. thought
7. saw
8. frozen
9. driven
10. taught

II.
1. hung
2. thrown
3. woven
4. slid
5. gone
6. lost
7. drank
8. lent
9. supposed
10. know

III.
1. had arranged
2. has arranged

3. were
4. is (The *present tense* is used to express a permanent fact.)
5. have waited

MODIFIERS

I. 1. (I) He gave the instructions only once.
2. (I) He rented the apartment with a large living room to an elderly couple.
3. (C)
4. (I) The sentence is best phrased as in sentence 3.
5. (I) Sentence 3 is still the clearest.
6. (I) He saw a painting in the dentist's office; it was of Venus lying on a couch.
7. (C)
8. (I) The letter that we received yesterday is on the desk.
9. (C)
10. (I) The sentence is best rephrased as "When she won the race, the crowd applauded."

II. 1. more honest
2. fewest
3. largest
4. worse
5. most ordinary
6. best
7. more
8. roundest
9. least
10. quieter

FRAGMENT AND RUN-ON SENTENCES

I. 1. C
2. I
3. C
4. I
5. C
6. I
7. I
8. I
9. C
10. C

II. There are many problems that we must face—one of which is pollution. And even pollution can be divided into several areas—noise pollution, chemical pollution, air pollution. I should like to address myself to the problem of air pollution, in the hope of finding ways of reducing this problem—a problem that will surely contaminate the world in our own lifetime, if we allow it. Therefore, it is vital to our interests to seek a solution. This is my opinion.

III. 1. A
2. B
3. B

      4. B
      5. A

IV.   **1.** First we will complete the test. Then we will review the material.
      2. The weather was perfect. There was a blue sky with bright sunshine, and a soft breeze.
      3. C
      4. C
      5. We insisted on his attending the graduation exercises; unfortunately he showed his displeasure to everyone.

CAPITALIZATION

I. Of all the seasons in the year, my favorite is spring. In the spring, the entire world seems to come to life. The poet says that April is the cruelest month, because he associates the pains of birth and life with this season. But I disagree. To me, April is filled with hope and is the gentlest time of the year.

II. We went to the Newark Public Library because we needed several articles for our French class. The librarian, Miss Brown, suggested that we look at two magazines, *Holiday* and *Travel*, and we did. The article I liked the best was called, "Touring Paris."

III.   **1.** Last May we visited the northern city of Buffalo.
      2. Roberta Carradine announced that *The Color Purple* had won another prize.
      3. We had lunch with Mr. Johnson on Unionport Road.
      4. The award will be presented to Dr. Slone next Tuesday at a meeting of the International Ladies Garment Workers Union in Boston.
      5. Your father is two inches taller than Cousin Robert.

CHAPTER 2

Proper Punctuation

Although most multiple-choice examinations stress punctuation less than other aspects of writing, the careful writer must know the principal rules governing punctuation. Certainly a knowledge of proper punctuation is essential for all essay examinations. The following section is not intended to give a definitive set of rules but rather to provide a basic framework for the writer.

The Apostrophe

The apostrophe has three major uses:

(1) To indicate the possessive case of nouns. (It is not used with pronouns, since such pronouns as *yours, hers, ours, theirs,* and *whose* indicate possession already.)

(2) To indicate a contraction—the omission of one or more letters.

(3) To indicate plurals of letters, abbreviations, and numbers.

The Possessive Case

If the noun does not end in *s*—whether singular or plural—add an *'s;* if the noun ends in *s,* simply add the '. (Some writers prefer to add *'s* to all nouns, even those that already end in *s.*)

Examples: The chef's knife was extremely sharp.
The child's room was painted yellow.
The children's room was painted yellow.
The chefs' knives were extremely sharp.
Keats' poetry is among the very finest in the English language.

Contractions

A good rule of thumb is to supply the missing letter or letters. If you cannot do this—especially with pronouns—then perhaps no contraction is called for.

Examples: can't = can not
it's = it is
We **can't** go to the show tonight.
It's a beautiful day.

Plurals of Letters, Abbreviations, and Numbers

Usually the apostrophe is used to form the plurals of lowercase letters (a's, b's, c's, etc.), plurals of abbreviations with periods (Ph.D.'s, R.N.'s), and numbers (3's, 6's). With capital letters, abbreviations without periods, and even with numbers when no confusion results, there is a choice. In either case, the writer's style should be consistent.

> *Examples:* How many **e's** are there in your name?
> Four **M.D.'s** shared the suite of offices.

Apostrophe Exercises

(Answers to the following exercises are on pages 52 and 53.)

EXERCISE I   Change the following phrases into possessives.

> *Example:* The books of the pupils = The pupils' books

1. the class of the students
2. the music of the choir
3. the flag of the nation
4. the choice of the people
5. the coat of Joseph

EXERCISE II   Are the following words in **boldface** contractions? If so, what letter(s) are missing?

1. The animal rested **its** head on her lap.
2. I **cant** abide his muttering.
3. This mistake is **yours**, not **ours.**
4. **Its** about time he appeared.
5. **Whos** coming to your home?

EXERCISE III   Each of the following sentences contains a word in **boldface** that requires an apostrophe. Rewrite the word with the apostrophe correctly placed.

1. **Johns** mother is running for the Senate.
2. The **teachers** responsibility is obvious.
3. She borrowed her **friends** scarf.
4. There are several people in the **doctors** waiting room.
5. All of his **paintings** vibrant colors revealed the **artists** ability.

EXERCISE IV   For each of the following sentences, circle the one correct word from the choices in parentheses.

1. (Whose, Who's, Whose's) paper was selected?
2. The (womans', women's, womans') movement gained a good deal of support in recent years.

3. There are several toys in the (childrens', childrens, children's) room.

4. Both women are (R.N.S., R.N.'s).

5. Watch your (p's and q's, p and q's, pease and queues).

6. The (men's, mens, mens') locker rooms are always crowded.

7. Jimmy always had trouble with writing 2's and (threes, 3, 3's).

8. I enjoy reading (Dicken's, Dickens, Dickens') novels.

9. The (stores, store's) owner was shot.

10. Both my (aunt's, aunts', aunts) cars were damaged.

EXERCISE V In each of the following sentences, decide whether an apostrophe is needed in the words in **boldface.**

1. The **students** entered the room filled with anxiety.

2. The **semesters** work was nearing completion.

3. The **cars** engine needed repair.

4. There are several reasons for the **chairmans** decision.

5. **Its** really a matter of great urgency and so it **cant** be delayed, even for several **hours.**

The Colon _____

The colon is used to introduce a list of three or more items or a long quotation.

> *Examples:* The examination is divided into four distinct sections:
> The anchorman used the following statement:

Caution! Avoid using the colon directly after a verb. Avoid using the colon to interrupt the natural flow of language.

> *Poor:* We consumed: pizza, soda, ice cream, and peanuts.
> *Better:* We consumed pizza, soda, ice cream, and peanuts.

The Comma _____

The comma is used:

(1) To set off words in a series.

Use a comma between words in a series when three or more elements are present. The elements may be words, phrases, or clauses. (Notice the use of the commas in this last sentence.)

> *Examples:* She smiled, laughed, and shrieked.
> Calvin is a good friend, a serious student, and a cooperative employee.
> Deborah wanted to go out to eat, see a movie, or stay home and watch television.

Note: It is acceptable to omit the comma before the final *and* or *or* in a series. However, the writer's style should be consistent.

(2) *Before coordinating conjunctions* (and, but, nor, or, for) *that join two independent clauses.*

> *Examples:* I hope that my suggestions will help you, **and** I am
> willing to meet with you to discuss your work.
> It snowed two days ago, **but** I couldn't go skiing until
> today.

Note: If the independent clauses are short, the separating comma may be omitted.

> *Example:* The bell rang and the contest began.

(3) *To set off nonrestrictive, parenthetical, and appositive elements.*

A nonrestrictive element, often signaled by *who* or *which,* supplies material not essential to the sentence and which, if removed, will not change the meaning of the original sentence.

> *Example:* Cynthia, who is a good talker, is head of the debating
> club.

A parenthetical element is one that is added to the sentence without changing the sentence's meaning. Some common parenthetical elements are *to tell the truth, believe me, it appears to me, I am sure,* and *as a matter of fact.*

An appositive element describes a noun or pronoun but is not grammatically necessary for the sentence.

> *Examples:* Norma, an industrious and hard-working student,
> will run for class treasurer.
> Shrill and loud, the alarm disturbed our sleep.

Note: In the first example, the appositive phrase follows the noun it describes *(Norma)*; in the second, the appositive phrase precedes the noun it describes *(alarm)*.

(4) *To set off introductory clauses and phrases.*

> *Examples:* After you deliver the letter, please join us for a game
> of cards.
> Smiling at the audience, he accepted the award.

(5) *To separate two coordinate adjectives that precede the noun they describe.*

Coordinate adjectives are adjectives of equal importance.

> *Examples:* He is a patient, caring parent.
> She is an intelligent, talented executive.

In both these examples, *and* can be substituted for the comma. If *and* cannot be substituted without the meaning being changed, the adjectives are not coordinate, and no comma is needed.

> *Example:* It is a funny old film.

(6)   *To set off nouns in direct address.*

The name of the person addressed is separated from the rest of the sentence by commas.

> *Examples:* Evelyn, you are terrific!
> It seems, Mr. President, that you are mistaken.

(7)   *With dates and addresses.*

The different parts of a date and an address are separated by commas, including a comma after the last item.

> *Examples:* She was born on July 9, 1908, just before midnight.
> Is it possible to drive from Peekskill, New York, to Jacksonville, Florida, in under twenty-four hours?

Note: Using a comma where it is not needed is as confusing as omitting one when it is required.

Comma Exercise

(Answers to the following exercise are on page 53.)

EXERCISE 1   Decide where commas are required in the following paragraph.

> I shall never forget July 10 1986. It was the day my brother Jim returned from Tuscaloosa Alabama where he had been working. I hadn't seen Jim for well over a year and to tell the truth I really missed him. Jim a young man several years older than I had always been a source of help of inspiration and of encouragement to me. Although I knew that times had changed I really wasn't prepared for what was to take place.

The Dash

A *dash* is used:

(1)   Before a word or word group which indicates a summation or reversal of what preceded it.

> *Examples:* Patience, sensitivity, understanding, empathy—these are the marks of a friend.
> To lose weight, set yourself realistic goals, do not eat between meals, eat only in the kitchen or dining room, avoid restaurants—and then go out and binge.

Note: The material following the *dash* usually directs the attention of the reader to the content preceding it.

(2)   Before and after abrupt material of a parenthetical nature.

> *Example:* He was not pleased with—in fact, he was completely hostile to—the take-over.

End-Stop Punctuation

There are three types of punctuation used to end a sentence: the period, the question mark, and the exclamation mark.

A period is used at the end of a sentence that makes a statement.

> *Examples:* Today is Monday.
> There are thirty days in September.

A question mark is used after a direct question. A period is used after an indirect question.

> *Examples: Direction Question:* Would you like to go home?
> *Indirect Question:* I want to know whether you would like to go home.

An exclamation mark is used after an expression that shows strong emotion or issues a command. It may follow a word, a phrase, or a sentence.

> *Examples:* Hooray! We won the game!
> Help! I have a splinter!

End-Stop Punctuation Exercises
(Answers to the following exercises are on page 53.)

EXERCISE I Add the necessary end-stop punctuation to the following sentences.

1. Stop that

2. Did he stop doing that

3. I wondered whether he stopped doing that

4. We called for help

5. Help

6. We waited for almost an hour and no one came to our assistance

7. We never found out whether anyone heard our call

8. Actually, no one did

9. How could something like this happen

10. I hope it will never happen again

The Hyphen

The hyphen is used:

(1) With a compound modifier that precedes the noun.

> *Examples:* They prepared a well-organized agenda.
> (*But:* The agenda they prepared was well organized.)
> She owns a five-speed bicycle.
> (*But:* She owns a bicycle with five speeds.)

(2)   With fractions that serve as adjectives or adverbs.

Example: The best hotel in town is one-third empty.

Quotation Marks _____

Quotation marks are used:

(1)   To enclose the actual words of the speaker or writer.

Example: "Are the pictures ready yet?" she asked.

(2)   To emphasize words used in a special or unusual sense.

Example: The teenagers told the adults to "chill out."

(3)   To set off titles of short works or parts of a large work.

Example: This section is titled "Quotation Marks."

When an entire sentence is quoted, use a comma before the opening quotation marks, capitalize the initial word of the quotation, and place end-stop punctuation or a comma inside the closed quotation marks.)

Examples: Sandy said, "The steps are very slippery."
"I just went to the supermarket," John explained.

Caution!   Do not use quotation marks for indirect quotations.

Incorrect: He answered that "he would like to go home."
Correct: He answered that he would like to go home.
Or: He answered, "I would like to go home."

Caution!   Do not use quotation marks to gain acceptance for a poor choice of words.

Incorrect: We decided to "furniture" our house.
Correct: We decided to furnish our house.

Caution!   Periods and commas are placed *inside* quotation marks; colons and semicolons are placed *outside* quotation marks.

Examples: Today we discussed "My Wood," an essay by E. M. Forster.
Today we discussed "My Wood"; this work is an essay by E. M. Forster.

Quotation Marks Exercises
(Answers to the following exercise are on page 53.)

EXERCISE I   Add quotation marks wherever necessary in the following sentences.

1.   We plan to make popcorn and watch a movie, Janet remarked.

2.   He asked whether you want to read The Birthmark, a story by Nathaniel Hawthorne.

3. They confused the words bad and badly in their compositions.

4. One chapter in **Walden** is entitled Neighbors.

5. Roses are red, violets are blue, the child had written on the card.

6. You must remember this, he sang, a kiss is still a kiss.

7. In her essay On Education, she reminds us of the old saying, If God didn't make you a genius, neither will the University of Salamanca.

8. Robert Frost wrote in Mending Wall that Good fences make good neighbors.

9. Catherine used the word gross to describe the bug floating in the birdbath.

10. My brother said that he would contact me over the weekend to discuss the income-tax returns.

The Semicolon

A semicolon may be used to separate two complete ideas (independent clauses) in a sentence when the two ideas have a close relationship and they are not connected with a coordinating conjunction.

> *Example:* She keeps the stuffed animals on her bed; she has done this for ten years.

The semicolon is often used between independent clauses connected by conjunctive adverbs such as *consequently, therefore, also, furthermore, for example, however, nevertheless, still, yet, moreover, otherwise.*

> *Example:* The show had received an excellent review; however, we didn't care for the acting.
> (Note the use of the comma after the conjunctive adverb.)

Caution! Do not use the semicolon between an independent clause and a phrase or subordinate clause.

> *Incorrect:* I'd like to go to the library again; next Tuesday.
> *Correct:* I'd like to go to the library again next Tuesday.

Semicolon Exercises

(Answers to the following exercises are on pages 53 and 54.)

EXERCISE I   Decide whether the semicolons are correctly placed in the following sentences or whether another punctuation mark—or no punctuation mark—would be preferable.

1. It was one of those heavy summer rains; the kind that frequently occurs during the month of July.

2. We stared out of the window, hoping that the rain would stop; never-

theless, we knew that the picnic would have to be cancelled, since the ground would be wet.

3. It was the time to make alternate plans; and try to salvage the remainder of the day.

4. A few suggestions came to mind; we could go to a movie; or a museum, since both were indoor activities.

5. I had opted for the museum; however, my friends voted for a movie and so I was overruled.

6. Because the film in the neighborhood theater had received so many excellent reviews; we were certain that there would be many people in line for tickets.

7. If we arrived for the first showing; we would have a better chance of getting good seats.

8. We decided to do without lunch; and take along some fruit to the film; in case we became hungry.

9. Suddenly we looked out the window; the rain had stopped and the sun was shining.

10. We scrapped all our plans and headed for the beach; knowing that the best plans often change.

Punctuation Review
(Answers to the following exercises are on page 54.)

EXERCISE I Rewrite the following paragraph. There are many missing punctuation marks as well as incorrectly placed marks of punctuation.

> Ms. Jayne Smythe a well known author was the guest speaker. She brought along a copy of her latest novel; My Life Among the Parisians. The setting was in Paris France during the years following the Second World War; a time of great hardship, and stress. An audience of well over a hundred people had gathered to hear what Ms. Smythe would say some of us had traveled a long distance, to hear the lecture. Once she began to speak everyone became fascinated. Ms. Smythe spoke in a clear resonant and well-modulated voice: enunciating each word clearly.

EXERCISE II   Insert colons, dashes, or hyphens as needed in the following sentences.

1. I asked the auto mechanic to perform the following work wheel alignment, oil change, lubrication, and tune-up.

2. The radio which had been set to 102.6 FM was covered with water.

3. We read a well written essay about the two year old civic center located just a block from our house.

4. What Professor Wilson said was this "It is entirely possible—although many critics refuse even to consider the possibility that the person who wrote the plays attributed to William Shakespeare was not really Shakespeare but rather another poet/playwright of the time Christopher Marlowe, for example.

5. Not only is it a stick shift sports car but it comes with many special accessories.

Answers

APOSTROPHE

I. 1. the students' class
    2. the choir's music
    3. the nation's flag
    4. the people's choice
    5. Joseph's coat

II. 1. *Its* is not a contraction; it is a possessive form.
     2. can't = can not
     3. *Yours* and *ours* are not contractions; they are possessive forms.
     4. it's = it is
     5. who's = who is

III. 1. John's
      2. teacher's (singular), or teachers' (plural)
      3. friend's (singular)
      4. doctor's (singular), or doctors' (plural)
      5. paintings', artist's

IV. 1. Whose
     2. women's
     3. children's
     4. R.N.'s
     5. p's and q's
     6. men's
     7. 3's
     8. Dickens'
     9. store's
     10. aunt's (singular), or aunts' (plural)

V.   1. *Students* is a plural form in this sentence, so no apostrophe is used.
2. semester's work
3. car's engine
4. chairman's
5. It's, can't, hours

COMMA

I.   I shall never forget July 10, 1986. It was the day my brother, Jim, returned from Tuscaloosa, Alabama, where he had been working. I hadn't seen Jim for well over a year, and, to tell the truth, I really missed him. Jim, a young man several years older than I, had always been a source of help, of inspiration, and of encouragement to me. Although I knew that times had changed, I really wasn't prepared for what was to take place.

END-STOP PUNCTUATION

I.   1. Stop that!
2. Did he stop doing that?
3. I wondered whether he stopped doing that.
4. We called for help.
5. Help!
6. We waited for almost an hour and no one came to our assistance.
7. We never found out whether anyone heard our call.
8. Actually, no one did.
9. How could something like this happen?
10. I hope it will never happen again.

QUOTATION MARKS

I.   1. "We plan to make popcorn and watch a movie," Janet remarked.
2. He asked whether you want to read "The Birthmark," a story by Nathaniel Hawthorne.
3. They confused the words "bad" and "badly" in their compositions.
4. One chapter in **Walden** is entitled "Neighbors."
5. "Roses are red, violets are blue," the child had written on the card.
6. "You must remember this," he sang, "a kiss is still a kiss."
7. In her essay "On Education," she reminds us of the old saying, "If God didn't make you a genius, neither will the University of Salamanca."
8. Robert Frost wrote in "Mending Wall" that "Good fences make good neighbors."
9. Catherine used the word "gross" to describe the bug floating in the birdbath.
10. The sentence is correct. No quotation marks are needed in an indirect quotation.

SEMICOLON

I.   1. Substitute a comma for the semicolon.
2. Correct
3. Eliminate the semicolon; no punctuation is required.
4. The first semicolon is correct, but the second is not required and should be deleted.

5. Correct
6. Change the semicolon to a comma in order to separate the dependent clause from the independent clause.
7. Remove the semicolon following the introductory dependent clause. Use a comma after *showing*.
8. Both semicolons are incorrect. No mark of punctuation is required following *lunch*; use a comma after *film*, preceding the prepositional phrase.
9. Correct
10. Substitute a comma for the semicolon.

PUNCTUATION REVIEW

I. Ms. Jayne Smythe, a well-known author, was the guest speaker. She brought along a copy of her latest novel, *My Life Among the Parisians*. The setting was Paris, France, during the years following the Second World War, a time of great hardship and stress. An audience of well over a hundred people had gathered to hear what Ms. Smythe would say. Some of us had traveled a long distance to hear the lecture. Once she began to speak, everyone became fascinated. Ms. Smythe spoke in a clear, resonant, and well-modulated voice, enunciating each word clearly.

II.
1. I asked the auto mechanic to perform the following work: wheel alignment, oil change, lubrication, and tune-up.
2. The radio—which had been set to 102.6 FM—was covered with water.
3. We read a well-written essay about the two-year-old civic center located just a block from our house.
4. What Professor Wilson said was this: "It is entirely possible—although many critics refuse even to consider the possibility—that the person who wrote the plays attributed to William Shakespeare was not really Shakespeare but rather another poet/playwright of the time—Christopher Marlowe, for example.
5. Not only is it a stick-shift sports car but it comes with many special accessories.

CHAPTER 3

Usage and Diction

The section that follows is not an English textbook; it is simply a guide. It has been carefully prepared to help the student who is about to take an examination in English, and it should also prove of great value to the college freshman who wants to gain better knowledge of standard English.

Do not try to master all the information at once. Study one section at a time. At the end of each section there is a practice drill. See how well you do on the drill by checking your answers against the answer key provided. If you do well, go on to the next part. If you find that you have made a number of errors, review the section. It is important that you master each section before moving on to the next and that you do not skip any section.

A thorough mastery of this guide will result in higher scores on English examinations, better grades in college English courses, and increased ability to write clear and effective essays.

Levels of Usage

Diction concerns choosing the right word to express a thought most effectively. The successful writer selects words that are appropriate and correct for his purpose. It is important for the writer to know the essential difference between standard and nonstandard English.

Standard English is acceptable for most educated writers and speakers. It is used to convey precise or exact meaning. This is the level of writing that the college student is expected to manage with ease. Basically, standard English is the language of instruction, scholarship, and public address.

Nonstandard English is unacceptable for formal writing and speaking. Because nonstandard English includes illiteracies, ungrammatical constructions, slang, jargon, and obsolete words, you should avoid using nonstandard English unless you are aware that you are using a word or phrase that will not be acceptable or understood by a majority of readers. Colloquialisms are sometimes called informalisms, and while they may be appropriate to relaxed conversation, they usually should be avoided in writing.

Most tests measure the student's ability to recognize the difference between standard and nonstandard writing. Nonstandard forms should be avoided in formal essay writing.

Confusing Word Groups: 1 _____

a	used before words that start with a consonant sound
an	used before words that start with a vowel sound

Put the flowers in **a** vase.

It is **an** amazing card trick.

My neighbors made **a** united effort to clean the basement. (*United* begins with a consonant sound, *y*.)

I'll return in **an** hour. (*Hour* begins with a vowel sound, since the *h* is silent.)

and	used to join words or ideas

I like cats **and** dogs.

We are going to the basketball game **and** we would like to take you with us.

accept	*to receive* or *to agree to* something
except	*to exclude* or *excluding*

Please **accept** my apology.

Everyone **except** her brother ran home.

Her brother was **excepted** from the group of runners.

advice	*counsel, opinion* (noun)
advise	*to offer advice* (verb)

Do you want my **advice?**

I would **advise** you to contact your instructor.

affect	*to influence* (verb)
effect	*to cause* or *bring about* (verb) or *a result* (noun)

Smoking will **affect** a person's health.

The legislation will **effect** a change in your activities.

What was the **effect** of the senator's speech?

all ready	*everybody* or *everything ready,* or *all prepared*
already	*previously*

They were **all ready** to go to the dance.

She had **already** gone to the dance.

all together	*everybody* or *everything together*
altogether	*completely*

Students and faculty stood **all together** in front of the cafeteria.

We were **altogether** stunned by her comments.

desert (DEZZ-ert)	an *arid area*
desert (di-ZERT)	*to abandon* (verb) or a *reward* or *punishment* (noun, usually plural)
dessert (di-ZERT)	the *final course of a meal*

He took a camel and a canteen and set off across the **desert.**

They did not **desert** their friends when danger appeared.

The judge said that a brief prison term was a just **desert** for his crime.
The twins ordered hot fudge sundaes for **dessert.**

in used to indicate *inclusion, location,* or *motion within limits*
into used for *motion toward one place from another*

Your essays are **in** the folder.
She was singing **in** the rain.
She left her office and walked **into** the classroom.

it's the contraction of *it is* or *it has*
its a possessive pronoun meaning *belonging to it*

It's a beautiful day!
The cat ate **its** food.
I looked at the painting but could not figure out **its** meaning.

lay *to put*
lie *to recline*
lie *to tell a falsehood*

to lay:

Present tense:	**I lay**	
Past tense:	**I laid**	the pen on the desk.
Present perfect tense:	**I have laid**	

to lie (recline):

Present tense:	**I lie**	
Past tense:	**I lay**	on a blanket in the park.
Present perfect tense:	**I have lain**	

to lie (tell a falsehood):

Present tense:	**I lie**	
Past tense:	**I lied**	in saying my mother was an astronaut.
Present perfect tense:	**I have lied**	

lets third person singular present of *let*
let's a contraction for *let us*

I hope she **lets** me sign her book.
Let's go out for lunch tomorrow.

loose *not fastened* or *restrained,* or *not tight-fitting*
lose *to mislay, to be unable to keep, to be defeated*

The legs were **loose,** so the table fell apart.
The horse got **loose** and galloped away.
Did you **lose** your notebook again?
Our team will not **lose** the game.

passed the past tense of *to pass*
past *just preceding* or *an earlier time*

They **passed** the course after taking a two-week workshop.
They have worked hard during the **past** two weeks.

principal   *chief* or *main* (adjective), or *a leader* or *a sum of money* (noun)
principle   *a fundamental truth or belief*

Our **principal** objective is to graduate next year.
Every teacher was observed by the **principal** of the school.
We spent the interest but did not use the **principal** we had invested.
As a matter of **principle**, there are certain foods I will not eat.

quiet   *silent, still*
quit   *to give up* or *discontinue*
quite   *very* or *exactly, to the greatest extent*

Although she is intelligent, she is very **quiet** in class.
My sister-in-law **quit** smoking last month.
Since you did not eat breakfast, you are probably **quite** hungry by now.

raise   *to lift, erect*
raze   *to tear down*
rise   *to get up, to move down from a lower to a higher position, to increase in value*

He worked so hard he could no longer **raise** his arms.
I hope they do not **raze** the abandoned hotel in the middle of the night.
Did the value of your stock **rise** again today?

set   *to place something down* (mainly)
sit   *to seat oneself* (mainly)

to set:

Present tense:	He **sets**	
Past tense:	He **set**	the package on the desk.
Present perfect tense:	He **has set**	

to sit:

Present tense:	He **sits**	
Past tense:	He **sat**	on the couch.
Present perfect tense:	He **has sat**	

stationary   *standing still*
stationery   *writing materials*

She remained in a **stationary** position for twenty minutes.
I bought a pen and a notebook at the **stationery** store.

suppose   *to assume* or *guess*
supposed   the past tense and also the past participle of *to suppose*
supposed to   *ought to* or *should*

I **suppose** you will sleep late tomorrow.
I **supposed** you would sleep late today.
I had **supposed** you would attend the reunion.
You are **supposed to** bake it at 375° for thirty minutes.

than used to express *comparison*
then used to express *time* or *a result* or *consequence*

This cabinet is newer **than** the other one.
First I visited one home, and **then** I visited another.
If you cook dinner, **then** I will wash the dishes.

their *belonging to them*
there *in that place*
they're the contraction for *they are*

They hung **their** coats on the hooks in the hall.
The coats are over **there** on the hooks in the hall.
Tell them **they're** welcome to join us.

though *although* or *as if*
thought the past tense of *to think,* or *an idea* (noun)
through *in one side and out another, by way of, finished*

Though I am on a diet, I can't resist having a piece of cake.
She **thought** he was taking her to see a play.
That's an interesting **thought.**
It was fun to walk **through** the field.
Are you **through** with the magazine?

to *in the direction of* (preposition); it is also used before a verb to indicate the *infinitive*
too *very, also*
two the number *2*

I'll walk you **to** the corner.
I like **to** eat ice cream.
Do you like ice cream, **too?**
It is **too** cold for me.
She has **two** exams this afternoon.

use *to employ, put into service*
used the past tense and the past participle of *to use*

Did you climb the stairs or **use** the elevator?
I **used** the elevator.

used *in the habit of* or *accustomed to;* is followed by *to*
used *not new*

She got **used to** climbing the stairs.
He purchased a **used** coat at the flea market.

weather *atmospheric conditions*
whether introduces a *choice;* it should not be preceded by *of* or *as to*

How do you like the **weather** in New York?
We don't know **whether** we'll visit our neighbors or go for a ride.

were a past tense of *to be*
we're a contraction of *we are*
where refers to *place* or *location*

They **were** my favorite actors.
I said that **we're** having lunch together.
Do you want to know **where** we are going?

who's the contraction for *who is*
whose *of whom;* implies ownership

Who's in the mood to order a pizza?
Whose drink is this?

your   *belonging to you* (possessive adjective)
you're is a contraction for *you are*

Share **your** candy with her.
I heard that **you're** having lunch together.

Confusing Word Groups: 1—Exercises
(Answers to the following exercises are on page 99.)

EXERCISE I   *Underline* the correct choice.

1. If you (loose, lose) this opportunity, it may be lost forever.
2. I must avoid ordering a rich (dessert, desert) while I am on this diet.
3. I believe that we have already (past, passed) our apartment house.
4. It was (all together, altogether) the best course of action.
5. Finish putting away the dishes before you (lay, lie) down.
6. Peter always chooses to (sit, set) next to Paul.
7. What do you consider to be the chief (affect, effect) of the Civil War?
8. Try to avoid purchasing such garish (stationary, stationery).
9. They are (all ready, already) to start on their trip.
10. There are few people who are more artistic (than, then) you.
11. The police officer neglected to (advise, advice) him of his rights.
12. Put the money (in, into) the envelope.
13. We listened to the (weather, whether) report on the radio.
14. We cannot (accept, except) your gracious invitation at this time.
15. The (principle, principal) reason for his refusal to purchase tickets to the opera was his lack of money.

EXERCISE II   Each of the following sentences may contain one or more errors. Check [✔] the space provided if the sentence is correct; if there are errors, write the correct form for each error.

1. Their are several errors in the sentence. _____

2. We're delighted that you did not miss the train. _____

3. The lion tried to reach it's paw through the bars of the cage. _____

4. They left their books back at the campsite. _____

5. Are they suppose to be here by nine o'clock? _____

6. It is better to raise a family in a quite neighborhood than in a tumultuous one. _____

7. I have forgotten who's book I borrowed. _____

8. Are they threw assembling the chair? _____

9. There has been a substantial raise in the cost-of-living index. _____

10. He forgot to take a umbrella with him. _____

11. He wished to purchase a use book. _____

12. It's too bad that you came so late to the theater. _____

13. If its appropriate, lets mention the two books in our speech. _____

14. I know that your trying very hard, but there are still problems. _____

15. His poor vision is certain to effect his performance. _____

Confusing Word Groups: 2 _____

allusion *an indirect reference*
illusion *an erroneous concept* or *perception*

The essay contained an **allusion** to an episode in the Bible.
The magician explained that the trick was only an **illusion.**

allude *to make a reference to*
elude *to escape from*

Does the essay **allude** to an episode in the Bible?
We helped the deer to **elude** the hunters.

angel *a heavenly creature*
angle *a point at which two lines meet,* or *an aspect seen from a particular point of view*

"One acts like an **angel**, the other like a devil," she said.
He checked every **angle** before he placed his bet.

ante a prefix meaning *before*
anti a prefix meaning *against*

Before I entered the doctor's office, I saw the nurse in the **ante**room.
The tobacco industry dislikes him because he belongs to an **anti**-smoking group.

breath   *an intake of air*
breathe *to draw air in and give it out*
breadth *width*

Push your chest against the x-ray plate and take a deep **breath.**
They cannot **breathe** comfortably during the allergy season.
The length of the mirror was twice as great as its **breadth.**

build   *to erect, construct* (verb), *or the physical makeup of a person or thing* (noun)
built   the past tense of *to build*

The architect was hired to design and **build** the house.
He has a gymnast's **build.**
The architect designed and **built** the house.

buy   *to purchase*
by   *near, by means of, or before*

Try to **buy** your books during the first week of classes.
We'll meet you **by** the main gate.
Meet us **by** noon.

capital   the *place of government;* or *wealth*
capitol   the *building* which houses the state or national legislatures

Nashville is the **capital** of Tennessee.
His employees wanted to raise **capital** to start their own business.
The Smithsonian Museum isn't too far from the **Capitol** in Washington, D.C.

cease   *to end*
seize   *to take hold of*

Please **cease** your chattering; we want to hear the actors.
The F.B.I. agents attempted to **seize** the kidnappers.

choice   *a selection*
choose   *to select*
chose   the past tense of *to choose*

I'll make my **choice** from the regular menu.
I'll **choose** the wine in a few minutes.
I **chose** my dessert with great care.

cite   *to quote*
sight *seeing, what is seen* (noun)
site   *a place where something is located or occurs*

She will **cite** your research to prove her point.
We were thrilled by the **sight** of the city at sunset.
They returned to the **site** of the crime.

cloth   *fabric or material*
clothe *to put on clothes, to dress*

Was the star wearing a **cloth** coat, or was it a fur?

Every morning, she spends a long time deciding how to **clothe** herself.

coarse	*vulgar* or *harsh*
course	*a path* or *a plan of study*

His language was **coarse** and impolite.
The wallpaper has a **coarse** texture.
The crew did not know that the plane was off **course.**
She is registering for a **course** in accounting.

complement	*a completing part*
compliment	*an expression of praise or admiration* (something given without charge is *complimentary*)

A 60° angle is the **complement** of a 30° angle.
They want to **compliment** us for our outstanding presentation.

conscience	*the awareness of the difference between right and wrong*
conscious	*aware*

His **conscience** bothered him, so he returned the book to the library.
The jurors were **conscious** of their great responsibility.

consul	*a government representative*
council	*an assembly that meets for deliberation* (*councillor*)
counsel	*advice* (*counselor*)

The **consul** at the embassy helped them to find an English-speaking
   dentist.
The faculty **council** met to evaluate the new curriculum.
We can always trust our attorney's wise **counsel.**

decent	*suitable*
descent	the process of *going down;* or *lineage*
dissent	*disagreement*

He wanted to know where to get a **decent** meal.
The **descent** of the jet made my ears ache.
They are of French-Canadian **descent.**
Because he could not agree with the others, one judge found it necessary
   to **dissent.**

farther	*more distant* (adjective or adverb)
further	*to a greater extent; more distant in time*

Now they live even **farther** from the train station.
If your comments go any **further,** we'll be forced to leave.

fine	*good, well, precise* (adjective); *a penalty* (noun); or *to penalize* (verb)
find	*to locate* or *discover*
fined	*penalized*

You wrote a **fine** paragraph!
Is there a $35 **fine** for double parking?
He can't **find** those important papers.
They were **fined** ten yards for an infraction of the rules.

knew   the past tense of *to know*
new   *of recent origin*

> I **knew** the correct answer.
> She got a brand **new** silver dollar.

know   *to have knowledge* or *understanding*
no   a negative used to express *denial, refusal,* or *complete lack*

> I **know** the correct answer.
> There is **no** more ice cream in the freezer.

later   *after a certain time*
latter   *the second of two*

> I'll do my homework **later.**
> Of the two buildings, the **latter** is far more modern.

mine   *belonging to me* (possessive adjective)
mind   *human consciousness* (noun); *to object, to watch out for* (verb)

> I told him that the car is **mine.**
> Will they **mind** if we take the bus?
> Her **mind** isn't what it used to be.

moral   *good* or *ethical* (adjective); *a lesson to be drawn* (noun)
morale (more-AL)   *spirit*

> Does the lawyer have a **moral** obligation to his client?
> What is the **moral** of the play?
> Her **morale** improved as soon as her pocketbook was returned.

personal   *related to an individual's character, conduct, private affairs* (adjective)
personnel   *an organized body of individuals* (noun)

> My secretary did not open the envelope, since it was marked "**personal** and confidential."
> In order to serve the public more efficiently, we will increase **personnel** by ten percent.

seem   *to appear*
seen   the past participle of *to see*

> Our new neighbors **seem** to be very friendly.
> We have **seen** this program.

Confusing Word Groups: 2—Exercises

(Answers to the following exercises are on page 100.)

EXERCISE I   *Underline* the correct choice.

1. That word does not require a (capital, capitol) letter.

2. We are responsible for the (moral, morale) of the sailors.

3. The doctor's (anteroom, antiroom) was filled with patients.

4. There was (know, no) evidence of plagiarism in the essay.

5. The frightened ewe tried to (allude, elude) the hunters.

6. The (clothe, cloth) was carefully woven by hand.

7. It is important to let the disease run its (coarse, course).

8. She resented the (personal, personnel) remarks that her employer made.

9. He (knew, new) that she would opt for the yellow dress.

10. Most of us would like to have an athletic (built, build).

11. (Later, Latter) on in the week we will visit the museum.

12. A fine wine is a good (compliment, complement) to the meal.

13. He completed the essay with an interesting historical (illusion, allusion).

14. I don't wish to (seen, seem) ungracious, but I will not attend the reception.

15. She didn't appear to be (conscience, conscious) of the effects of her remarks.

EXERCISE II Check [✔] the space provided if the sentence is correct; if there is an error, write the correct form.

1. It is important that you cite the source of the article. _____

2. I will cloth you in beautiful garments. _____

3. He hasn't seem any of his friends at the game. _____

4. It would be valuable to cease every opportunity. _____

5. We decided to buy his present well in advance of his birthday. _____

6. She walked much further than any of her friends. _____

7. We thought that this was the descent thing to do. _____

8. We followed his counsel very strictly. _____

9. He choose very formal attire to wear to the party. _____

10. Suddenly, and without any apparent warning, his breathe returned. _____

11. Everyone enjoys hearing a compliment. _____

12. We will always remember the site of her standing at the door. _____

13. I have the feeling that I shall never fined the ring. _____

14. The lamp was hung on a very poor angel. _____

15. I suppose we should let him make his own choice. _____

Confusing Word Groups: 3 _____

accede   *to agree with*
exceed   *to be more than*
concede   *to yield* or *agree* (not necessarily willingly)

The judge will **accede** to their request that the jury be polled.
You will get a ticket if you **exceed** the speed limit.
He could not avoid being checkmated, so the player decided to **concede** the game.

access   *ability to enter or communicate with*
excess   *a portion of something which surpasses specified limits* (noun); or *more than usual* (adjective)

We need a key to gain **access** to the basement.
He got a ticket for driving in **excess** of the speed limit.
The butcher trimmed the **excess** fat from the meat.

adapt   *to adjust* or *change*
adept   *skillful*
adopt   *to take as one's own*

They cannot **adapt** to the difference in weather.
We admired your **adept** cross-examination of the witness.
Our friends want to **adopt** another child.

adverse   *unfavorable*
averse   *having a feeling of repugnance or dislike*

The **adverse** publicity made him withdraw his candidacy.
I am not **averse** to allowing the I.R.S. to examine my records.

assistance   *the act of help or assisting; aid*
assistants   *helpers, aides*

Her expert **assistance** enabled me to complete the work on time.
I was not able to meet with the supervisor, but I did get to see two of his **assistants**.

canvas   *a heavy, coarse material*
canvass   *to solicit, conduct a survey*

That couch has a **canvas** slipcover.
I'll **canvass** the faculty members to see what they think of the administration.

carat   *a unit of weight*
caret   *a proofreading symbol, indicating where something is to be inserted*
carrot   *a vegetable*

For their engagement, he gave her a two-**carat** diamond ring.
Use a **caret** to indicate where the word should be inserted in the sentence.
For a quick snack, she keeps **carrot** sticks in the refrigerator.

click	*a brief, sharp sound*
clique	*an exclusive group, circle,* or *set of people*

When I heard the **click**, I knew I was being photographed.
In order to provide support, her **clique** sat together at the opera.

confidant	*one to whom private matters are confided* (noun)
confidence	*a feeling of assurance or certainty, trust* (noun)
confident	*being sure, having confidence* (adjective)

She tells everything to her sister, her favorite **confidant.**
I have developed greater **confidence** in my ability to pass the course.
His **confident** attitude inspired trust in his ability to perform the job.

disburse	*to pay out*
disperse	*to scatter, distribute widely*

The business office plans to **disburse** the funds next Friday.
The crowd will **disperse** as soon as the policemen arrive.

discomfit	*to upset*
discomfort	*lack of ease*

We have some news that will probably **discomfit** you.
The class complained that the hard chairs caused much **discomfort.**

dual	*double*
duel	*a contest between two persons or groups*

Her **dual** nature makes it difficult to trust her.
At the end of the story, the pirates and the soldiers engage in a **duel** to
the death.

elicit	*to draw forth, evoke*
illicit	*illegal, unlawful*

The joke will **elicit** a laugh, or at least a smile.
The headline mentioned a series of **illicit** stock purchases for which he
will be tried in court next month.

emigrate	*to leave a country*
immigrate	*to enter a country*

They plan to **emigrate** from Russia in two days.
They hope to **immigrate** to the United States.

eminent	*of high rank, prominent, outstanding*
imminent	*about to occur, impending*

We need an **eminent** attorney to chair the investigating committee.
Her appointment as head of the committee is **imminent.**

epitaph	*a memorial inscription on a tombstone or monument*
epithet	*a term used to describe or characterize the nature of a person or thing*

They composed a poetic **epitaph** for her monument.
He was arrested after shouting an **epithet** and throwing a rock.

expand　*to spread out*
expend　*to use up*

Next year we plan to **expand** the garden to include raspberries and asparagus.
Boxers are careful not to **expend** too much energy in the early rounds.

fair　*light in color, reasonable, pretty*
fare　*price*, usually for admission or transportation

Considering the crime, we thought that the punishment was **fair.**
Service has not improved, but the **fare** has been raised to $1.

faze　*to worry* or *to disturb*
phase　*an aspect*

The snowy roads did not **faze** him, since he owns a four-wheel-drive truck.
She is going through a new **phase** of emotional development.

formally　*in a formal way*
formerly　*at an earlier time;* used to describe a condition that no longer exists

It became official when he was **formally** offered the ambassadorship.
Now he plays for New York; **formerly** he was with the San Diego team.

fort　*a fortified place*
forte (fort)　*a strong point*
forte (for-tay)　*loudly* (a musical term)

With the small logs the boys were able to build a **fort.**
Her **forte** is baking cream-filled tarts.
It is more dramatic when the concluding section is played **forte.**

idle　*unemployed* or *unoccupied*
idol　*image* or *object of worship*

It is his responsibility to make certain that the workers do not remain **idle** for too long.
The story is about a golden **idol** that is stolen from a shrine in Mexico.

incidence　*the frequency of an occurrence*
incidents　*occurrences, events*

The **incidence** of crime has decreased since the guards began to check I.D. cards at the gate.
After two disturbing **incidents,** the team was barred from playing in the tournament.

lightening　*making less heavy* (from *to lighten*)
lightning　*electric discharge in the atmosphere; flashes of light; moving with great speed*

Our use of aluminum and plastic had resulted in the **lightening** of the racing car.
We got out of the pool as soon as we saw the **lightning.**

patience	*calm endurance; tolerance* (noun)
patients	*people under medical treatment*

She explained the subject matter with **patience** and a friendly demeanor.
The doctor will see **patients** this afternoon.

precede	*to come before*
proceed	*to go ahead*

The meal will **precede** the speeches.
Please **proceed** now that the light is green.

prophecy	*prediction* (noun, rhymes with *sea*)
prophesy	*to predict* (verb, rhymes with *sigh*)

Do you really expect the **prophecy** to come true?
I **prophesy** that he will be our next president.

Confusing Word Groups: 3—Exercises

(Answers to the following exercises are on page 100 and 101.)

EXERCISE I *Underline* the correct choice.

1. His (prophecy, prophesy) was gloomy and pessimistic.
2. I dislike the (click, clique) of people that you associate with.
3. He pleaded with the government to allow his family to (emigrate, immigrate) from the Soviet Union to the United States.
4. His pursuit of money was tantamount to (idle, idol) worship.
5. I felt a great deal of (discomfit, discomfort) when she entered the office.
6. It is really not necessary to (expand, expend) that much energy on the project.
7. There is a (dual, duel) purpose for making the call.
8. The (incidents, incidence) of contamination is alarming.
9. Are you (adverse, averse) to writing a letter of condolence?
10. We were all requested to dress (formally, formerly) for the party.
11. The police were asked to (disburse, disperse) the crowd.
12. My (fort, forte) is not diplomacy, as you will readily notice.
13. I think that we should (precede, proceed) with the agenda.
14. His remuneration will be in (access, excess) of a thousand dollars.
15. Reading about the famine didn't seem to (faze, phase) him one bit.

EXERCISE II Check [✔] the space provided if the sentence is correct; if there is an error, write the correct form.

1. He tried to be confidant about the success of the enterprise. _____

2. When Cassandra attempted to prophecy concerning future events, no one believed her. _____

3. There are people who have made a study of the epitaphs that are written on tombstones. _____

4. The discomfit that you are suffering as a result of your fall is only temporary. _____

5. We wish the division of work to be fare and just. _____

6. Browning wrote that a "man's grasp must accede his reach." _____

7. When it comes to revealing my innermost feelings, he is my most trustworthy confidant. _____

8. A good teacher attempts to illicit information from his students. _____

9. Sometimes it is difficult for immigrants to adopt to our culture. _____

10. He placed himself in eminent danger. _____

11. We fully realize that a good deal of patients and understanding will be required. _____

12. He placed the canvass on the balcony, hoping that it would dry during the day. _____

13. The lightening illuminated the house and created a strange feeling. _____

14. If you require any assistance in completing the task, simply let me know. _____

15. Her five-carat diamond ring attracted a good deal of attention. _____

Glossary of Usage: 1

abbreviate   *to shorten by omitting*
abridge   *to shorten by condensing*

Do you know how to **abbreviate** the term **et cetera?**
It is permissible to check your spelling in an **abridged** dictionary.

advantage	*a superior position*
benefit	*a favor conferred or earned* (as a profit)

It was the server's **advantage;** he needed one more point to win the game.
The boundaries were re-drawn for your **benefit.**

aggravate	*to make worse*
annoy	*to bother* or *to irritate*

The long hike **aggravated** my swollen ankle.
The buzzing of the fly **annoyed** her.
(*not:* The buzzing of the fly **aggravated** her.)

alibi	*an explanation on the basis of being in another place*
excuse	*an explanation on any basis*

If you were playing cards with him at the time of the robbery, then you can support his **alibi.**
Is there an **excuse** for your rude behavior?

all ways	*in every possible way*
always	*at all times*

They want to help us in **all ways** possible.
I am **always** willing to share a good dessert.

almost	*nearly, not quite*
most	*the greatest amount or number* or *to the largest part, a majority*

The sun has **almost** set.
You should offer her **most** of the stamp collection.

alongside of	*side by side with*
alongside	*parallel to the side*

Should they be allowed to build a store **alongside of** the church?
The bus pulled up **alongside** my car.

allot	*to give* or *apportion*
a lot	*many* (used with *of*); *alot* is a misspelling of *a lot*

Ask her to **allot** a few minutes for feeding the hamster.
There are **a lot** of toys in the baby's room. (*better:* There are **many** toys. . . .)

alright	now often employed in common usage to mean *all right* (In formal usage *all right* is still preferred by most authorities.)
all right	*satisfactory, very well, uninjured,* or *without doubt*

Are you **alright?**
He really did **all right** on the examination.
That is our car, **all right.**

alternate	(noun) *a substitute or second choice*
alternate	(verb) *to perform by turns*
alternative	*a choice between two things, only one of which may be accepted*

In case no tickets are available for the date you prefer, please choose an **alternate.**

He will **alternate** between the Celtics and the Knicks next season.

I am looking for an **alternative** to disbanding the commission.

(In less formal usage, *alternative* is not always limited to a choice between *two*.)

alumna	*a female graduate* (plural: *alumnae; ae* rhymes with *key*)
alumnus	*a male graduate* (plural: *alumni; ni* rhymes with *high*)

She is a Barnard **alumna.**
He is a Columbia **alumnus.**

among	*used to discuss more than two items*
between	*used to discuss two items only*

The property was divided **among** the five children.
It was a debate **between** the two major candidates.

amount	*used to refer to a quantity not individually countable*
number	*used to refer to items that can be counted individually*

There is a great **amount** of snow to be cleared.
A **number** of students will register for another English course.

annual	*yearly*
biannual	*twice a year* (also *semiannual*)
biennial	*once in two years* or *every two years*

It's time for my **annual** meeting with the tax accountant.
We pay our insurance on a **biannual** basis, in January and in July.
She gets a complete medical examination **biennially.**

anxious	*worried*
eager	*keenly desirous*

She was **anxious** about the opening of her new play.
We are **eager** to dine at that fine restaurant.

anyways	an incorrect form for *anyway*
anywheres	an incorrect form for *anywhere*

He can't be home that early **anyway.**
They couldn't find him **anywhere** in the gymnasium.

aren't I   used informally, but in formal usage *am I not* is correct.

Am I not a member in good standing?

around   should not be used in formal writing as a substitute for *about* or *near*

You live near [not **around**] my house.

as   not always as clear as *because, for,* or *since* (also see *like*)

He is going home, **because** he needs his sleep.

as	when used as a conjunction, is followed by a verb
like	when used as a preposition, is not followed by a verb

"Do **as** I say, not **as** I do," he said.
Try to behave **like** an adult.

as . . . as	used in an affirmative statement
so . . . as	used in a negative statement

He is **as** productive **as** anyone else in the film business.
She is not **so** cheerful today **as** she was yesterday.

as good as	used for comparisons, not to mean *practically*

This office is **as good as** the one next door.
You **practically** ran right into him.
(*not:* You **as good as** ran right into him.)

astonish	*to strike with sudden wonder*
surprise	*to catch unaware*

The power of his acting will **astonish** you.
Your appearance will **surprise** her.

at	should be avoided when it does not contribute to the meaning of an idea

Where do you live **at?** may be heard in informal usage, but Where do you live? is the correct form.

I'll call for you **about** nine o'clock. (*not:* **at about** nine o'clock.)

awfully	sometimes heard in informal usage. In formal usage, *very* is correct.

He is a very good player. (*not:* an **awfully** good player.)

a while	(noun) used after a preposition
awhile	(adverb) used in other cases

We watched television for **a while.**
We watched television **awhile.**

backward	(adjective) *slow in learning*
backward, backwards	both may be used as adverbs

When I tried to teach him how to dance, I saw that he was a **backward** pupil.
The boxer jogs **backward** at the end of every workout. (*or:* The boxer jogs **backwards.** . . .)

bad	(adjective) used after verbs that refer to the senses, such as *look, feel*
badly	(adverb) *greatly, in a bad manner*

We feel **bad** that you were not reappointed to the committee.
They performed the skit very **badly.**

been	the past participle of *to be,* used after helping verbs *have, has,* or *had*

being the *-ing* form of *to be,* usually used after helping verbs *is, am, are, was, were*

We have **been** close friends for twenty years.
Our friendship is **being** tested by this situation.

being as and **being that** should not be used in standard English. *Because* and *since* are preferable.

Since it is her birthday, he is taking her out this evening. (*not:* **Being as** it is her birthday. . . .)
Because the show starts early, we won't have time to eat supper together. (*not:* **Being that** the show. . . .)

Glossary of Usage: 1—Exercises
(Answers to the following exercises are on page 101.)

EXERCISE I Check [✓] the space provided if the sentence is correct; if there is an error in usage, write the correct form.

1. He stopped the bus alongside of the curb. _____

2. Whenever she forgets her homework, she makes up another alibi. _____

3. The volume contains three abridged novels. _____

4. He is the college's most successful alumna. _____

5. He wondered why the cat wanted to aggravate the parakeet. _____

6. When will she be alright? _____

7. The minister decided to present his alternate sermon. _____

8. He practices his jump shot most every day. _____

9. Rob said that he ain't coming to class next week. _____

10. It was difficult to count the amount of steps on the escalator. _____

11. The combination of pictures and brief description of the product made the advertisement very effective. _____

12. I would not purchase that car, because it needs alot of repairs. _____

13. We changed the day and time of the meeting for her advantage. _____

14. They are all ways attempting to improve themselves by taking adult-education courses in the evening. _____

15. He divided the ice cream between Abbie, Emily, Jordan, and Paul. _____

EXERCISE II Check [✓] the space provided if the sentence is correct; if there is an error in usage, write the correct form.

1. Is the new telephone as good as the old one was? _____

2. They ended the game around midnight. _____

3. As far as learning to drive was concerned, he was a very backwards student. _____

4. I am going upstairs to sleep a while. _____

5. "Am I not going to be allowed to present my case?" he asked. _____

6. Her uncle is an awfully famous actor. _____

7. They played as much music as possible in the three-hour period. _____

8. Stop doing that! You are acting just as a baby. _____

9. They said that they felt badly that they could not visit us today. _____

10. Where would you like to eat lunch at? _____

11. He will meet you anywheres you desire. _____

12. We been working out with the weights for fifteen minutes. _____

13. Next week we plan to surprise her with a luncheon in her honor. _____

14. He is anxious to go to the zoo with you. _____

15. Being as there are no more cookies, would you accept a piece of fruit? _____

Glossary of Usage: 2 _____

beside   *at the side of*
besides   *in addition to*

She stood **beside** him at the hearing.
Besides being a fabulous dancer, he is an outstanding singer.

better   *recovering*
well   *completely recovered*
better   used with the verb *had* to show desirability

She is **better** today than she was yesterday.
By next week, she will be **well**.
We had better [not **We better**] call the doctor immediately.

between you and I   an incorrect form, since the object of the preposition *between* should be the objective case *me*, not the subjective case *I*.

Between you and me, she is no longer doing her work very carefully.

both   *two, considered together*
each   *one of two or more*

Both of the youngsters ran in the race.
Each youngster received a certificate of merit.

bring *to carry toward the speaker*
take *to carry away from the speaker*

Bring the tape recorder over here.
Take your books and go home.

bunch used informally to describe *a group of people;* in formal usage *group* is preferred

A **group** of patients wanted to speak to the surgeon about his fees.

burst used in present and past tenses to mean *to explode* or *to break*
bust and busted incorrect forms of *burst*

Is she going to **burst** the bubble?
She laughed when the bubble **burst.**

but that sometimes heard in informal usage, but in formal usage *that* is correct

I never doubted **that** you would pass the examination.

can *being able to do something*
may *having permission to do something;* or *having the possibility* (used interchangeably with *might*)

I **can** eat two pieces of pie.
May I go with you?
I **may** be home late.

cannot seem
or can't seem sometimes used informally, but in formal usage *seems unable* is correct

My sister **seems unable** to learn how to divide fractions.

complexioned regularly used instead of *complected.*

The **fair-complexioned** woman carried an umbrella as protection against the noon-day sun.

consistently *in harmony*
constantly *regularly, steadily*

We reminded her to act **consistently** with the rules she had established.
We **constantly** reminded her to follow those guidelines.

continual *happening again and again at short intervals*
continuous *without interruption*

The **continual** beeping means that it is time for us to replace the battery.
The city was unprepared for two days of **continuous** snowfall.

could of an incorrect form of *could have,* which can be contracted to *could've* in informal usage

I wish I **could've** been there.
(*Better:* I wish that I **could have** been there.)

couple	*two*
several or **a few**	*more than two*

George and Gracie were a hilarious **couple.**
The show presented the work of **a few** very funny actors—Groucho Marx, W. C. Fields, Charlie Chaplin, and Buster Keaton.

data   the Latin plural of *datum,* meaning *information* (*data* is preferred with plural verbs and pronouns but is now acceptable in the singular)

We presented the **data** to the media.
These **data** were important.
(*or:* This **data** was important.)

did	the past tense of *to do*
done	the past participle of *to do*

I **did** my homework before I went out.
I **have done** my homework as the teacher suggested.

different than   often used informally, but in formal usage *different from* is correct

This painting is certainly **different from** that one.

disinterested	*impartial*
uninterested	*not interested*

The referee is supposed to be a **disinterested** official.
Since we were **uninterested** bystanders, we found the game very unexciting.

doesn't	a contraction of *does not* (third person singular)
don't	a contraction of *do not,* and is not a substitute for *doesn't*

The round peg **doesn't** fit in the square hole.
He **doesn't** play poker.
I **don't** drink beer.
They **don't** care for sushi.

doubt whether   often heard in informal usage, but *doubt that* is the correct form

I **doubt that** they will win the pennant again this year.

due to   sometimes used informally at the beginning of a sentence, but in formal usage *because of, on account of,* or similar expression is preferred

Because of [not **due to**] the President's speech, my favorite program will not be broadcast.
(*But:* My favorite program will not be broadcast **due to** the President's speech.)

each other	refers to *two persons*
one another	refers to *more than two persons*

Peter and Janine have known **each other** for fifteen years.
Four of the teammates have known **one another** since they played together in high school.

either . . . or	refers to *choices*
neither . . . nor	the negative form

Either Leigh **or** Angie will paint the bathroom.
Neither Leigh **nor** Angie will paint the bathroom.

else than	sometimes heard in informal usage; in formal usage *other than* is correct

It is a mistake to consider Benjamin Franklin nothing **other than** a politician.
The woman who knocked at the door was none **other than** my mother.

enthuse or enthused	should be avoided; *enthusiastic* is preferred

I was **enthusiastic** about going backstage after the play.

equally as good	an incorrect form; *equally good* or *just as good* is correct

This turntable is **just as good** as that one.
This turntable and that one are **equally good.**

etc.	the abbreviation for the Latin term *et cetera*, meaning *and so forth*, and *other things*. (In general, it is better to be specific and not use *etc.*)

She says that oranges, peaches, cherries, **etc.**, are healthful. (*etc.* is not
   preceded by *and*)
She says that oranges, peaches, cherries, **and other fruits** are healthful.

everyone	(pronoun) *all of the people in the context being discussed*
every one	used to refer to *each individual person or thing*

A silver medallion was presented to **everyone** at the convention.
The manager praised **every one** of the starting players.

every bit as	incorrect usage for *just as*

The blue chair is **just as** solid as the red chair.

ever so often	*frequently* or *repeatedly*
every so often	*occasionally* or *now and again*

Ever so often, at least once a week, I think about being back home in
   Indiana.
Because of my busy work schedule, I can only return home **every so often.**

expect	sometimes used incorrectly to mean *assume* or *presume*

I **assume** (not **expect**) that the cost of living index will be changed.

Glossary of Usage: 2—Exercises
(Answers to the following exercises are on page 102.)

EXERCISE I Check [✔] the space provided if the sentence is correct; if there is an error
in usage, write the correct form.

1. He consistently forgets to bring in his assignments. _____

2. She cannot seem to be on time for her appointments. _____

3. I hope you will take the battery to me as soon as possible. _____

4. We did not know the light-complected newcomer. _____

5. We know that both men will do a very good job. _____

6. Can I please leave the room for a few minutes? _____

7. She never doubted but that she would earn excellent grades in high school. _____

8. He was sitting besides me in the auditorium. _____

9. The continual barking of the dog was extremely annoying. _____

10. Between you and I, I think it is time for her to get a haircut. _____

11. I ate a couple of apples for lunch; both were delicious. _____

12. When the balloon busted, the infant began to cry hysterically. _____

13. You better do what she says if you want to get your allowance. _____

14. I wish I could of been with you when you were in California. _____

15. A bunch of tourists went to stand in line for tickets. _____

EXERCISE II Check [✓] the space provided if the sentence is correct; if there is an error in usage, write the correct form.

1. We enjoy sweet desserts, such as ice cream, cake, cookies, and etc. _____

2. Every one of the players was wearing a red sash around his waist. _____

3. Natalie, Cathy, Ellie, and Mary have sung with each other for many years. _____

4. This basketball is equally as good as the one you used to have. _____

5. Due to the heavy snowfall, the concert was postponed until Sunday. _____

6. We doubt whether the doctor is in yet. _____

7. Adam is every bit as hungry as Scott is. _____

8. She don't intend to go directly home after work. _____

9. We are really disinterested in attending the ballet next week. _____

10. Every so often, I enjoy playing poker with my friends. _____

11. My view of the situation is very different than yours. _____

12. It is too bad that neither Harold or Robert will be playing tonight. _____

13. They are not very enthused about coming to live in the city. _____

14. She claims that she done the entire crossword puzzle this morning.

_____

15. I expect that he was able to install the lock without too much difficulty.

_____

Glossary of Usage: 3 _____

fewer refers to items that can be counted
less refers to something viewed as a mass, not as a series of individual items

There are **fewer** books on the floor now that the shelves have been installed.
There was **less** snow this year than in the past two years.

finalized used to mean *concluded* or *completed*, usually in informal usage; in formal usage, *completed* is preferred

When the merger was **completed**, they drank champagne to celebrate.

flaunt *to make a display of*
flout *to show contempt, scorn*

She was foolish to **flaunt** her wealth by wearing a mink coat on such a hot evening.
If you **flout** his authority, you will be detained by the border patrol.

former *the first of two items*
latter *the second of two or more items*

The **former** half of the conference had been devoted to philosophical discussions.
The **latter** half of the conference was devoted to applications of theory.
Mr. Green and Ms. Scarlet attended the ball; the **former** wore a tuxedo, the **latter** a gown designed by a famous couturier.

good an adjective; *good* is often used informally as an adverb, but the correct word is *well*

She is a very **good** golfer.
She plays golf very **well**.

graduated followed by the preposition *from* when it indicates *completion of a course of study*
graduated also means *divided into categories* or *marked intervals*

We **graduated from** college two years ago. (*or:* We **were graduated from** college two years ago.)
I use a **graduated** measuring cup to calculate how much of each ingredient I need to make the pancake mix.

guess sometimes used informally to mean *think* or *suppose,* but it is incorrect in formal usage

I **think** [not **guess**] the speech was very successful.

habit   *an individual tendency to repeat a thing*
custom   *group habit*

What does she think of his **habit** of squeezing the toothpaste from the middle of the tube?

It is her family's **custom** to have pancakes for breakfast on Christmas Day.

had ought   an incorrect form for *ought* or *should*
hadn't ought   an incorrect form for *should not* or *ought not*

The women **ought** [*not* **had ought**] to let the men do the cooking.
She **ought not** [*not* **hadn't ought**] to have run in the marathon.
She **should not** [*not* **hadn't ought**] have run in the marathon.

hanged   used in reference to *a person*
hung   used in reference to *a thing*

The criminal was **hanged** in front of the courthouse.
The pictures were **hung** on every wall in the apartment.

have got   incorrect usage; *got* should be omitted

We **have** [*not* **have got**] a box of handkerchiefs.

healthful   (adjective) *giving health*
healthy   (adjective) *having health*

She is doing her best to stick to a **healthful** diet.
I am happy to report that the child is **healthy** now.

hisself   a misspelling of *himself*

He said that he did it **himself.**

human   adjective; used informally as a noun, but in formal usage *human beings* is correct

Is it true that love is a basic need of all **human beings?**
(*But:* Is it true that love is a basic **human** need?)

if   introduces a *condition*
whether   introduces a *choice*

We can go for a walk **if** it isn't too cold.
I asked **whether** we could go for a walk.

if it was   implies that *something might have been true in the past*
if it were   implies *doubt* or indicates *something that is contrary to fact*

If the cat **was** inside this morning, it is inside now.
If it were earlier, I would drive you to the shopping center.

imply   *to suggest* or *hint at* (the speaker *implies*)
infer   *to deduce* or *conclude* (the listener *infers*)

Did you mean to **imply** that he should have listened more carefully?
Should I **infer** that you are displeased?

in back of
in the back of
(or at the back of)

behind
in the rear of

The outlet is **in back of** the television set.
They sat **in the back of** the auditorium.

in regards to   an incorrect form for *in regard to*

I am calling **in regard to** your application.

instance where   sometimes used informally, but the correct term is *instance in which*

I can't think of one **instance in which** he ever helped us.

irregardless   an incorrect form for *regardless*

Regardless of the weather, the parade will begin at noon.

is when and **is where**   sometimes used informally, but in formal usage *occurs when* and *is a place where* are correct

The saddest scene **occurs when** the lovers are separated.
His favorite dining spot **is a place where** there are booths and checkered table cloths.

kind of and **sort of**   informal expressions that should be rephrased

By midnight he was **rather** (*not* **kind of**) sleepy.
She was **somewhat** (*not* **sort of**) bothered by the loud music.

kid   used informally to mean *child* (noun) or *to make fun of* (verb), but is incorrect in formal usage

We'll be happy to babysit for your **child** (*not* **kid**).
I don't always laugh when you **make fun of** (*not* **kid**) me.

learn   *to acquire knowledge*
teach   *to give knowledge*

Can an old dog **learn** new tricks?
I can **teach** you how to throw a curveball.

least   *smallest in degree* or *lowest in rank*
less   *smaller* or *lower*

That is the **least** enjoyable of all the books on the shelf.
The film version is **less** enjoyable than the original book.

leave   *to go away from* (a verb is not used with *leave*)
let   *to permit* (a verb is used with *let*)

We plan to **leave** town on the afternoon bus.
Let me purchase the tickets before we meet to have lunch.

lend	(verb) *to give to*
loan	(noun) *that which is given*
borrow	*to take from*

The bank will **lend** you $1000.
You were approved for a **loan** of $1000.
You said you want to **borrow** $1000 from the bank.

| liable | *responsible according to the law* |
| likely | *probable* |

The town government was **liable** for damages when she tripped on the broken sidewalk.
Unless the toddler gets a snack right now, he is **likely** to become cranky.

| libel | *a written and published statement injurious to a person's character* |
| slander | *a spoken statement* of the same sort |

The publisher claims that since he can prove the assertions in the book, he will not be exposed to a **libel** suit.
If you cannot prove those mean things you have been saying, you may be liable in a **slander** suit.

like	a preposition used to introduce a phrase
as if	used to introduce a clause (a subject and a verb)
as	a conjunction used to introduce a clause
like if	an incorrect form for *like, as,* or *as if*

It seems **like** a good idea.
It seems **as if** he thinks it is a good idea.
She did **as** she was ordered to do.

| many | refers to a *number* |
| much | refers to a *quantity* or *amount* |

How **many** pounds of feed are stored in the barn?
There is **much** feed stored in the barn.

| may of | an incorrect form for *may have* |
| might of | an incorrect form for *might have* |

She **may have** been at home, but I don't recall.
She **might have** gone home if we hadn't arrived.
(*Note:* Contractions of these terms are unacceptable in formal usage.)

Glossary of Usage: 3—Exercises

(Answers to the following exercises are on pages 102 and 103.)

EXERCISE 1 Check [✔] the space provided if the sentence is correct; if there is an error in usage, write the correct form.

1. We have got your letters in our mailbox. _____

2. They write good. _____

3. My former residence had a sunken living room. _____

4. Since the operation, he has been eating healthy foods. _____

5. I was pleased to see the students who had graduated college last year. _____

6. He hung the lamp from the hook in the center of the bedroom ceiling. _____

7. It was unpleasant to see how the private flaunted the captain's orders. _____

8. He cleaned the room all by hisself. _____

9. It is my custom to walk the dog at sunrise. _____

10. They are attempting to finalize the transaction at this very moment. _____

11. You hadn't ought to have written your name on the desk. _____

12. I guess that we will be able to appear in person to present our case. _____

13. It is terrible when they stop acting like humans and start acting like animals. _____

14. The second floor contains less light-switches and outlets than the architect recommended. _____

15. She wants to know if he is asleep yet. _____

EXERCISE II Check [✓] the space provided if the sentence is correct; if there is an error in usage, write the correct form.

1. The funniest line in the play is when the third act is nearly over. _____

2. We're not liable to go out with you tonight. _____

3. They will gladly loan you their typewriter for as long as you need it. _____

4. She treats her kitten like if it were a human being. _____

5. I am going to carry an umbrella, irregardless of what the weatherman predicts. _____

6. I hope that you will let us visit you once the matter has been settled. _____

7. Does your kid attend religious school in the afternoon? _____

8. In regards to your trip, it would be best for you to make a reservation right now. _____

9. Based on what he wrote in the magazine article, she is suing him for slander. _____

10. The air-conditioning system is in the back of those bushes. _____

11. The doctor wants to know exactly how much pounds you would like to lose on this diet. _____

12. Because of the leaks, he is less eager to water the lawn while you are away. _____

13. We are certain that your guide will be able to learn you a few important things. _____

14. Should he imply from your comments that you are being promoted? _____

15. They might of left their reports in your mailbox. _____

Glossary of Usage: 4 _____

maybe   *perhaps, possibly* (adverb)
may be   shows *possibility* (verb)

> **Maybe** they are in the restaurant.
> They **may be** in the restaurant.

mighty   *powerful* or *great;* should not be used in formal writing to mean *very*

> He was **very** (*not* **mighty**) hungry.

media   the Latin plural of *medium;* it refers to a *means of mass communication* or *artistic expression* and is used with a plural verb

> The news **media** have retained their freedom.
> What is the most significant achievement of the **medium** of television?

must of   incorrect form for *must have;* a contraction of this term is unacceptable in formal usage)

> You **must have** forgotten to return the book when it was due.

myself   used as an *intensifier* if the subject of the verb is *I*
myself   not correct when used instead of *I* or *me*

> I bought **myself** [*not* **me**] a new sweater.
> My father and **I** [*not* **myself**] went to the show.
> They asked my mother and **me** [*not* **myself**] for assistance.

nice used informally to mean *pleasing, good, fine* but a more exact, less over-used word is preferred

We had a **good** [*not* **nice**] time at the party.
She prepared a **delicious** [*not* **nice**] meal.

nowheres incorrect usage for *nowhere*

The package is **nowhere** in the house.

off of sometimes used informally, but *off* is correct in formal usage

The car was taken **off** [*not* **off of**] the auction list.

okay (O.K.) used informally, but is to be avoided in formal writing

This essay is **acceptable** [*not* **okay**].

on account of an incorrect form for *because*

He did not pass the course **because** [*not* **on account of**] he failed every examination.

oral *spoken*
verbal *expressed in words,* either spoken or written

She spoke clearly when presenting the **oral** report to the class.
During the war, he developed a code to transfer **verbal** messages into mathematical patterns.

outdoor *an adjective*
outdoors *an adverb*

We're going to have a drink at the **outdoor** bar.
In warm weather, they set up the bar **outdoors.**

owing to used informally, but in formal usage *because* is preferred

Because it is an informal event, we will not be wearing business suits.

people *a united or collective group of individuals*
persons *individuals that are separate and unrelated*

The **people** voted to establish a new council.
The police spotted four **persons** hitchhiking last night.

per a Latin term used mainly in business: *per diem* (by the day), *per hour* (by the hour)
as per used informally to mean *according to* or *by the;* avoid this term in formal writing

According to [*not* **as per**] your request, I have paid the bill.

plan on used informally, but in formal usage *plan to* is correct

I **plan to go** [*not* **plan on going**] to the concert.

plenty (noun) *abundance;* incorrect as an adverb or adjective

There are **plenty** of flowers on the tree.
The auditorium is very **full** [*not* **plenty full**].

prefer that than	incorrect form for *prefer that to*

We **prefer that to** any other couch in the showroom.

put in	incorrect form for *spend, make,* or *devote*

Her lawyer will **devote** [*not* **put in**] many hours this week to preparing the brief.
He should **make** [*not* **put in**] a brief appearance at the fundraiser.

quit	sometimes used informally to mean *stop,* but in formal usage *stop* is preferred

I hope he will **stop** [*not* **quit**] bothering us.

quite	used to mean *very* in informal usage, but in formal usage *very* is preferred

The article was **very** [*not* **quite**] informative.

quite a few	used to mean *many* in informal usage, but in formal usage *many* is preferred

The owner of the building has sold **many** [*not* **quite a few**] apartments this month.

read where	an incorrect form for *read that*

I **read that** he is favored to win a special award for his excellent new documentary film.

real	an incorrect form for *really* or *very*

He is a **really** good cook. (Better: He is a **very good** cook.)
He performed **really well** on the test.

reason is because	used informally in speech, but in formal usage *the reason is that* is correct

The reason I prefer his painting **is that** [*not* **because**] it makes more sense to me.
(*Or:* I prefer his painting **because** it makes more sense to me.)

refer back/report back	since *re* means *back* or *again,* the word *back* is redundant and should be omitted

The President was asked to **refer** to his notes.
Did his advisors **report** to the President as often as necessary?

repeat again	redundant; *again* should be omitted

I hope they will **repeat** the phone number.

respectfully **respectively**	*with respect and decency* *as relating to each, in the order given*

We listened **respectfully** to the sermon.

President Smith and Vice-President Jones are, **respectively,** the most powerful government leaders.

run   used informally to mean *conduct, manage,* but in formal usage *conduct* or a similar word is preferred

The computer system helps us to **manage** [*not* **run**] our business in a more efficient manner.

said   sometimes used in business or law to mean *the* or *this;* in formal usage, *the* or *this* is correct

said   also used incorrectly to mean *told someone*

When **the** defendant [*not* **said** defendant] was arraigned in court, the judge made a serious error.

The judge **told** me [*not* **said**] to file another affidavit.

same as   an incorrect form for *in the same way as* or *just as*

Was the district attorney's son treated in the same way as any other suspect?

says   third-person-singular present tense of *say*

said   past tense of *say* (*goes* or *went* should not be used instead of *says* or *said*)

She **says** what she means.
She **said** what she meant.

Glossary of Usage: 4—Exercises

(Answers to the following exercises are on page 103.)

EXERCISE I   Check [✔] the space provided if the sentence is correct; if there is an error in usage, insert the correct form.

1. When his grades dropped, the basketball player was taken off of the starting team. _____

2. The report is okay so far, but it should be more detailed. _____

3. Judging by the level of the water, it must of been raining all week. _____

4. I may be able to visit you in London next year. _____

5. There is nowheres I would rather be than here. _____

6. Owing to the pessimistic weather forecast, we decided to cancel the expedition. _____

7. The company appreciated their excellent oral presentation. _____

8. The media is providing comprehensive coverage of the hearings. _____

9. The opera will be performed outdoor in the park. _____

10. My friend and myself repaired the fence while you were away. _____

11. When interviewed on the evening news, he appeared mighty intelligent.

_____

12. They are some of my favorite persons. _____

13. We were late on account of the traffic jams. _____

14. He maybe one of the best poets in the world. _____

15. She had a very nice experience at the library today. _____

EXERCISE II Check [✓] the space provided if the sentence is correct; if there is an error in usage, insert the correct form.

1. I read in the magazine where the product is being discounted in drug-stores. _____

2. She will run the company while her father is on vacation. _____

3. They put in an appearance at the party in order to appease their family.

_____

4. If the exercises are confusing, you will be able to refer back to the lists.

_____

5. Do you prefer that to any other possibility? _____

6. The reason I am going downstairs is because I want to pick up the mail.

_____

7. They are a real serious group of students. _____

8. We watched respectfully as the flag was lowered. _____

9. By the time the job had been completed, they were plenty tired.

_____

10. She has been raised same as her brother was raised. _____

11. The report strongly advises you to quit eating so many dairy products.

_____

12. He was pleased when his friend went, "I've got an extra ticket for you."

_____

13. Do you plan on going to the football game? _____

14. When will the program be repeated again? _____

15. It was quite interesting to read the review of her book. _____

Glossary of Usage: 5 _____

saw the past tense of *to see*
seen the past participle of *to see*

I **saw** you in the library yesterday.
I have **seen** you in the library every day this week.

seem used informally in the expressions *I can't seem to* and *I don't seem to,* but in formal usage the sentence should be rephrased

I **can't find** [*not* **can't seem to find**] a parking spot.

seldom ever used informally, but in formal usage *ever* is redundant and should be omitted, or *if* should be inserted

They **seldom** drive to New York City on Sunday.
They **seldom if ever** drive to New York City on Sunday.

shall used with *I* and *we* in formal usage; informally, *I will (would)* may be used

will used with *you, he, she, it, they;* when an emphatic statement is intended, the rule is reversed

I **shall** meet you at the attorney's office.
We **shall** dine at eight o'clock.
I definitely **will** help you move your furniture.
They **shall** not pass.

shape incorrectly used to mean *state* or *condition*

Since he exercises regularly, he is in very good **condition.** (*not* **shape**)

should of an incorrect form for *should have,* which can be contracted to *should've* in informal usage

You **should've** played bingo with us last night.
Better: You **should have** played bingo with us last night.

sink down sometimes heard in informal usage, but *down* is redundant and should be omitted

Did you see him **sink** into the quicksand and disappear?

some time *a segment of time*
sometime *at an indefinite time in the future*
sometimes *occasionally*

They need **some time** to repair the tire.
The car will be ready **sometime** tomorrow.
We **sometimes** meet to discuss her child's progress.

stayed *remained*
stood *took* or *remained in an upright position or erect*

He **stayed** in bed until the doctor told him to go for a walk.
She **stood** in front of the store for twenty minutes.

still more yet redundant; *yet* should be omitted

There are **still more** patients to be examined.

sure   used informally to mean *surely* or *certainly,* but in formal usage *surely* or *certainly* is preferred

You **certainly** are intelligent!
Since the traffic is so heavy, we will **surely** be late.

testimony   *information given orally*
evidence   *information given orally or in writing; an object which is presented as proof*

She gave **testimony** to the county clerk.
They presented the gun as **evidence** of his guilt.

than any   used informally in a comparison, but in formal usage *than any other* is preferred

She is younger **than any other** child in the play group.

the both   used informally, but in formal usage *the* should be omitted

I hope to meet **both** of you again in the near future.

their   in informal usage, often appears in the construction, ''Anyone can forget *their* umbrella,'' but since *anyone* takes a singular personal pronoun, *his* is the correct form

Anyone can forget **his** umbrella.

theirselves   an incorrect form for *themselves*

They agreed to drive **themselves** home right after the lesson.

them   the objective case of *they;* it is not used instead of *those* (the plural of *that*) before a noun

How do you like **those** [*not* **them**] odds?

try and   sometimes used informally instead of *try to,* but in formal usage *try to* is correct

From now on, we are going to **try to** behave more appropriately in the theater.

unbeknownst to   incorrect form for *without the knowledge of*

Without the knowledge of [*not* **Unbeknownst to**] his parents, John had a wild party at his home last week.

upwards of   an incorrect form for *more than*

His personal library contains **more than** [*not* **upwards of**] two thousand volumes.

valuable   *of great worth*
valued   *held in high regard*
invaluable   *priceless*

Her gold watch is **valuable.**
He is a highly **valued** colleague.
A good name is an **invaluable** possession.

wait on   sometimes used informally, but in formal usage *wait for* is correct.

I waited **for** [*not* **waited on**] you for nearly thirty-five minutes.

which   refers to *things,* not *people*
who   refers to *people*
that   refers to *things* or *people*

I have read all the articles **which** he has written.
They asked for the name of the woman **who** had waited on them.
I have read all the articles **that** he has written.
They asked for the name of the woman **that** had waited on them.

while   unacceptable for *and, but, whereas, though,* or *although*

He resides in New York, **whereas** [*not* **while**] she resides in London.
Although [*not* **While**] we can understand his viewpoint, we cannot condone the use of violence.

who is, who am   note these constructions:

It is I **who am** the most experienced.
It is he **who is** . . .
It is he or I **who am** . . .
It is I or he **who is** . .
It is he and I **who are** . . .

who, whom   to determine whether to use *who* or *whom* (without grammar rules):

(Who, Whom) do you think should receive the extra dessert?

Step One: Change the *who-whom* part of the sentence to its natural order:

Do you think **(who, whom)** should receive the extra dessert?

Step Two: Substitute *he* for *who,* and *him* for *whom:*

Do you think **(he, him)** should receive the extra dessert?

Step Three: Since *he* would be used in this instance, the correct form is the subjective, not the objective case:

Who do you think should receive the extra dessert?

whoever, whomever   see *who, whom* above

Pass the salad to **whoever** wants it. (subject of verb *wants*)
Pass to **whomever** you see downfield. (object of preposition *to*)

win   you *win* a game
beat   you *beat* another player

If I jump one more piece, I will **win** the game of checkers.
I can **beat** [*not* **win**] him in a race.

(Beat is incorrect usage for *swindle:* The con artist **swindled** the woman out of her savings.)

without   incorrect usage for *unless*

They will not receive a good education **unless** [*not* **without**] they work hard for it.

worst kind
and worst way   incorrect usages for terms such as *very badly* or *extremely*

The city is **badly** in need of more policemen. (*not:* The city **needs more policemen in the worst way**.)

would of   an incorrect form for *would have,* which can be contracted to *would've* in informal usage

I **would've** played bingo with you last night. (Better: I **would have** played bingo with you last night.)

Glossary of Usage: 5—Exercises
(Answers to the following exercises are on page 104.)

EXERCISE I   Check [✔] the space provided if the sentence is correct; if there is an error in usage, insert the correct form.

1. She sounded very nervous as she presented her testimony. _____

2. Sometime when he is expecting a package, he puts up a sign for the mailman. _____

3. Your brother shall do his homework tomorrow. _____

4. They donated more money than any members of the board. _____

5. I seldom see him on campus. _____

6. The both of you are being seated in the front row of the auditorium. _____

7. They should of visited their grandmother last week. _____

8. The fishing rod will sink down to the bottom of the pond. _____

9. There are still more essays yet to be revised. _____

10. He can't seem to locate the letter. _____

11. Anyone who is going to attend the Tuesday performance will be able to pick up their ticket on Monday. _____

12. On our trip to Maine we plan to spend sometime with our grandparents in Bar Harbor. _____

13. I seen my former teacher in the shopping center last night. _____

14. For a man of his age, he is in very good shape. _____

15. They sure made a great hit with the audience. _____

EXERCISE II   Check [✓] the space provided if the sentence is correct; if there is an error in usage, insert the correct form.

1. I have been waiting on you for forty-five minutes. _____

2. The students won the faculty in the volleyball competition. _____

3. He'll pass the ball to whoever reaches the goal line first. _____

4. We won't fix the buzzer without you pay us in advance. _____

5. The demonstration was attended by upwards of 50,000 people. _____

6. Unbeknownst to the skipper, the ship changed its course. _____

7. She is a highly valuable friend. _____

8. He is the man which won the lottery last month. _____

9. We want to purchase an automobile in the worst way. _____

10. Will you try and get your room cleaned up by lunchtime? _____

11. You should have stood in bed! _____

12. She will return them books to the library on Monday. _____

13. If I had had the time, I would of gone to the park this morning. _____

14. After inviting forty guests to the party, they cooked a lavish meal all by theirselves. _____

15. My car is gray while yours is red. _____

Cliches

A cliché is an expression that seems tired and worn out because of its frequent use. As a result, the effectiveness and originality that it once possessed are no longer present and all its freshness is gone. Perhaps the first time someone wrote "busy as a bee" or "blushing bride" the expressions were clever and well-turned, but by now we are so used to hearing these phrases that all the sparkle is gone and they have become clichés. The careful writer will try his best to avoid using these trite phrases. However, we are all aware that from time to time one may creep into our writing, *sad to relate*. Oops!

A List of Clichés:

abreast of the times

acid test

after all is said and done

agony of suspense

all in all

all work and no play

along these lines

as luck would have it

at a loss for words

at one fell swoop

at the tender age of

bathed in tears

beat a hasty retreat
beauties of nature
better half (wife)
better late than never
bitter end
blood is thicker than water
blushing bride
bolt from the blue
brave as a lion
bright and early
brown as a berry
budding genius
burning the midnight oil
busy as a bee
by and large
by leaps and bounds
center of attraction
checkered career
clear as crystal
clinging vine
cold as ice
conspicuous by its absence
cool as a cucumber
covers a multitude of sins
deadly earnest
deep, dark secret
die laughing
doomed to disappointment
drastic action
easier said than done
equal to the occasion
eyes like stars
fair sex
favor with a selection
few and far between
fiber of his (my) being
filthy lucre
footprints on the sands of time
force of circumstances
generous to a fault
goes without saying
goodly number
good points
green with envy
hanging in the balance
heartfelt thanks
heated argument
heavy as lead
herculean efforts
hungry as bears
ignorance is bliss
in great profusion

in the last analysis
institution of higher learning
it stands to reason
last but not least
last straw
life's little ironies
lion's share
mantle of snow
meets the eye
method in his madness
motley throng
neat as a pin
needs no introduction
never got to first base
nipped in the bud
none the worse for wear
on the ball
paramount issue
partake of refreshment
poor but honest
powers that be
promising future
pure and simple
quick as a flash
rear its ugly head
reigns supreme
riot of color
rotten to the core
sad to relate
sadder but wiser
sea of faces
self-made man
short but sweet
sigh of relief
simple life
skeleton in the closet
slow but sure
snow-capped mountains
soul of honor
steady as a rock
straight from the shoulder
strong, silent man
strong as a lion
struggle for existence
sturdy as an oak
sweat of his brow
take my word for it
thereby hangs a tale
the time of my life
the weaker sex
the worse for wear
this day and age

thunderous applause	wee, small hours
time marches on	wend his way
tiny tots	wheel of fortune
tired but happy	white as a sheet
too funny for words	white as snow
untiring efforts	with bated breath
veritable mine of information	words fail me
view with alarm	work like a dog
walk of life	wreathed in smiles

Idioms

Each language has phrases or expressions peculiar to itself, its own way of expressing an idea. Sometimes these idioms do not follow rules of logic or conform to standard grammatical principles. Custom and local usage often dictate the construction of the idiomatic phrase. Special care must be taken to use the correct preposition in the idiomatic phrase.

List of Idioms

abound in	(or *with*) This letter **abounds in** mistakes.
accompanied by	(a person) The salesman was **accompanied by** the buyer.
accompanied with	(a present) He **accompanied** the closing of the contract with a gift.
acquiesce in	The executives were compelled to **acquiesce in** the director's policy.
acquit of	The manager was **acquitted of** the charges against him.
adept in	(or *at*) He is **adept in** typing.
agree to	(an offer) The firm **agrees to** your payment in settlement of the claim.
agree upon	(or *on*) (a plan) We must **agree upon** the best method.
agree with	(a person) I **agree with** the doctor.
allergic to	The patient is **allergic to** dust.
angry about	(an event, situation) I am very **angry about** the high unemployment rate.
angry at	(a thing, an animal) The child is **angry at** his stuffed animals.
angry with	(a person) We were **angry with** the careless attendant. (*Mad* is used informally to mean *angry,* but, more properly, it means *insane.*)
appropriate for	(meaning *suitable to*) The gown is also **appropriate for** a dinner dance.
available for	(a purpose) The specialist is **available for** a consultation now.
available to	(a person) What course of action is **available to** you at this time?
averse to	The President is **averse to** increasing his staff.
cognizant of	He was not **cognizant of** dissension among the workers.

coincide with	Your wishes **coincide with** mine in this situation.
commensurate with	What you earn will be **commensurate with** the amount of effort you apply to your task.
compare to	(shows similarity between things that have different forms) In one sonnet, Shakespeare **compares** a woman's hair **to** wire.
compare with	(shows similarity or difference between things of like form) The assignment was to **compare** Thoreau's essays **with** Emerson's.
compatible with	The ideas of the section manager should be **compatible with** those of the buyer.
comply with	If you do not wish to **comply with** his request, please notify him at once.
conducive to	The employer's kindness is **conducive to** good work.
conform to	(or *with*) The average person **conforms to** the vote of the majority.
conversant with	We need a salesman who is fully **conversant with** what he is selling.
desirous of	We are not **desirous of** a price increase.
different from	This new machine is **different from** the old one.
differ from	(a thing in appearance) A coat **differs from** a cape.
differ with	(an opinion) I **differ with** your views on public affairs.
dissuade from	She will **dissuade** him **from** making that investment.
employed at	(a definite salary) The student aide is **employed at** the minimum wage.
employed in	(certain work) His brother is **employed in** reading blueprints.
envious of	Some of the employees are **envious of** his good fortune.
identical to	(or *with*) These stockings are **identical to** those I showed you last week.
in accordance with	Act **in accordance with** the regulations.
infer from	I **infer from** his remarks that he is dissatisfied.
in search of	He set out **in search of** fame and fortune.
listen to	We will **listen to** the broadcast this evening.
necessary to	Your help is **necessary to** the success of the project.
oblivious of	(or *to*) The typist is **oblivious of** the construction noise outside.
opposite to	(or *from*) (meaning *contrary*) Your viewpoint is **opposite to** mine.
pertinent to	Your comment is not really **pertinent to** the discussion.
plan to	Do you **plan to** go to the play tonight?
prefer to	She **prefers** silk **to** polyester.
prior to	You will receive a deposit **prior to** the final settlement.
required of	The letter states what is **required of** you.
stay at	He wants to **stay at** home this evening.
vie with	The salesmen are **vying with** one another for this week's prize.

Mixed Metaphors _____

A *metaphor* is a figure of speech that implies a comparison. Unlike a *simile,* which is a comparison using *like* or *as* as indicators, the metaphor does not use indicators. If used correctly, metaphors and similes may add vividness and color to writing, but if used incorrectly, the opposite effect may result and the writing can become trite and even silly. The writer should be careful to use metaphors that are appropriate to the style of the essay and logical in construction. If the logic is faulty, a *mixed metaphor* may result.

Good: James Joyce once wrote, "My body was like a harp and her words and gestures like fingers running upon wires."
Poor: The lovely ocean beat against the shore with its strident voice clawing at the sands.

Good: The ballet dancer floated through space, her feet tracing arabesques on the stage.
Poor: The ballet dancer's feet moved with hushed grace, flapping their wings with flowery movements.

Wordiness _____

Wordiness involves needless repetition of words or phrases which do not add meaning or give called-for emphasis to the sentence. Very often a sentence can be made more effective by eliminating needless repetitions or *redundancies* and expressing the thought in a more compact way. Wordiness often involves errors in usage.

_____ Examples of Wordiness

Repeating meaning:

the honest truth
blue in color
same exact
the month of June
new innovation
pie a la mode with ice cream
consensus of opinion

Repeating words:

In which pool did he swim **in?**
From what school did you graduate **from?**
At which position are you working **at?**

Unnecessary use of pronouns after a noun:

My aunt **she** is a social worker.
The boy and girl **they** will both be here.
The teacher **he** gave a difficult assignment.

Unnecessary expressions:

> In my opinion, I believe that . . . (I believe that . . .)
> In the event of an emergency . . . (In an emergency, . . .)
> On the possibility that it may . . . (Since it may . . .)

Wordy phrases:

> close to the point of (close to)
> have need for (need)
> with a view to (to)
> in view of the fact that (because)
> give consideration to (consider)
> means to imply (imply)
> disappear from view (disappear)
> in this day and age (today)
> the issue in question (issue)
> come in contact with (meet)

Answers _____

CONFUSING WORD GROUPS: 1

I.
1. lose
2. dessert
3. passed
4. altogether
5. lie
6. sit
7. effect
8. stationery
9. all ready
10. than
11. advise
12. into
13. weather
14. accept
15. principal

II.
1. There
2. ✔
3. its
4. ✔
5. supposed
6. quiet
7. whose
8. through
9. rise
10. an
11. used
12. ✔
13. it's, let's
14. you're
15. affect

CONFUSING WORD GROUPS: 2

I.
1. capital
2. morale
3. anteroom
4. no
5. elude
6. cloth
7. course
8. personal
9. knew
10. build
11. later
12. complement
13. allusion
14. seem
15. conscious

II.
1. ✔
2. clothe
3. seen
4. seize
5. ✔
6. farther
7. decent
8. ✔
9. chose
10. breath
11. ✔
12. sight
13. find
14. angle
15. ✔

CONFUSING WORD GROUPS: 3

I.
1. prophecy
2. clique
3. emigrate
4. idol
5. discomfort
6. expend
7. dual
8. incidence
9. averse
10. formally
11. disperse
12. forte
13. proceed
14. excess
15. faze

II. 1. confident
2. prophesy
3. ✔
4. discomfort
5. fair
6. exceed
7. ✔
8. elicit
9. adapt
10. imminent
11. patience
12. canvas
13. lightning
14. ✔
15. ✔

GLOSSARY OF USAGE: 1

I. 1. alongside the curb
2. another excuse
3. ✔
4. alumnus
5. to annoy the
6. all right
7. ✔
8. almost every day
9. he isn't (or: is not)
10. number of steps
11. ✔
12. a lot
13. her benefit
14. are always
15. divided . . . among

II. 1. ✔
2. about midnight
3. very backward
4. sleep awhile
5. ✔
6. a very famous
7. ✔
8. just like a
9. felt bad
10. delete at
11. anywhere
12. We have been
13. ✔
14. is eager to
15. Since there

GLOSSARY OF USAGE: 2

I.
1. constantly forgets
2. she seems unable to
3. bring the battery
4. light-complexioned
5. ✔
6. May I
7. delete but
8. beside me
9. continuous barking
10. Between you and me
11. ✔
12. balloon burst
13. You had better
14. could have
15. group of tourists

II.
1. delete and
2. ✔
3. with one another
4. just as good
5. Because of the heavy (or: The concert was postponed . . . due to. . . .)
6. doubt that the doctor
7. is just as
8. She doesn't
9. uninterested in attending
10. ✔
11. different from
12. neither . . . nor
13. enthusiastic about
14. she did
15. I assume

GLOSSARY OF USAGE: 3

I.
1. delete got
2. write well
3. ✔
4. healthful foods
5. graduated from
6. ✔
7. flouted the captain's
8. himself
9. my habit
10. to conclude
11. You should not have
12. I suppose
13. like human beings
14. fewer light-switches
15. whether he is asleep

II.
1. occurs when
2. not likely
3. lend you
4. as if
5. regardless of
6. ✔
7. your child
8. In regard to
9. for libel
10. is in back of
11. how many
12. ✔
13. to teach you
14. he infer
15. might have

GLOSSARY OF USAGE: 4

I.
1. delete of
2. report is acceptable [or a similar word] so far
3. must have
4. ✔
5. is nowhere
6. Because of the
7. ✔
8. media are
9. performed outdoors
10. friend and I
11. very intelligent
12. favorite people
13. late because of
14. he may be
15. a very good [or enjoyable, or a similar word] experience

II.
1. read . . . that the product
2. will manage
3. made an appearance
4. delete back
5. ✔
6. The reason is that (or: I am going downstairs, because. . . .)
7. really serious
8. ✔
9. very tired
10. raised in the same way as
11. stop eating
12. friend said
13. plan to go
14. delete again
15. very interesting

GLOSSARY OF USAGE: 5

I.
1. ✔
2. Sometimes when
3. will do
4. than any other members
5. ✔
6. delete The (Both . . .)
7. should have
8. delete down
9. delete yet
10. delete seem to
11. pick up his (or her) ticket
12. some time
13. I saw
14. good condition
15. they certainly (or surely)

II.
1. waiting for you
2. beat the faculty
3. ✔
4. unless you pay
5. more than 50,000
6. Without the knowledge of the skipper
7. highly valued
8. man who
9. replace in the worst way with very badly (or: We are eager to purchase an automobile.)
10. try to
11. have stayed
12. those books
13. would have
14. themselves
15. but, not while (or add a semicolon and delete while)

CHAPTER 4

Spelling

Recently a survey was taken in a college freshman English class. Students were asked to list their greatest problems in writing. When the results were tabulated, the biggest problem that they had indicated was *spelling*.

Yet when their professor was asked to cite what he considered to be the area of greatest weakness among his students, spelling was not on the list.

Obviously the students and the instructor had different perceptions. Follow-up discussions indicated that student writers are worried about their ability to spell correctly—perhaps more than they need to be. As a result, they avoid using certain words and even "freeze" on certain phrases. This hurts the entire writing process and interrupts the smooth flowing of ideas.

Five Spelling Pitfalls

Pitfall One

When does *i* come before *e* and when does the *e* come before the *i*?

RULE: *I* before *e*,
Except after *c*,
Or when sounded like *ay*,
As in *neighbor* and *weigh*.

Exceptions: 1. Words in which both vowels are pronounced use *ie* after *c* as in *society*

2. Words with a *shen* sound use *ie* after *c* as in *sufficient*

3. Other exceptions: *either* or *neither, foreign, height, seize, their, weird*

Pitfall Two

When adding suffixes such as *-ing* and *-ed*, when do I double final consonants?

RULE: When a word of *one* syllable ends in *one* consonant preceded by *one* vowel, then double the consonant before:

-ing
-ed
-er or **-ar**

Examples: bar   ba**rr**ed
beg   be**gg**ar
stop   sto**pp**ing

Note: *This applies only if the suffix added begins with a vowel.*

RULE: In a word of more than one syllable, listen very carefully. Pronounce the word aloud. If the accent is on the final syllable, and that syllable ends in one consonant preceded by one vowel, the final consonant is doubled. If the accent is not on the final syllable, do not double the consonant. *This only applies if the suffix begins with a vowel.*

Examples: begin   beginning
prefer   preferred
But: worship   worshiping
color   coloring

When the suffix begins with a consonant, do not double the last letter of the word.

Examples: commit   commitment
prefer   preferment

Pitfall Three

When is the silent *e* at the end of a word dropped?

RULE: Drop the silent *e* at the end of a word before a suffix beginning with a vowel. Keep the silent *e* before adding a suffix beginning with a consonant.

Examples: shine   shining
hope   hopeful

Exceptions: Words ending in *c* or *g* maintain the *e* before endings beginning with a vowel. This is done to maintain the original sound of the *c* or the *g*. Verbs ending in *ie* often drop the *e* and change the *i* to *y* before joining with *ing*.

Examples: changeable
peaceable
dying

Exceptions: Keep the *e* to keep the meaning clear

shoe + ing = shoeing
toe + ing = toeing

Exceptions: Before *able,* sometimes the *e* is retained

love + able = loveable
move + able = moveable

Exceptions: There are always exceptions!

true + ly = truly
due + ly = duly
argue + ment = argument
whole + ly = wholly

Pitfall Four

What do I do with a word ending in *y* before I add an ending?

RULE: Change the *y* to *i* if the letter *before* the *y* is a consonant. Keep the final *y* if the letter before the final *y* is a vowel.

Examples: busy   busily
cloudy   cloudiness
donkey   donkeys
stay   staying

Exceptions: Keep the *y* in words like the following:

babyish
carrying
studying

Pitfall Five

How can I spell suffixes correctly when they all sound alike?

RULE: *-able* or *-ible*?

If you can form a word ending in *-ation* or *-ance,* choose *-able*.

irritable (irritation)
durable (duration)
variable (variance or variation)

If you can form a related word that ends in *-tion* or *-sion,* choose *-ible*.

admissible (admission)
digestible (digestion)

RULE: *-ceed, -cede,* or *-sede*?

1. Only one word ends in *-sede—supersede*

2. Only three words end in *-ceed—exceed, proceed, succeed*

3. All other words end in *-cede*

RULE: *-ful* or *full*?

The only word that ends in full is *full*. All other words end in *ful*.

Ten Special Spelling Hints

1. Keep a record of words that you misspell. Be certain that you spell the words correctly on your list. Review the list periodically.

2. Always proofread your essays to discover careless or inadvertent misspellings. Sometimes these misspellings are simply slips of the pen.

3. Consult a dictionary if you are not certain about a correct spelling.

4. Do not allow mispronunciation to cause you to misspell. Often your ear is an excellent guide for good spelling, but there are times that you may be pronouncing a word incorrectly and either adding extra sounds or omitting sounds.

Examples:

February	*not*	Febuary
athlete	*not*	athelete
government	*not*	goverment
modern	*not*	modren
everyone	*not*	everone
gratitude	*not*	graditure

5. Study the list of words that confuse you. Distinguish between words of similar sound.

Examples:

affect	effect
were	where
forth	fourth
sole	soul
wholly	holy

6. Do not drop a final *l* when you add *-ly*.

Examples:

real	+	ly	=	really
formal	+	ly	=	formally

7. Be careful when you add a prefix to the stem of the word that you don't omit a letter or add a letter.

Examples:

ir	+	rational	=	irrational
mis	+	spell	=	misspell
dis	+	agree	=	disagree
mis	+	spent	=	misspent
dis	+	appear	=	disappear

8. Use the apostrophe correctly when forming contractions.

Examples:

do not	=	don't
could not	=	couldn't
they are	=	they're
it is	=	it's

9. Be careful not to use the apostrophe when you form the ordinary plural of nouns.

Examples: The bo**ys** are here.
not: The bo**ys'** are here.
not: The boy**'s** are here.

10. Use capital letters only when required. It is just as incorrect to spell a word with a capital letter when it is not needed as it is to omit a needed capital letter.

Spelling Exercises

(Answers to the following exercises are on pages 111 to 113.)

EXERCISE I Fill in the missing letters (ie or ei).

1. f____ld

2. conc____t

3. sl____gh

4. v_____n

5. c_____ling

6. n_____ce

7. sc_____ntific

8. s_____zure

9. consc_____ntious

10. anc_____nt

EXERCISE II   Add the ending to the following words:

1. fib + ing   = _____

2. beg + ing   = _____

3. control + able   = _____

4. commit + ment   = _____

5. color + ful   = _____

6. stop + ing   = _____

7. big + est   = _____

8. quit + ing   = _____

9. rob + ing   = _____

10. glad + ly   = _____

EXERCISE III   Add the suffix indicated to the following words:

1. bride + al   = _____

2. force + ible   = _____

3. force + ful   = _____

4. imagine + ary   = _____

5. hope + less   = _____

6. true + ly   = _____

7. remove + ing   = _____

8. life + like   = _____

9. like + ly   = _____

10. service + able   = _____

EXERCISE IV   Add endings to the following words:

1. fly + er   = _____

2. rely + able   = _____

3. noisy + ly   = _____

4. worry + some   = _____

   5. betray + ing = _____

   6. healthy + est = _____

   7. mercy + ful = _____

   8. study + ing = _____

   9. easy + est = _____

   10. study + ed = _____

EXERCISE V If a word is misspelled, correct it. If it is spelled correctly, make a check [✓] in the space provided.

   1. beautiful _____

   2. collectable _____

   3. convertable _____

   4. irritible _____

   5. bountiful _____

   6. commendible _____

   7. preceed _____

   8. procede _____

   9. sucede _____

   10. intersede _____

EXERCISE VI The following three spelling drills are based on words drawn from several lists of "spelling demons" as well as a study of words most frequently misspelled by college freshmen. The words in *Level One* are words in constant use by the average person; the words in *Level Two* are words often used but certainly of greater difficulty; the words in Level Three are words occasionally used by students and of greatest difficulty.

In each group of three words, there is one misspelling. Find the misspelled word and spell it correctly on the line provided.

Level One

1. carriage	consceince	association	_____
2. achievement	chief	aviater	_____
3. alltogether	almost	already	_____
4. annual	desireable	despair	_____
5. independance	ninety	nevertheless	_____
6. billian	weather	rhyme	_____
7. quiet	lying	naturaly	_____
8. speach	straight	valleys	_____
9. transfered	tragedy	reference	_____
10. received	reciept	reception	_____

Level Two

1.	calender	appropriately	casualties	_____
2.	affidavid	colossal	development	_____
3.	diptheria	competent	bigoted	_____
4.	prevelent	precipice	nauseous	_____
5.	fundamentally	obedience	bookeeper	_____
6.	tenant	repetetious	serviceable	_____
7.	cloudiness	donkies	babyish	_____
8.	wholly	wirey	strenuous	_____
9.	successfully	renowned	propagander	_____
10.	recuperate	vacuum	specificaly	_____

Level Three

1.	innoculate	aeronautics	saboteur	_____
2.	prejudice	panacea	amethist	_____
3.	laringytis	recipe	psychological	_____
4.	scissors	supremacy	cinamon	_____
5.	rarify	rescind	thousandth	_____
6.	superstitious	surgeon	irresistably	_____
7.	sophomore	brocoli	synonym	_____
8.	questionnaire	mayonaise	prophecy	_____
9.	jeoperdy	narrative	monotonous	_____
10.	primitive	obedience	mocassin	_____

Answers

Spelling

I.
1. ie
2. ei
3. ei
4. ei
5. ie
6. ie
7. ie
8. ei
9. ie
10. ie

II.
1. fibbing
2. begging
3. controllable
4. commitment

    5. colorful
    6. stopping
    7. biggest
    8. quitting
    9. robbing
  10. gladly

III.
    1. bridal
    2. forcible
    3. forceful
    4. imaginary
    5. hopeless
    6. truly
    7. removing
    8. lifelike
    9. likely
  10. serviceable

IV.
    1. flyer
    2. reliable
    3. noisily
    4. worrisome
    5. betraying
    6. healthiest
    7. merciful
    8. studying
    9. easiest
  10. studied

V.
    1. correct
    2. collectible
    3. convertible
    4. irritable
    5. correct
    6. commendable
    7. precede
    8. proceed
    9. succeed
  10. intercede

VI. **Level One:**
    1. conscience
    2. aviator
    3. altogether
    4. desirable
    5. independence
    6. billion
    7. naturally
    8. speech
    9. transferred
  10. received

Level Two:

1. calendar
2. affidavit
3. diphtheria
4. prevalent
5. bookkeeper
6. repetitious
7. donkeys
8. wiry
9. propaganda
10. specifically

Level Three:

1. inoculate
2. amethyst
3. laryngitis
4. cinnamon
5. rarefy
6. irresistibly
7. broccoli
8. mayonnaise
9. jeopardy
10. moccasin

CHAPTER 5

How to Take an Essay Test

Pre-Writing

Before you begin to write your essay, read the question several times so that you are familiar with the material. You might wish to underline key words or phrases. Do not spend too much time—only two or three minutes—on this planning. What you hope to accomplish during this pre-writing stage is:

1. to gain familiarity with the essay question;

2. to develop a point of view, deciding if you are in agreement or disagreement with the statement given; and

3. to develop a thesis statement that is the essential idea of your essay.

The Thesis

The first step in planning an essay is to decide on a *thesis,* the point you intend to make in your essay. It is often of great value to try to state the thesis of your composition in a single sentence during the pre-writing time. When developing a thesis, bear the following ideas in mind:

1. The thesis must be neither too broad nor too narrow.

2. The thesis must be clear to you and to the reader of your essay.

3. Everything in the essay must support the thesis. To introduce material that "drifts away" might well result in a confusing essay and a low score.

4. Use specific details rather than vague generalizations to support your thesis.

Limiting the Subject

A youngster once wanted to learn a little bit about penguins. A librarian suggested a book of well over a thousand pages called *Penguins.* When he returned the book, the librarian asked him if he had enjoyed reading the volume. "Well," he replied, "I really didn't need to know so much about penguins."

Most essay tests require compositions of 250 to 500 words. Therefore, you cannot write a thousand pages on "Penguins," so you must learn to limit your topic in order to discuss it fully in the time allowed. In fact, the more you limit your topic, the more successful your essay is likely to be, since you will be better able to supply the specific details that give an essay interest and life.

Organizing the Essay _____

Decide how many paragraphs you are going to write. Unless specifically indicated, there is no set rule concerning length. We are often told that "length is not a valid substitute for strength." Therefore, do not write furiously to fill up several pages, so that it will appear that you have many ideas. Actually, this can result in needless repetition, rambling, lack of organization, and muddled thinking. By the same token, you don't want your essay to appear to be skimpy. Obviously, if you write only four or five sentences, the examiner may not be able to get an adequate picture of your writing ability and may penalize you as a result. Many high school teachers and college instructors indicate that a three or four paragraph development is usually desirable for a twenty-minute essay test. This is not to say that some students may not wish to attempt an additional paragraph in the designated time. Here is where practice before the examination can be of great help to you. But remember to time yourself during the practice sessions. If you can only write one paragraph in twenty minutes, then you must continue to write—and perhaps a bit more rapidly—to develop the three-paragraph organization.

The Introduction _____

There are students who get bogged down before they begin to write. They stare at the blank paper and "choke up," unable to get going. The secret to beginning to write is to *write!*

Start right in. You have analyzed the question in your pre-planning. Now, in your introduction, you want to set down in clear sentences the topic you are going to write about, indicating to the reader perhaps why the topic has value or is cause for concern, giving if you can some background to the situation, and pointing the reader in the general direction that your essay is going to move.

Since you have only four or five minutes for this introduction, it is often sufficient to accomplish one or two of these tasks in three to six sentences.

_____ Five Items to Bear in Mind

1. In writing your introduction, keep in mind the key words of the question.

2. Avoid being "cute" or funny, ironic or satiric, overly emotional or too dramatic. Set the tone or attitude in your first sentence. You may well wish to appear sincere, clear, and straightforward.

3. Don't bother repeating the question word for word. A paraphrase in your own words is far better than just copying the words of the exam question.

4. Try in your first paragraph to let the reader know what your essay is going to deal with and what your controlling idea is. This can be accomplished in a clear topic sentence.

5. Each sentence should advance your topic and be interesting to your reader.

Test Yourself: Here are four sentences. Which one do you feel is the best topic sentence for an opening paragraph?

1. I have an aunt who is quite old, past eighty, and she lives alone in a very run-down neighborhood.

2. Old age can be a real problem.

3. I am going to do my best in the next fifty minutes to try to let you know what I really and truly believe about this problem that was stated in the essay question assigned to us.

4. Since people are living to a more advanced age, we might do well to examine how we can utilize the wisdom and experience that our senior citizens have to offer instead of just disregarding them.

Answer:

Sentence 4 is the best opening sentence since it states the topic clearly, limits the scope of the essay, and even presents the attitude of the writer.

Recognizing Effective Introductions

An *effective* introduction often refers to the subject of the essay, explains the value of the topic or attracts the attention of the reader by giving a pertinent illustration. Ineffective beginnings often contain unrelated material, ramble, and lack clarity.

Test Yourself: Examine the following five introductory paragraphs and decide whether each is effective or ineffective. Be able to defend your decision.

1. I agree that older people have many problems just as young people do. Adolescents often say that it's tough being young and I guess I agree.

2. Today more than ever before child abuse is coming under careful scrutiny. Although it is true that children have been abused in the past, the focus has never been clearer and that is all for the better.

3. It's really very important to think about and discuss such things. I know many people are very concerned about it.

4. Corruption in government must be everyone's concern. We can no longer hide behind the old saying, "You can't fight City Hall." Actually we can and we must.

5. I'm tired of hearing about dirty politics. It was always there just like sickness and other problems only now we read more about it. Sometimes I get disgusted because with all my school work I can't pay attention to taking care of other matters. And then I'm criticized.

Answers

1. *Ineffective.* The conclusion is not clear. The writer confuses the reader by discussing young people, older people, and adolescents.

2. *Effective.* The writer presents a strong statement on the need for writing the essay and addressing himself to the topic.

3. *Ineffective.* The paragraph is not clear. The use of the phrase "such things" and the pronoun "it" without an appropriate antecedent tend to confuse the reader.

4. *Effective.* The initial sentence contains a strong and valid thesis. The use of a quotation tends to re-enforce the subject under discussion. The paragraph is clear and the tone is strong.

5. *Ineffective.* The paragraph is rambling and muddled. The writer never presents a clear thesis statement.

The Development

The heart of the essay is the development, or the middle paragraph or paragraphs. Here the writer must attempt, in one or two paragraphs, to support the main idea of the essay through illustrations, details, and examples. The developmental paragraphs must serve as a link in the chain of ideas and contribute directly to the essay's central thought. All the sentences of the development must explain the essential truth of the thesis or topic sentence without digression.

In the limited time available on most essay tests, you can take only about ten minutes to produce six to ten sentences that will support the main thesis of the essay and prove the reality of your point of view. You may do this through a style that is descriptive, narrative, or expository, using a factual approach or an anecdotal one. Whatever approach you choose and whatever style you adopt, your writing must be coherent, logical, unified, and well ordered.

Caution!   Avoid the following pitfalls in the development of your essay:

1. Using sentences that are irrelevant and contain extraneous material

2. Using sentences that have no sequence of thought but seem to jump from one idea to another

3. Using sentences that do not relate to the topic sentence or do not flow from the preceding sentence

The good writer makes use of transitional words or phrases to connect thoughts and to provide for a logical sequence of ideas. Therefore, you would be wise to examine the following list of transitional ideas so that you might select those that you feel are most helpful in developing your middle paragraphs:

therefore	first of all	then
moreover	secondly	indeed
however	for example	in any case

consequently   for instance   on the other hand
of course   finally   nevertheless

Many other good linking expressions can be added to the above list, but if you choose judiciously from these fifteen expressions, you will find that your development will be more coherent and well ordered.

Test Yourself: In the following three samples, the transition is missing. Supply a transitional word or phrase that will allow the second sentence to follow smoothly or logically from the first.

1. He is an excellent piano player. There are times when his technique seems weak.

2. Generally, I believe doctors are very dedicated to helping people. There are exceptions to this.

3. He arrived late to take the examination. He dropped his pen and book when he finally got to his seat.

Answers

1. Choose one of the following transitional expressions to indicate a contrast: and yet, but, however, nevertheless, still, yet

> He is an excellent piano player; however, there are times when his technique seems weak.

2. Choose an expression from the following list to indicate concession: although this may be true, at the same time, granted that, I concede, no doubt, doubtless

> Generally, I believe doctors are very dedicated to helping people. No doubt, there are exceptions.

3. Use one of the following expressions to start your second sentence to indicate the idea of "in addition": furthermore, in addition, however, also, equally important, then

> He arrived late to take the examination. Furthermore, he dropped his pen and book when he finally got to his seat.

Effective Writing _____

There are three important factors that should be considered in writing an essay:

1. Unity
2. Coherence
3. Support

Essays are judged by how well they meet these three basic requirements.

To improve an essay you are writing, ask yourself these questions:

Unity

1. Do all the details in the essay support and develop the main thesis?

2. Do all the illustrations relate to the main point and add to the general effectiveness of the essay?

3. Have irrelevant ideas been deleted?

Coherence

1. Does the essay show a sense of organization?

2. Is the material presented logically?

3. Does the essay include transitional words or phrases that allow the reader to move easily from one idea to the next?

Support

1. Does the essay use details that make it interesting and vivid?

2. Is the main idea supported with concrete and specific illustrations?

3. Does the essay contain sufficient supporting details to clarify and persuade?

The Conclusion

Lewis Carroll once gave some very good advice. He said, "When you come to the end, stop!" The successful writer, like the wise guest, knows that he must not prolong his stay; when he comes to the end of his essay, he must draw his comments together in a strong, clear concluding paragraph.

A good concluding paragraph should give the reader the feeling that the essay has made its point, that the thesis has been explained, that a point of view has been established. This can be accomplished in about four to six sentences in one of the following ways:

1. Through a *restatement* of the main idea

2. Through a *summary* of the material covered in the essay

3. Through a *clear statement of* the *writer's opinion* of the issue(s) involved

Of course, if you had a good deal of time, there would be many additional techniques that you could employ to conclude your composition. But on an essay test, your time is limited, and you will have only five minutes or so to write a conclusion that will leave the reader feeling that you are a competent writer.

Caution! Just as there are good techniques, there are also some very ineffective methods that students are tempted to use in drawing a composition to a close. Try to avoid falling into the following traps:

1. Apologizing for your inability to discuss all the issues in the allotted time

2. Complaining that the topics did not interest you or that you don't think it was fair to be asked to write on so broad a topic

3. Introducing material that you will not develop, rambling on about non-pertinent matters, or using material that is trite or unrelated

Keep in mind that a good conclusion is related to the thesis of the essay and is an integral part of the essay. It may be a review or a restatement or it may lead the reader to do thinking on his own, but the conclusion must be strong, clear, and effective.

Recognizing Effective Conclusions

Remember that an *effective* concluding paragraph may restate the thesis statement, summarize the main idea of the essay, draw a logical conclusion, or offer a strong opinion of what the future holds. An *ineffective* final paragraph often introduces new material in a scanty fashion, apologizes for the ineffectiveness of the material presented, or is illogical or unclear.

Exercise I: Why are the following sentences ineffective in a concluding paragraph?

1. I wish I had more time to write a more convincing paper, but I find that in the allotted time this is all that I could do.

2. Although I have not mentioned this before, many senior citizens centers are being set up all over the country.

3. Now that I have explained my point of view, perhaps you would care to share your ideas with me on this topic.

Answers

1. Avoid using a complaining or apologetic tone in your conclusion. This detracts from the strength of your conclusion and serves to point out your inability to communicate ideas.

2. Do not add an idea that is completely new in your conclusion unless you are prepared to justify its inclusion and to develop it before you end your essay.

3. This kind of sentence is unrealistic and trite. The reader is not going to be able to share his ideas nor is he required to do so in this examination. This sentence seems to indicate that the writer was unable to find a satisfactory conclusion and resorted to a shop-worn comment.

EXERCISE II Examine the following five conclusions and decide whether each is effective or ineffective.

1. That's all I have to say about the topic. I know I'm not an expert, but at least this is my opinion and what I believe.

2. Certainly we can conclude that we are affected by the media. The advertisers are beginning to control our thinking and our decision making. The alert consumer must recognize this and act accordingly.

3. We must find other solutions to this problem. I know in England they have developed hospices to handle the terminally ill. But we can't discuss that here because of lack of time.

4. From all evidence we have, smoking presents a clear and present danger to the young person. The best cure for the habit appears to be to stop before beginning.

5. So be careful not to skip school. You must realize that a good education is important for you and so you should take advantage of your teachers when you are young. You won't be sorry.

Answers

1. *Ineffective.* This statement is a repetitious apology.

2. *Effective.* The paragraph is strong and clear. The conclusion is logical and the writer's opinion is well stated.

3. *Ineffective.* New material is presented but not developed.

4. *Effective.* The conclusion drawn appears to be logical. The phrasing is concise and to the point.

5. *Ineffective.* The tone is preachy; it is preferable to avoid addressing the reader directly or give commands. It would be better to use the third person.

Proofreading

Proofreading is an essential part of the writing experience. At least five to ten minutes of an essay test should be reserved for proofreading your work and making any needed corrections. There are certain "errors" that you may discover during the proofreading period:

1. Omission of words—especially *the, a, an*

2. Careless spelling errors

3. Final letters on words

4. Incorrect use of capital letters

5. Faulty punctuation

In addition, as you proofread you may change a word or adjust a phrase to make your essay more effective. However, remember that you will not have time to revise your entire essay or rewrite a paragraph.

Proofreading Exercises

(Answers to the following exercises are on pages 129 to 131.)

The following drills will help you recognize and correct common errors. The first six drills each focus on one error such as the fragment, comma-splice or run-on, homonym confusion, omission of final letters, etc., and the seventh drill presents a paragraph with a combination of errors. Rewrite each paragraph, correcting all the errors you find. You can check your response with the corrected paragraphs following the drills.

EXERCISE I Perhaps the most important person in his life was his mother. A beautiful woman who devoted her life to her family. She had married his father when she was quite young. Not quite eighteen. And hardly out of high school. As a result, her plans to enter college had to be deferred for a while. "It's all a matter of priorities," she said. Feeling that she was in love and wanted to start a family. "I'll get back to my schooling one day," she told her friends. She did. Although it took over fifty years.

EXERCISE II Everybody seems to be on a diet nowadays perhaps it's because we all want to be youthful. All you have to do is pick up a newspaper or magazine, the pictures of slim, athletic men and women look back at you, challenging you to lose weight the easy way. Actually there is no easy way, I discovered after going on diets for over five years. First I'd stare, and then I'd stuff, the result was I lost thirty pounds, and I gained thirty-five pounds, as a consequence, I'm now five pounds heavier than I was last year.

EXERCISE III There are some people who cant seem to concentrate in a quiet room. "Its too quiet," they complain. They seem to thrive on some low level of noise, and so while theyre studying, they turn on the radio or the television set. Their parents, not understanding the situation, may ask, "Whats going on here? Youre never going to be able to do your assignment with all that noise!" Yet its precisely the "noise" that helps them to do the homework. A radios music provides the accompaniment to start the days work. As my friends brother once said, "Everyone has the right to choose his own place to work. Whats important is that the professors assignment gets completed."

EXERCISE IV I much prefer city life to country life. I remember I once spent my vacation in a sleepy town in Tennessee where my uncle live. It was so quiet! Perhaps some people will think I could have relax there but actually I was bore because I was not interest in any of the things or activities that took place there. Whenn I arrive at my uncle's home, I thought that I would enjoy the change. But my enjoyment last only one day. Then I start to feel restless and I count the days until I would return to the "big city" with its excitement and bustle.

EXERCISE V Their are many reasons for students to go too college. First of all, college has a definite affect on our lives, since its a place were we are exposed to people of diverse backgrounds and also to many different branches of learning. Then too, at college students have a choice of extracurricular activities that they can choose to attend and to farther they're interests and abilities. All considered, people should follow the advise of those who advocate a college education.

EXERCISE VI　　We have been told that there has alway been a generation gap between the old and the young. As a result, communication between children and parent is at best difficult. My own mother often tell me that when she was young she could not discuss many important subject with her parents and so she relied on her few close friend for these discussion. Yet today she does not fully understand why it so difficult for me to bridge this gap and communicate openly. She feel that now it different and she is more understanding than either of her parent was. Oh well, let see what happen when I have children.

EXERCISE VII　　Everyone should have a hobby. A special interest to cultivate during spare time. For some individual Sports and Athletic are good way to keep themself amuse and occupy, other people prefer the theater more and attending various Culture Event. In my opinion a hobby should be a way to develop your personality. And also to make you a more interesting person. Someone who is well round and who will be appreciate by others, therefore, I urge each and everyone to make good use of there leisure time and spend free hour widely.

Analysis of Two Sample Essay Questions _____

Two sample essay questions appear below. Following each question are two student responses and an analysis of the strengths and weaknesses of each response.

_____ Sample Essay Question A

Essay Topic

In a recent article, a major university asked several faculty members to discuss what they considered the most important problem plaguing our country and the world. The professors spoke of the widespread hunger confronting half of the people on earth, the extinction of hundreds and even thousands of species because of the destruction of tropical forests, and the overwhelming poverty in many countries.

There are other concerns that might be mentioned: the prejudice and lack of understanding among people and nations, the inadequate distribution of wealth, and the threat of nuclear annihilation.

Choose at least one problem that you feel should be the prime concern of mankind and discuss how it should be addressed in the remaining years of the twentieth century.

Sample Response 1

As we near the turn of the century there are so many major problems plaguing humanity that it is hard to know where to begin to solve them. It is terribly sad to see so much hunger and poverty throughout the world—in our country and elsewhere. But perhaps the most frightening problem we face is what to do to avoid nuclear annihilation.

Destruction will not come with a "whimper" but with a "bang" I'm afraid. So many countries possess nuclear weapons—superpowers and smaller countries as well—that the likelihood of a catastrophe, accidental or otherwise is great. Events in the United States and in Russia have proven that nuclear reactors are not all that safe. Then there are the threats made by smaller nations at war against other small nations. The prospect is possible and terrible.

Many people do not even bother to have children or get married nowadays. They say it's better to just enjoy the little time they have left before the world is blown up. It's a very depressing situation and not easy to explain to youngsters. Also, some people say that they can't trust politicians to do the right thing.

Therefore, this is a very serious problem that must be addressed before the end of the century—as soon as possible in fact. But intelligent answers to this very difficult problem do not seem to be at hand.

Analysis of Sample Response 1
Strengths

1. The essay is well organized, keeping to the subject and developing its arguments in a logical progression.

2. The introduction is well developed as it moves from the general to the specific—from "many major problems" to the problem of the avoidance of nuclear annihilation.

3. The second paragraph begins with an *allusion,* the technique of making indirect reference to an author or work of literature. In this case, the writer alludes to T. S. Eliot's famous line, "This is how the world ends, not with a bang but a whimper"—a most appropriate way to suggest a point of view.

4. The concluding paragraph is signalled by a transition ("Therefore") that prepares the reader for a summation of the preceding arguments and uses some of the language of the topic that the writer has chosen to discuss.

Suggestions for Improvement

1. The essay might be revised to address or elaborate on certain ideas. First, the writer should suggest how the problems noted might be addressed, since that is what the question required. Second, the discussion of the breakdown of social values and family life needs specific development and details so that it would be more germane to the central issue.

2. In the second paragraph, specific examples of conflicts between nations might have provided illustration of the thesis.

3. Revisions are needed to make the tone more consistent. In the third paragraph, the tone becomes informal and the argument wanders.

4. In the opening sentence of the concluding paragraph, the word "this" is vague and its antecedent is not clear. If the author means "the possibility of nuclear annihilation," he should state so.

5. Several commas might be added for appropriate pauses:

> *Paragraph 1:* "As we near the turn of the century,"
>
> *Paragraph 2:* "but with a 'bang,' I'm afraid."
>
> *Paragraph 2:* "a catastrophe, accidental or otherwise, is great."
>
> *Paragraph 4:* "as soon as possible, in fact."

Sample Response 2

Over the past years there has been an area of concern that people have forgotten, and yet I feel that this should be our cheif concern. The area is that of pollution. Our entire world is suffering from various forms of pollution and I feel that if we do not open our eyes to this problem we will soon see the general break-down of our universe.

Because of the increasing number of cars on our streets and the various forms of mass transportation, our air is becoming polluted. All sorts of harmful gasses are being given off into the air, and we are breathing in fumes that will surely cause us many kinds of diseases. We pollute our bodies with cigarete smoke and drugs but we also pollute our bodies with gasoline fumes and taken together we are shortening our lives.

Garbage and poisons are polluting our soil and our streams. Newspaper articles always point out that all the chemicals that we use to grow bigger and more delicious fruits and vegetables and to destroy the bugs are going to destroy us as well. The chemicals get into our foods and then we eat them, and soon we will suffer the affects. Garbage is thrown into the waters and rivers and our fish become contaminated.

Of course, poverty, nuclear war, and hunger are problems, but so is pollution, and pollution is a problem that people overlook; that is why it is so dangerous. I think that over the next few years laws should be passed to regulate air pollution, to solve the problem of garbage disposal, and to deal with the use of chemicals and agriculture. In my opinion, this should be our major concern.

Analysis of Sample Response 2

Strengths

1. The writer shows an intelligent handling of the topic. Choosing an area not mentioned in the question, the problem of pollution is a thoughtful alternative approach.

2. The four paragraphs are well organized and well developed. Specific examples are provided in the body of the essay.

3. The essay is clear, generally well written, and consistent with the writer's thesis statement. The reader feels that the author strongly believes in the point of view presented.

Suggestions for Improvement

1. The author's suggestions for addressing the problem should be stated clearly and developed specifically earlier in the essay, not merely in a brief concluding comment.

2. The author appears to overstate the case in writing in the introduction that "people have forgotten" pollution and in the conclusion "people overlook" this problem.

3. More careful proofreading might result in the correction of usage and spelling errors: in paragraph one, "cheif" should be "chief"; in paragraph two "cigarete" should be "cigarette"; in paragraph three "affects" should be "effects."

4. In Paragraph three, the concluding sentence might well be eliminated since it adds no new idea and simply repeats what has been stated earlier in the paragraph.

Sample Essay Question B

Essay Topic

Were the good old days actually that good? We must remember that our grandparents did not have all the modern conveniences to make life easier. There were no airplanes or cars, no washing machines, no television, no computers. Therefore, it is better to live today in the modern world than to look back to the last century.

Agree or disagree with this statement, drawing upon your personal experiences, your observations of others, or your reading.

Sample Response 1

I prefer to be living today rather than when my grandparents were born in the last century or before that even. Today young people can really enjoy themselves they have TV and discos and movies and all sorts of entertainment. Not like long ago when all you did all day was work and then at night you were to tired to do anything accept sleep.

Today we have greater opportunities to do things and to get ahead. There is less prejudism against people because of there race or color or religion. You can go to more kinds of colleges like a two year school or a four year school and there are even many programs to help you if you are financially unable to pay the tuition costs and payments.

I don't believe that the good old days were really that good. I'm very happy to be living today in today world. These are the good days.

Analysis of Sample Response 1
Strengths

1. There is a sense of organization. The essay is divided into three paragraphs—an introduction, a development, and a conclusion.

2. The author attempts to stick to the topic and provide examples.

3. Although there are technical errors in the third paragraph, the conclusion provides an interesting summary.

Suggestions for Improvement

1. The essay lacks clarity and is wordy. The opening sentence could have been concluded after "born." In paragraph 2, the first sentence is vague; "to do things" and "to get ahead" should be explained and clarified. The third sentence of the second paragraph needs to be tightened: "There are two and four year colleges with various programs to assist those in financial need."

2. There are sentence structure problems. The second sentence of the first paragraph is a run-on sentence. A period should follow "themselves." The sentence that follows is a fragment. "Not like long ago" could be changed to add clarity and also to provide a subject for the sentence: "This is different from times past when all people did . . ."

3. There are several errors in word choice. In the last sentence of the first paragraph, "to tired" should be changed to "too tired" and "accept" should be "except." In the second sentence of the second paragraph, "prejudism" should be "prejudice" and "there race" should be "their race."

4. There is an error in the use of the possessive form. In the second sentence of the third paragraph, "today world" should be "today's world."

Sample Response 2

Someone once said that for everything you gain you have to give up something. I agree. We gained the subway, but we have to put up with being crowded like sardines and herded like cattle, being pushed and shoved. We gained large buildings and big cities, but we lost our privacy and we are forced to live in little cubby holes. We gained airplanes and automobiles and with it comes all the dirty air and pollution.

Our grandparents worked hard and didn't have time to relax but maybe they got real pleasure from their work. At least they ate the food that they grew and weren't concerned about all the chemicals and sprays and sickness that came from the fruit and vegetables. Maybe they developed a real feeling of accomplishment too. They didn't have TV or radios but they had good neighbors and they would enjoy visiting with friends and family. We gained television but we lost the ability to have a good conversation and to enjoy the company of other people.

Every century has its good points and its problems. I don't want to go back to living a hundred years ago but I do feel that we could learn from the way they lived. Maybe we could adopt some of their customs and bring some of the good old days into today's world.

Analysis of Sample Response 2
Strengths

1. There is an excellent three-paragraph organization. The introduction is fully developed with several pertinent illustrations. The body provides several additional points that support the writer's contention. The conclusion is a thought-provoking summary of the essay.

2. The use of contrast between past and present provides a fine frame for the essay. The theme of "gain and loss" is carried through with appropriate illustrations and a mature vocabulary.

3. There are no errors in sentence structure and the writer reveals that he can use both simple and complex sentences effectively.

Suggestions for Improvement

1. The second sentence of the opening paragraph seems ineffective in the context of so many mature comments. It could be rewritten: "This is especially true in comparing our world with the world of our grandparents."

2. There is a problem with pronouns and antecedents; this results in a lack of clarity. In the last sentence of the first paragraph, the singular pronoun "it" is incorrect since it does not agree with the plural "airplanes and automobiles." It would be better to write: "We gained airplanes and automobiles, but with modern means of travel we must suffer dirty air and pollution." So too, the second sentence of the concluding paragraph could be rewritten to clarify the pronoun "they": ". . . but I do feel that we could learn from the way our grandparents lived." This change clarifies the use of the pronoun "their" in the subsequent sentence.

Answers

Proofreading

EXERCISE I Perhaps the most important person in his life was his ~~mother. A~~ *mother, a* beautiful woman who devoted her life to her family. She had married his father when she was quite ~~young. Not quite eighteen. And~~ *young, not eighteen, and* hardly out of high school. As a result, her plans to enter college had to be deferred for a while. "It's all a matter of priorities," she ~~said. Feeling~~ *said, feeling* that she was in love and wanted to start a family. "I'll get back to my schooling one day," she told her friends. She ~~did. Although~~ *did, although* it took over fifty years.

EXERCISE II Everybody seems to be on a diet ~~nowadays perhaps~~ *nowadays. Perhaps* it's because we all want to be youthful. All you have to do is pick up a newspaper or magazine; the pictures of slim, athletic men and women look back at you, challenging you to lose weight the easy way. Actually there is no easy way, I discovered after going on diets for over five years. First I'd ~~stare,~~ *starve,* and then I'd ~~stuff. the~~ *stuff. The* result was I lost thirty pounds, and I gained thirty-five ~~pounds, as~~ *pounds. As* a consequence, I'm now five pounds heavier than I was last year.

EXERCISE III There are some people who ~~cant~~ *can't* seem to concentrate in a quiet room. "~~Its~~ *It's* too quiet," they complain. They seem to thrive on some low level of noise, and so while ~~theyre~~ *they're* studying, they turn on the radio or the television set. Their parents, not understanding the situation, may ask, "~~Whats~~ *What's* going on here? ~~Youre~~ *You're* never going to be able to do your assignment with all that noise!" Yet ~~its~~ *it's* precisely the "noise" that helps them to do the homework. A ~~radios~~ *radio's* music provides the accompaniment to start the ~~days~~ *day's* work. As my ~~friends~~ *friend's* brother once said, "Everyone has the right to choose his own place to work." ~~Whats~~ *What's* important is that the ~~professors~~ *professor's* assignment gets completed."

EXERCISE IV I much prefer city life to country life. I remember I once spent my vacation in a sleepy town in Tennessee where my uncle ~~live.~~ *lived.* It was so quiet! Perhaps some people will think I could have ~~relax~~ *relaxed* there but actually I was ~~bore~~ *bored* because I was not ~~interest~~ *interested* in any of the things or activities that took place there. ~~Whenn~~ *When* I ~~arrive~~ *arrived* at my uncle's home, I thought that I would enjoy the change. But my enjoyment ~~last~~ *lasted* only one day. Then I ~~start~~ *started* to feel restless, and I ~~count~~ *counted* the days until I would return to the "big city" with its excitement and bustle.

EXERCISE V ~~Their~~ *There* are many reasons for students to go ~~too~~ *to* college. First of all, college has a definite ~~affect~~ *effect* on our lives, since ~~its~~ *it's* a place ~~were~~ *where* we are exposed to people of diverse backgrounds and also to many different branches of learning. Then too, at college students have a choice of extracurricular activities that they can choose to attend ~~and~~ to ~~farther~~ *further* ~~they're~~ *their* interests and abilities. All considered, people should follow the ~~advise~~ *advice* of those who advocate a college education.

EXERCISE VI We have been told that there has always been a generation gap between the old and the young. As a result, communication between children and parents is at best difficult. My own mother often tells me that when she was young she could not discuss many important subjects with her parents, and so she relied on her few close friends for these discussions. Yet today she does not fully understand why it *is* so difficult for me to bridge this gap and communicate openly. She feels that now it *is* different and she is more understanding than either of her parents was. Oh well, let's see what happens when I have children.

EXERCISE VII   Everyone should have a hobby, ~~A~~ special interest to cultivate during
spare time. For some individuals, ~~S~~ports ~~and Athletic are~~ good way to
keep ~~themself~~ amuse and occupy; ~~o~~ther people prefer the theater ~~more
and attending various~~ Culture ~~Event?~~ In my opinion, a hobby ~~should~~ be a
way to develop ~~your~~ personality, ~~A~~nd ~~also to~~ make ~~you a~~ more interesting, ~~person.~~ ~~Someone who is~~ well-round and ~~who will be~~ appreciated
by others, therefore, ~~I urge each and everyone to~~ make ~~good~~ use of
~~there~~ leisure time, ~~and spend free hour widely.~~

EXERCISE VII
(retyped)   Everyone should have a hobby, a special interest to cultivate during spare
time. For some individuals, participating in sports is a good way to keep
themselves amused and occupied. Other people prefer to attend the theater
or other cultural events. In my opinion, a hobby can be a way to develop the
personality and make people more interesting, well-rounded, and appreciated by others. Therefore, people should make use of their leisure time.

CHAPTER 6

The Business Letter

In writing business letters it is important that the correct form be followed. Business letters serve a variety of purposes, from letters of application to letters of complaint or praise. But whether a person is writing to seek admission to a school, to order merchandise, to reserve a room in a hotel, to apply for a position, or to complain that a product was misrepresented, there are certain formats to which the writer must conform.

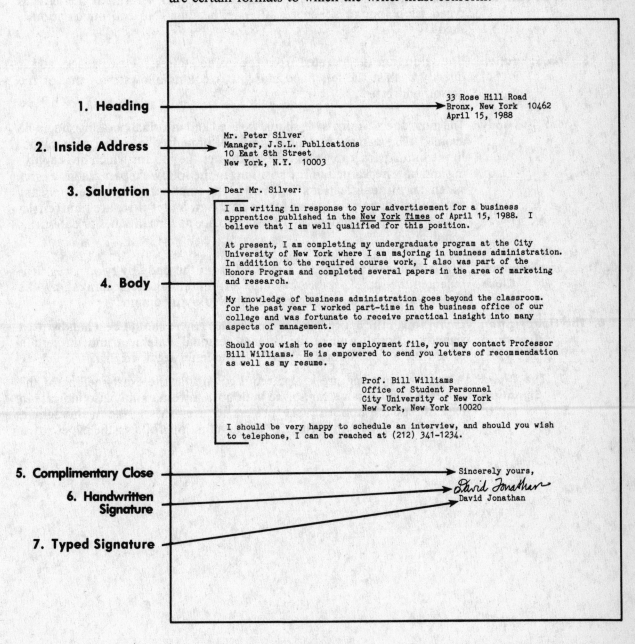

1. **Heading** → 33 Rose Hill Road
Bronx, New York 10462
April 15, 1988

2. **Inside Address** → Mr. Peter Silver
Manager, J.S.L. Publications
10 East 8th Street
New York, N.Y. 10003

3. **Salutation** → Dear Mr. Silver:

4. **Body**

I am writing in response to your advertisement for a business apprentice published in the New York Times of April 15, 1988. I believe that I am well qualified for this position.

At present, I am completing my undergraduate program at the City University of New York where I am majoring in business administration. In addition to the required course work, I also was part of the Honors Program and completed several papers in the area of marketing and research.

My knowledge of business administration goes beyond the classroom. for the past year I worked part-time in the business office of our college and was fortunate to receive practical insight into many aspects of management.

Should you wish to see my employment file, you may contact Professor Bill Williams. He is empowered to send you letters of recommendation as well as my resume.

Prof. Bill Williams
Office of Student Personnel
City University of New York
New York, New York 10020

I should be very happy to schedule an interview, and should you wish to telephone, I can be reached at (212) 341-1234.

5. **Complimentary Close** → Sincerely yours,

6. **Handwritten Signature** → *David Jonathan*

7. **Typed Signature** → David Jonathan

1. In a business letter, neatness is very important. If you can, type the letter on good paper. If you must write the letter in your own handwriting, use good cursive penmanship.

2. Proofread very carefully so that you avoid careless errors and spelling mistakes.

3. Be brief and to the point. Don't wander off the topic or repeat yourself.

4. Observe the acceptable format.

1. The Heading There is no end punctuation and no indentation in this three-line heading. If the letter is typed, the lines are single-spaced.

2. The Inside Address Just like the heading, the inside address is in block form. If the letter is typed, skip four to six spaces after its heading. No end punctuation is used.

3. The Salutation The salutation is separated from the inside address by two spaces and is directly against the left hand margin. A colon follows the name of the person addressed.

4. The Body The most direct writing style should be used and informal phrasing should be avoided. The material presented should be organized into clear paragraphs. In the initial paragraph, the writer indicates the job for which he is applying and how he learned of the position. In the following paragraphs a brief statement of qualifications is given. In the final paragraph, the applicant states a willingness to appear for an interview and if there are time restrictions so that an interview can only take place at certain times or dates, this is indicated.

5. The Complimentary Close The complimentary close is separated from the body by two spaces. It is indented the same distance from the left margin as the heading. Only the first word is capitalized, and it is followed by a comma.

6. The Handwritten Signature Even though the entire letter is typewritten, there should be a handwritten signature, both to make the letter a personal statement and, in certain cases (like a price quotation), to give the letter legal weight.

7. The Typed Signature A typewritten signature is also required so that the exact spelling of the correspondent's name cannot be in doubt. A woman may also indicate in parentheses the honorific she prefers to use—(Ms.) Naomi Snodgrass, (Mrs.) Sophonisbe Ingelfinger. No punctuation follows the typewritten signature.

TESTS
OF
ENGLISH
COMPOSITION

CHAPTER 7

SAT I: Verbal Reasoning

Colleges use a number of techniques to choose prospective students. Some colleges rely heavily upon what they consider objective criteria such as short answer tests. Those who favor this technique claim that it is a fair and impartial way to select students, since there is relative anonymity and exams may be scored mechanically. Other colleges prefer more personal involvement. They wish to see and interview candidates. In this way, students have the opportunity to present themselves, answer questions, and perhaps ask a few as well. In addition, colleges usually review past academic records and consider extracurricular activities, community service, special talents and interests, and personality. Some form of ability testing is nearly always part of the mix; SAT I: Verbal Reasoning Test is one widely used measure of verbal ability.

Format of SAT I: Verbal Reasoning Test

The Verbal Reasoning Test requires 75 or 80 minutes and consists of 75 to 85 questions.

Three kinds of questions appear on the Verbal Reasoning Test: critical reading; sentence completion; and analogies. The approximate distribution is:

Critical Reading—40 questions

Sentence Completion—19 questions

Analogies—19 questions

Overview of SAT I: Verbal Reasoning Test Questions

Critical Reading

Several passages are presented; each is followed by a number of questions about the material it presents. The topics of the passages may include humanities, social sciences, natural sciences, or narrative (either fiction or nonfiction). Two of the passages, referred to as the "double passage," are on the same or related topics. One selection offers a viewpoint that opposes, supports, or somehow complements the view expressed in the other selection.

There are four passages in all:

1 @ 400–550 words
1 @ 550–700 words
2 @ 700–850 words, total.

Since each passage contains all the information necessary to answer the questions, the test-taker need not be an ''expert'' in the subject matter.

Critical reading questions generally ask for the following kinds of information:

1. The main idea of the passage.
2. The author's opinion or point of view.
3. A definition of vocabulary in context.
4. An inference from content or tone.
5. An interpretation of words or concepts.
6. In the double passage, a comparison or contrast of material.

Each passage must be read carefully. If the passage is based on unfamiliar material, it may be helpful to scan the questions first, then read the passage. A close reading of the passage involves paying attention not only to the subject matter, but also to style, attitude, and tone. When an answer is chosen from the choices presented, it must be selected on the basis of what is stated or implied in the passage, not on the reader's own knowledge and personal background. A choice is not necessarily correct because it is a true statement. The student must be certain that a choice is based on what is required in the question and not be misled by material that is partially true or material that may be accurate but is not of primary importance in relation to the point of the reading.

Sentence Completion

In this section of the SAT I, a sentence is presented with either one or two blanks. Each blank indicates that there is a missing word. The student must then decide which word or words among the choices presented best completes the sentence by fitting into the other parts of the sentence. This requires knowledge of word meaning and an ability to work with contextual clues. Often the sentences are gathered from published material, so the student who has read widely has a decided edge in tackling this section of the examination. However, it is sufficient to read each sentence closely, paying attention to the tone, to prepositions and conjunctions, and to the content.

In approaching this type of question, the test-taker should read the entire sentence carefully so that the idea presented is completely understood. All the choices presented must be considered, and if there are two blanks the entire set of words must be valid, not simply one. Once the decision has been made, it is wise to reread the entire sentence to determine whether it makes good sense.

Analogies

Analogies require the student to see a relationship in a pair of words and then to see a similar relationship in another pair. To answer this type of question, the test-taker determines the precise relationship that exists in the first set of words and then attempts to discover which of the following sets of words has a parallel relationship. Obviously, this type of test requires the student to think carefully about the precise meaning of words and not be fooled by word pairs that have a close but not a parallel relationship.

Test-Taking Hints for the SAT I

When you take the SAT I, keep in mind three essentials: timing, guessing, and evaluating.

Timing

The amount of time required for answering a question depends on its degree of difficulty. A question which takes one person three or four minutes to answer may take another only thirty seconds—and vice versa. Since every question on the exam has the same weight in the final score, be sure to work on the more difficult questions *only after you have finished all the easier ones*. Pass over the hard ones and concentrate on the easy ones until you have reached the last question.

One time-saver is to keep one eye on the choices while working through the steps of a solution. Depending on the selection, a glance at the choices may reveal a likely answer or one or more eliminations. If you first solve the problem and *then* search for the answer among the choices, you will waste time. You should notice that the instructions always tell you to *find*, rather than *formulate*, the best choice.

Guessing

You will be cautioned against "wild" guessing. You receive a credit of one point for each correct choice; no credit for an unanswered question. However, you receive a *penalty* of ¼ point for every wrong choice you select. When you have no idea at all which choice is correct, you must leave the question blank; a wild guess will cost you more than it will profit you. If, on the other hand, you don't know the correct choice but can be sure that one or more choices can be eliminated from consideration, your calculated guess will bring the odds into your favor; you should, in these cases, make your selection. These calculated guesses are a critically important factor for success.

Evaluating

In order to use your time most wisely and to turn the maximum number of *doubtful* questions into good calculated guesses—or answers—you must adopt a method of evaluating the amount of time needed for each question. One method that has met with success has been that of a "quick sort" into one of three categories: (1) easy, (2) difficult but feasible with extra time, and (3) very difficult or seemingly impossible. An investment of ten or fifteen seconds per question will enable you to sort the questions. Then, you should answer the easy questions immediately. If it is in the second category (''difficult but feasible with extra time''), mark it with a circle. Work on it when you have dealt with all the easy questions. If it is in the third category (''very difficult or seemingly impossible''), mark it with a cross and plan to tackle it *only if and after you have finished everything in the second category.*

Above all, remember that this is a test of good judgment and common sense.

Hints for Taking Objective Tests

The form of the objective test on the SAT I and SAT II is multiple-choice questions. These questions call for a definite answer. Here are five hints to aid you in getting credit for all you know.

1. Scan the entire test before you begin. Become comfortable with the format, the number of questions, and the time allocated for responding.

2. Read the directions carefully and make certain you know what is required.

3. Begin the test. Answer all the questions you are certain you know. Don't waste time on doubtful items. Return to those later, *but be certain you leave spaces on the answer sheets for the answers you skip.*

4. Read *all* the choices before selecting the correct response. Eliminate all the obviously incorrect choices and then choose the *best.*

5. Look for clues in the wording that will help you select the best answer: words like *sometimes, always,* or *never.*

Hints for Answering Critical Reading Questions

Critical Reading Tests a Variety of Skills

*   Your ability to read for *facts*
*   Your ability to understand what is said
*   Your ability to recognize or apply authors' views (inferences)
*   Your skill at finding the main idea
*   Your understanding of words in context
*   Your ability to relate what you already know to what is in the passage

Steps to Follow in the Critical Reading Section

1. Scan the passage for a general idea.
2. Read the questions *but not the answers.*
3. Read the passage and underline key parts.
4. Read and answer questions.

Do's and Don'ts for Reading Comprehension

- *Do* answer questions only on the basis of what is in the passage and not on what else you know.

- *Do* stay away from answers that seem too easy or that are taken word for word from the passage.

- *Do* answer the easy questions first.

- *Do* be suspicious of answers with absolute words such as *never, always,* and *forever.* Usually these answers are too limiting.

- *Do* save the reading comprehension passages for last.

- *Do* underline key words in the passages such as *not, rather than, except,* and *never.*

- *Do* use context clues to determine the meaning of words you do not know.

- *Do* determine the kind of question being asked and *do* realize that some kinds are easier than others. The four major kinds of questions in reading comprehension are:

    1. details or facts (ability to recall what you've read)
    2. inference and implications
    3. author's tone or mood
    4. main idea (What is this passage about? What would be a good title for this passage?)

- *Don't* waste time rereading passages again and again.

- *Don't* expect the questions to follow the order of the passage.

- *Don't* select an answer just because it is a true statement unless it is also the answer to the question.

- In answering questions for the main idea, *don't* be distracted by answers that may be true according to the passage but may not be the main idea.

- *Don't* look in just one section for the answer unless you are directed to do so.

Following each Critical Reading passage, a number of questions challenge the reader's

I. Verbal reasoning skills

II. Knowledge of vocabulary in context

I. Verbal Reasoning Skills

These skills are often necessary to determine the value of the written material, to decide what is fact and what is opinion, and to discover faulty logic. In other words, verbal reasoning skills are those skills that the educated reader calls upon to analyze and to evaluate what is read.

When the educated person reads critically, the following four criteria must be kept in mind:

1. the purpose of the selection

2. the use of emotional words as a technique to persuade

3. the material as fact or opinion

4. when the selection was written

Examples

1. Joey is just such a child. He came to my attention a week before summer recess.

   What is the purpose of these sentences?

   (A) to explain
   (B) to compare
   (C) to contrast
   (D) to provide an illustration
   (E) to entertain

   The correct response is (D). These two sentences serve to introduce an illustration. The author uses an example to highlight his main idea.

2. We feel very strongly that it is the patriotic duty of each citizen to exercise his right to vote in all elections, not just presidential ones.

   Which of the following words is based on an appeal to the emotions?

   (A) citizen
   (B) patriotic
   (C) exercise
   (D) right
   (E) just

   Choice (B) is best. Words like *patriotic, oppressed, liberty,* and *freedom* are all emotionally charged and help convey the message that the author intends the reader to receive.

3. Alice is the most intelligent girl I know.

   This statement is

   (A) factual
   (B) negative
   (C) incorrect
   (D) opinion
   (E) accurate

   Choice (D) is correct. The statement is the opinion of the writer. It may indeed be accurate or incorrect, but it needs to be proved. The concept of intelligence might convey different ideas to different people.

II. Knowledge of Vocabulary in Context

Often the meaning of an unfamiliar word can be figured out by the way it is used in a sentence. The sentence itself offers the clues. Likewise, contextual clues often make clear the intent of a word that may have a number of different meanings.

Examples:

1. The *diverse* personalities of the students made the teacher's job more challenging since he didn't know which reaction he would receive.

   Diverse means

      (A) pleasant
      (B) varied
      (C) emotional
      (D) hostile
      (E) boring

   Choice **(B)** is correct. The students' personalities were diverse, varied, and, therefore, unpredictable.

2. This house is much too *commodious* for me, since I live alone.

   Commodious means

      (A) comfortable
      (B) architectural
      (C) spacious
      (D) urban
      (E) congested

   Choice **(C)** is best. A spacious house may not be good for a single person.

3. Bill is *gregarious* by nature, not at all withdrawn.

   Gregarious means

      (A) sociable
      (B) introverted
      (C) quiet
      (D) hostile
      (E) thrifty

   Choice **(A)** is best. The context clue is "not at all *withdrawn*," the opposite of sociable.

Hints for Answering Sentence Completion Questions

Sentence Completion questions test

- Your understanding of words in context
- Your knowledge of grammatical structures
- Your awareness of style

Sentence completions present you with a sentence with one or two missing words represented by blanks. You are to complete the sentence by choosing the most appropriate word or pair of words from the list of choices.

Do's and Don'ts for Sentence Completion

- *Do* remember four things when choosing words to fill in blanks: The words must (a) make sense, (b) carry out the meaning of the sentence, (c) be grammatically correct, and (d) continue the *style* of the passage or sentence.

- If there are two blanks, *do* make sure both words fit.

- *Do* look for *key words* in the sentence that serve as clues.

Examples: *although, by contrast, but, because, since.*

- *Do* notice what part of speech is called for.

Example: At its present rate of _____ , the business will have to move to larger quarters.

       (A) accord
       (B) accordingly
       (C) accretion
       (D) accuracy
       (E) accrue

Choice (**C**) is correct. Accretion is growth. As the business grows, it will need more space.

- *Do* notice whether a positive or a negative word is called for. Contextual clues in the form of connotations of the words used can be very helpful.

Example: Liberty and slavery differ only in the nature of the controlling authority, so freedom can easily be perverted into _____ .

       (A) humility
       (B) abrogation
       (C) servitude
       (D) emancipation
       (E) defense

Consider the negative connotation of *perverted* and choose a completion with an equally negative connotation. Choice (**C**) is best. Liberty and slavery are contrasted; freedom and servitude represent a similar contrast.

- *Do* (in one-blank questions) eliminate answer choices that are synonyms of each other.

Example: There is no chance of _____ in a society where everyone thinks alike.

       (A) consensus
       (B) agreement
       (C) monotony
       (D) tranquillity
       (E) innovation

Choice (E) is best. Since (A) and (B) have the same meaning, neither can be the answer. Turn the sentence around. If everyone thinks alike, there is no chance of innovation.

- *Don't* choose paired complementary words when the sentence cries out for contrast.

Example: Despite her _____ nature, Molly was capable of tactful negotiation

and even won praise for her patient efforts toward _____ .

    (A) diplomatic . . . amity
    (B) congenial . . . accord
    (C) altruistic . . . dissension
    (D) rebellious . . . insurrection
    (E) tempestuous . . . reconciliation

Choice (E) is best. Only (C) and (E) offer the contrast required by "Despite." Choice (C) makes no sense.

- *Don't* choose words that contradict each other if the sentence implies causation.

Example: She is so _____ that she has been _____ all day.

    (A) serene . . . nervous
    (B) anxiety ridden . . . calm
    (C) nervous . . . anxiety
    (D) ecstatic . . . lamenting
    (E) nervous . . . anxious

Choice (E) is best. A nervous person is anxious.

- Your choice must be grammatically correct.
- *Don't* skip any part of the sentence.
- *Don't* select an answer because it is a cliché or because it sounds good.

Hints for Answering Analogy Questions

Analogy questions test your ability to see a relationship in a pair of words, to understand the ideas expressed in the relationship, and to recognize another relationship that may be similar or parallel.

Analogy questions present you with a pair of words followed by five more pairs of words. You must select from those five pairs the one pair that bears the same internal relationship as do the words of the first pair to one another.

Question pair :: Answer pair
seldom : frequently :: never : always

Seldom has the same relationship to *frequently* that *never* has to *always*.

Rules for Parts of Speech in Analogies

If the words in the given pair are matching parts of speech, then the words in the answer pair must also be matching parts of speech. In other words, if the words in the given pair match each other, then the words in the answer pair must match each other, but they don't have to match the given pair.

Example: hot : cold :: day : night   adj. : adj. :: noun : noun

If the words in the given pair do not match (if they are different parts of speech), then the words in the answer pair must be *exactly* the same parts of speech as the given pair and in exactly the same order.

Examples: adult : big :: child : small   noun : adj. :: noun : adj.
                  when : time :: where : locale   adv. : noun :: adv. : noun
                  doctor : operates :: professor : teaches   noun : verb :: noun : verb

Do's and Don'ts for Analogies

- *Do* be aware that the order of the answer pair must be the same as that of the question pair. An otherwise correct answer choice in which the order is reversed is incorrect.

  father : son :: daughter : mother IS INCORRECT

- *Do* consider each pair of words as a unit that represents a particular relationship. *Don't* look for the relationship between an individual word in the first pair with any one word in any of the other pairs.

Example: KEY : DOOR

         (A)   lock : glass
         (B)   wine : cellar
         (C)   skeleton : trap
         (D)   stack : book
         (E)   combination : lock

The answer, of course, is **(E)**. A combination opens a lock as a key opens a door. If you had tried relating individual words, you might have chosen **(C)** while thinking of a skeleton key.

- *Do* notice the parts of speech of the words in each pair. These serve to help you eliminate wrong answers and are good clues to the right answers.

- *Do* watch out for superficial relationships.

Example: MUSIC : CLARINET

         (A)   wood : furniture
         (B)   symphony : piano
         (C)   furniture : carpentry tools
         (D)   notes : composer
         (E)   class : students

You might be tempted to pick **(B)** or **(D)** because they are about music, but they are not correct because they do not express the same relationship. Do not pick an answer pair that concerns the same subject matter as the given words unless that pair also expresses the same relationship as the given pair. Here the answer is **(C)**. Carpentry tools are used to create furniture as a clarinet is used to create music.

- *Don't* spend too much time on one question. If you do not know the meaning of one of the words in the first pair or if you cannot see any relationship between the words in that pair, skip the question and go on to the next.

● *Don't* be too quick to choose an answer pair that seems overly simple or obvious. Refine to the narrowest, most specific analogy.

Example: HELMET : HEAD

> **(A)** sword : soldier
> **(B)** umbrella : clothing
> **(C)** thimble : finger
> **(D)** stocking : shoe
> **(E)** watch : wrist

(E) is possible, but **(C)** is the correct answer. Consider how a helmet fits over the entire top part of the head, protecting it. So, likewise, does a thimble fit over the end of a finger to protect it. The watch, while worn around the wrist, does not entirely cover the hand nor does it protect it.

Kinds of Analogies

1. part : whole / whole : part
    leg : body :: wheel : car / poem : stanza :: symphony : movement

2. cause : effect
    cloud : rain :: sun : heat

3. broad category : specific category :: a variety of whole : part
    tree : elm :: flower : daisy

4. word : synonym or definition
    happy : content :: scared : afraid

5. word : antonym
    slavery : freedom :: happiness : sadness

6. degree
    anxiety : panic :: dislike : hate

7. worker : tool
    dentist : drill :: farmer : plow

8. creator : creation
    poet : poem :: artist : picture

9. professional : profession
    teacher : education :: doctor : medicine

10. characteristic
    baby : small :: genius : intelligent

11. tool : function
    camera : photography :: stove : cooking

12. symbol : what is symbolized
    Cross : Christianity :: Star of David : Judaism

13. need : that which satisfies the need
    thirst : water :: hunger : food

14. place
    airplane : sky :: boat : water

15. sequence
    acorn : oak :: egg : turtle

SAT I Mini-Test

The Mini-Test that follows is designed to help you to discover your strengths and weaknesses in areas tested on the verbal portion of SAT I. It is modeled after the actual examination, but it contains fewer questions in each of the categories. Following the test are an answer key and an explanation of the answers. Use this material to guide your study in those areas in which you need the most practice. A full-length practice test follows the Mini-Test.

Critical Reading

Directions: In the following excerpt on language development, the author discusses the importance of context clues in learning the meanings of words. Answer all questions on the basis of what is *stated* or *implied* in the passage.

Since the relation between a word and its referent is a mental one, we can think of different referents for the same word. Thus *spring* may be a season, a source of drinking water, or a metal bar or coil. This multiple use of the same word allows us to describe a limitless number of experiences with a limited number of words. The people to whom we are speaking or writing can usually tell which meaning we have in mind by noticing the whole statement or situation in which we use a word—"I'll be glad when spring comes"; "Fill this bottle at the spring"; "The car has a broken spring." The whole statement or situation in which a word is used is called its *context.*

In practice we learn the meanings of words by their contexts. When we are learning our language, we do not meet the word "run" by itself; we always meet it in some situation—a man running for a bus, a child running a temperature, a quarterback running a team, and so on. We learn the meanings of "run" by repeatedly experiencing it in context. This is exactly how the writers of dictionaries get their definitions. They gather sample contexts and write the definitions to describe the meanings these convey, so that when a dictionary lists different meanings of the word "spring," it is recording the contexts in which "spring" most frequently occurs.

1.　This passage would be particularly interesting to

　　(A) a student studying the writing process
　　(B) a historian
　　(C) a physicist
　　(D) a person trying to improve his ability to use non-verbal communication
　　(E) a consumer　　　　**1.** Ⓐ Ⓑ Ⓒ Ⓓ Ⓔ

2.　Using contextual clues

　　(A) is not useful when studying a foreign language
　　(B) is a valuable reading skill
　　(C) is frequently misleading
　　(D) has no relation to referents　　**2.** Ⓐ Ⓑ Ⓒ Ⓓ Ⓔ
　　(E) is more valuable with phrases than with full statements

3.　"Context" is

　　(A) opposed to meaning
　　(B) a limitless number of experiences
　　(C) of no use to writers of dictionaries
　　(D) the entire situation in which a word is employed
　　(E) a limited number of experiences　　**3.** Ⓐ Ⓑ Ⓒ Ⓓ Ⓔ

4. It can be inferred from the content of the passage that a non-native speaker of a language

    (A) has an advantage over a native speaker
    (B) will have more difficulty writing than speaking his new language
    (C) will depend heavily on referents
    (D) has less need for dictionary study than a native speaker
    (E) experiences difficulty because of a lack of contextual experiences

    4. Ⓐ Ⓑ Ⓒ Ⓓ Ⓔ

Sentence Completion

Directions: Each sentence below has one or two blanks, each blank indicating that something has been omitted. Beneath the sentence are five lettered words or sets of words. Choose the word or set of words that *best* fits the meaning of the sentence as a whole.

5. There are phenomena that, even after the most _____ and painstaking investigations, cannot be _____ .

    (A) happy—obliterated
    (B) felicitious—rationalized
    (C) fortuitous—managed
    (D) oblique—handled
    (E) cautious—explained

    5. Ⓐ Ⓑ Ⓒ Ⓓ Ⓔ

6. If a plant cannot live according to its _____ it dies; and so a man.

    (A) pleasure
    (B) nature
    (C) roots
    (D) leaves
    (E) foliage

    6. Ⓐ Ⓑ Ⓒ Ⓓ Ⓔ

7. The press must not only be _____ ; it must be completely _____ .

    (A) free—independent
    (B) read—self-supporting
    (C) distributed—frugal
    (D) criticized—democratic
    (E) evaluated—critical

    7. Ⓐ Ⓑ Ⓒ Ⓓ Ⓔ

Analogies

Directions: Each question below contains a pair of words in capital letters, followed by five pairs of words. Select the pair that *best* expresses a relationship similar to the one expressed by the capitalized pair.

8. ARIA: DUET

    (A) opera: drama
    (B) soliloquy: speech
    (C) monologue: dialogue
    (D) repartee: actor
    (E) song: lyric

    8. Ⓐ Ⓑ Ⓒ Ⓓ Ⓔ

9. PENNY: DIME

    (A) cent: dollar
    (B) silver: gold
    (C) year: decade
    (D) lira: shekel
    (E) coin: mint

9. Ⓐ Ⓑ Ⓒ Ⓓ Ⓔ

10. TREASURER: FINANCES

    (A) secretary: minutes
    (B) president: chairman
    (C) vice-president: congress
    (D) senator: representative
    (E) agenda: meeting

10. Ⓐ Ⓑ Ⓒ Ⓓ Ⓔ

Answers

SAT I Mini-Test

Critical Reading	1.	A
	2.	B
	3.	D
	4.	E
Sentence Completion	5.	E
	6.	B
	7.	A
Analogies	8.	C
	9.	C
	10.	A

Explanatory Answers for SAT I Mini-Test

Critical Reading

1. **(A)** Since the passage is concerned with the meaning of words, only choice **(A)** is appropriate.
2. **(B)** Since "we learn the meaning of words by their contexts," using contextual clues is a definite way for the reader to comprehend the message of the writer.
3. **(D)** The last sentence of the first paragraph supplies the meaning of *context*, "the whole statement or situation in which a word is used . . . ."
4. **(E)** Since non-native speakers may not be familiar with the various ways words are used in a language not their own, they often lack experience in using contextual clues to interpret material.

_____ ## Sentence Completion

5. **(E)** Only choice **(E)**, *cautious*, is in harmony with *painstaking* as a modifier of *investigations*; and even after these investigations, some phenomena cannot be *explained*.

6. **(B)** A comparison is being made between a plant and a man and so the word sought must apply to both. *Roots, leaves,* and *foliage* apply only to plants, and *pleasure* does not convey the sense of the sentence; therefore, only choice **(B)** is correct.

7. **(A)** The structure of the sentence suggests that the two missing words should be closely related. Since *free* and *independent* are synonyms and are often associated with the media, choice **(A)** is the most suitable.

_____ ## Analogies

8. **(C)** An *aria* is a melody for a single voice in an opera; a *duet* is a composition for two voices. A *monologue* is spoken by a single person; a *dialogue* is a conversation which is spoken by at least two people.

9. **(C)** The relationship between *penny* and *dime* is one to ten, just as is the relationship between *year* and *decade*.

10. **(A)** Just as a *treasurer* is responsible for the *finances* of an organization, a *secretary* is responsible for the *minutes,* the record of a meeting's proceedings.

Answer Sheet for Sample Test 1: SAT I

1. Ⓐ Ⓑ Ⓒ Ⓓ Ⓔ
2. Ⓐ Ⓑ Ⓒ Ⓓ Ⓔ
3. Ⓐ Ⓑ Ⓒ Ⓓ Ⓔ
4. Ⓐ Ⓑ Ⓒ Ⓓ Ⓔ
5. Ⓐ Ⓑ Ⓒ Ⓓ Ⓔ
6. Ⓐ Ⓑ Ⓒ Ⓓ Ⓔ
7. Ⓐ Ⓑ Ⓒ Ⓓ Ⓔ
8. Ⓐ Ⓑ Ⓒ Ⓓ Ⓔ
9. Ⓐ Ⓑ Ⓒ Ⓓ Ⓔ
10. Ⓐ Ⓑ Ⓒ Ⓓ Ⓔ
11. Ⓐ Ⓑ Ⓒ Ⓓ Ⓔ
12. Ⓐ Ⓑ Ⓒ Ⓓ Ⓔ
13. Ⓐ Ⓑ Ⓒ Ⓓ Ⓔ
14. Ⓐ Ⓑ Ⓒ Ⓓ Ⓔ
15. Ⓐ Ⓑ Ⓒ Ⓓ Ⓔ
16. Ⓐ Ⓑ Ⓒ Ⓓ Ⓔ
17. Ⓐ Ⓑ Ⓒ Ⓓ Ⓔ
18. Ⓐ Ⓑ Ⓒ Ⓓ Ⓔ
19. Ⓐ Ⓑ Ⓒ Ⓓ Ⓔ
20. Ⓐ Ⓑ Ⓒ Ⓓ Ⓔ
21. Ⓐ Ⓑ Ⓒ Ⓓ Ⓔ
22. Ⓐ Ⓑ Ⓒ Ⓓ Ⓔ
23. Ⓐ Ⓑ Ⓒ Ⓓ Ⓔ
24. Ⓐ Ⓑ Ⓒ Ⓓ Ⓔ
25. Ⓐ Ⓑ Ⓒ Ⓓ Ⓔ
26. Ⓐ Ⓑ Ⓒ Ⓓ Ⓔ

27. Ⓐ Ⓑ Ⓒ Ⓓ Ⓔ
28. Ⓐ Ⓑ Ⓒ Ⓓ Ⓔ
29. Ⓐ Ⓑ Ⓒ Ⓓ Ⓔ
30. Ⓐ Ⓑ Ⓒ Ⓓ Ⓔ
31. Ⓐ Ⓑ Ⓒ Ⓓ Ⓔ
32. Ⓐ Ⓑ Ⓒ Ⓓ Ⓔ
33. Ⓐ Ⓑ Ⓒ Ⓓ Ⓔ
34. Ⓐ Ⓑ Ⓒ Ⓓ Ⓔ
35. Ⓐ Ⓑ Ⓒ Ⓓ Ⓔ
36. Ⓐ Ⓑ Ⓒ Ⓓ Ⓔ
37. Ⓐ Ⓑ Ⓒ Ⓓ Ⓔ
38. Ⓐ Ⓑ Ⓒ Ⓓ Ⓔ
39. Ⓐ Ⓑ Ⓒ Ⓓ Ⓔ
40. Ⓐ Ⓑ Ⓒ Ⓓ Ⓔ
41. Ⓐ Ⓑ Ⓒ Ⓓ Ⓔ
42. Ⓐ Ⓑ Ⓒ Ⓓ Ⓔ
43. Ⓐ Ⓑ Ⓒ Ⓓ Ⓔ
44. Ⓐ Ⓑ Ⓒ Ⓓ Ⓔ
45. Ⓐ Ⓑ Ⓒ Ⓓ Ⓔ
46. Ⓐ Ⓑ Ⓒ Ⓓ Ⓔ
47. Ⓐ Ⓑ Ⓒ Ⓓ Ⓔ
48. Ⓐ Ⓑ Ⓒ Ⓓ Ⓔ
49. Ⓐ Ⓑ Ⓒ Ⓓ Ⓔ
50. Ⓐ Ⓑ Ⓒ Ⓓ Ⓔ
51. Ⓐ Ⓑ Ⓒ Ⓓ Ⓔ
52. Ⓐ Ⓑ Ⓒ Ⓓ Ⓔ

53. Ⓐ Ⓑ Ⓒ Ⓓ Ⓔ
54. Ⓐ Ⓑ Ⓒ Ⓓ Ⓔ
55. Ⓐ Ⓑ Ⓒ Ⓓ Ⓔ
56. Ⓐ Ⓑ Ⓒ Ⓓ Ⓔ
57. Ⓐ Ⓑ Ⓒ Ⓓ Ⓔ
58. Ⓐ Ⓑ Ⓒ Ⓓ Ⓔ
59. Ⓐ Ⓑ Ⓒ Ⓓ Ⓔ
60. Ⓐ Ⓑ Ⓒ Ⓓ Ⓔ
61. Ⓐ Ⓑ Ⓒ Ⓓ Ⓔ
62. Ⓐ Ⓑ Ⓒ Ⓓ Ⓔ
63. Ⓐ Ⓑ Ⓒ Ⓓ Ⓔ
64. Ⓐ Ⓑ Ⓒ Ⓓ Ⓔ
65. Ⓐ Ⓑ Ⓒ Ⓓ Ⓔ
66. Ⓐ Ⓑ Ⓒ Ⓓ Ⓔ
67. Ⓐ Ⓑ Ⓒ Ⓓ Ⓔ
68. Ⓐ Ⓑ Ⓒ Ⓓ Ⓔ
69. Ⓐ Ⓑ Ⓒ Ⓓ Ⓔ
70. Ⓐ Ⓑ Ⓒ Ⓓ Ⓔ
71. Ⓐ Ⓑ Ⓒ Ⓓ Ⓔ
72. Ⓐ Ⓑ Ⓒ Ⓓ Ⓔ
73. Ⓐ Ⓑ Ⓒ Ⓓ Ⓔ
74. Ⓐ Ⓑ Ⓒ Ⓓ Ⓔ
75. Ⓐ Ⓑ Ⓒ Ⓓ Ⓔ
76. Ⓐ Ⓑ Ⓒ Ⓓ Ⓔ
77. Ⓐ Ⓑ Ⓒ Ⓓ Ⓔ
78. Ⓐ Ⓑ Ⓒ Ⓓ Ⓔ

(Answers appear on page 168)

CHAPTER 8

Sample Test 1:
SAT I: Verbal Reasoning

78 Questions—75 Minutes

Questions 1–7:

Directions: In the following excerpt, the author discusses contemporary material on animal extinction. Answer all questions on the basis of what is *stated* or *implied* in the passage.

Line

The smaller the remnant population of some organism, the more difficult it is to study. Still, bit by bit, over the past several decades, the biological evidence of dwindling species has been brought together in the files of the Survival Service Commission of the International Union for the Conservation of Nat-
(5) ural Resources. A few years ago the information on birds and mammals threatened with extinction was published in two *Red Data Books*. For each such animal, there is a page of condensed information on biology and status. As new information comes in, a new page is printed to replace the old.

The organization of the *Red Data Books* is taxonomic, so that it is a simple
(10) matter, for example, to scan the parrots for threatened forms.

The present volume, too, is based on the files of the Survival Service Commission. Its authors include those of the *Red Data Books* and, like those books, it consists of accounts of threatened organisms taxonomically arranged. These accounts, however, are really individual essays. Each stands
(15) alone, yet the threat of extinction constitutes a theme which links them all together. Each is clearly written, logically organized, and packed with interesting information. Abundant, well-executed illustrations enliven the text. To the large sections on mammals and birds are added shorter ones on the much less intensively studied reptiles, amphibians, fishes, and plants. The
(20) book is introduced with a preface, a foreword, and an introduction—it really introduces the subject of the volume, which is the natural history of biotic extinction.

Biotic extinction is, of course, nothing new. Fisher, from the fossil record, places the mean life of a bird species at about two million years, and of a
(25) mammal at not much over 600,000. After that a species evolves into other species or becomes extinct. The pace of evolution—and of extinction—is much more rapid for island populations. Island forms, therefore, are prominent among species both extinct and threatened with extinction. In the West Indies the life of a bird species before colonization by man was only 180,000
(30) years. But—and here is Fisher's main point—this figure dropped to 30,000 with colonization by aboriginal man and to 12,000 with colonization from Europe.

The various major causes of biotic extinction can be grouped into natural causes (that is, changing through adaptation or being unable to adapt or
(35) compete) and effects of man, including hunting, introduced predators, introduced competitors, introduced diseases, and habitat alteration. Focusing on the period since 1600, which marked the beginning both of a rather definite knowledge of bird and mammal species and of the age of colonization, Fisher estimates that about 70 to 80 percent of both extinctions and serious
(40) population declines can be attributed to man's actions.

1. The author's main purpose for having written this article was to

    (A) relate the history of animal extinction
    (B) urge the need to practice good conservation
    (C) list animals that face extinction
    (D) explain the Survival Service Commission and its duties
    (E) review a book

2. It can be inferred from the passage that the animals most difficult to study would be

    (A) moles
    (B) buffalo
    (C) deer
    (D) sharks
    (E) rattlesnakes

3. It can be expected that with the colonization of an island by modern man the life of a bird species would be cut by at least

    (A) 10%
    (B) 35%
    (C) 50%
    (D) 70%
    (E) 85%

4. From the information presented in the passage, it can be said that animal species have been faced with extinction for

    (A) almost 400 years
    (B) nearly 12,000 years
    (C) about 180,000 years
    (D) about 2 million years
    (E) more than 2 million years

5. All of the following are mentioned as a cause of biotic extinction EXCEPT

    (A) man-made change to living areas
    (B) change through adaptation
    (C) widespread natural catastrophes
    (D) the transport of animals by man
    (E) failure to compete with natural enemies

6. From contextual clues, we can deduce that "taxonomic" (line 9) means

    (A) alphabetic
    (B) classification
    (C) mechanical
    (D) haphazard
    (E) careful

7. Human beings are responsible for

    (A) almost half of all population declines
    (B) establishing fossil records which show biotic extinction
    (C) well over half of all population declines
    (D) island colonization by aboriginal tribes
    (E) the pace of evolution

Questions 8–17:

Directions: In the following excerpt, the author discusses the significance of science and technology for our lives. Answer all questions on the basis of what is *stated* or *implied* in the passage.

Line
The American university is a direct descendant from the ancient universities in Europe. These are the oldest institutions, aside from the church itself, in Western civilization. They have survived many periods of trouble, of revolution, and of persecution. But the tradition of learning and of scholarly in-
(5) quiry has lived on.

Yet there are shortsighted people today who are saying that the modern university has outlived its usefulness; that it must be overthrown and replaced by something else whose nature is unspecified.

Remember, however, that there have been many occasions during the last
(10) 700 years when people said that universities were irrelevant or that it was wrong for them to pursue long-term goals in the face of immediate and pressuring problems. Fortunately, there have been stouthearted souls who insisted that the search for knowledge would never be outdated by current events, and we can all be eternally thankful that the forces of ignorance were
(15) so often defeated. They must be defeated again.

Knowledge and the search for knowledge have persisted through the centuries to the enormous benefit of human beings. The world may be troubled and distressed today, but think how much better off the people in this country are now than they were 50 years ago or 100 years ago and how much better
(20) off they are than the millions of people in countries which have not benefited from the progress of knowledge. We in the Western world have encouraged scientific discovery and its application intensively for 200 years to our vast material benefit. Today we are at a turning point. We can now use our stores of wealth and of knowledge as tools to solve the new problems which now
(25) beset our modern society.

What are those of us who have chosen careers in science and engineering able to do about meeting our current problems?

First, we can help destroy the false impression that science and engineering have caused the current world troubles. Quite the contrary, science and en-
(30) gineering have made vast contributions to better living for more people.

Second, we can identify the many areas in which science and technology, more considerately used, can be of greater service in the future than in the past to improve the quality of life. While we can make many speeches and pass many laws, the quality of our environment will be improved only through
(35) better knowledge and better application of that knowledge.

Third, we can recognize that much of the dissatisfaction which we suffer today results from our very successes of former years. We have been so eminently successful in attaining material goals that we are deeply dissatisfied that we cannot attain other goals more rapidly. We have achieved a better life for
(40) most people, but we are unhappy that we have not spread it to all people. We have illuminated many sources of environmental deterioration, but we are unhappy that we have not conquered all of them. It is our rising expectations rather than our failures which now cause our distress.

(45) Granted that many of our current problems must be cured more by social, political, and economic instruments than by science and technology, yet science and technology must still be the tools to make further advances in such things as clean air, clean water, better transportation, better housing, better medical care, more adequate welfare programs, purer foods, conservation of resources, and many other areas.

(50) The discovery and use of knowledge have always been relevant to a humane future. They are equally relevant today.

8. The author is primarily concerned with the

    (A) answers to current problems
    (B) defense of the search for scientific knowledge
    (C) problems of our nation's universities
    (D) moral obligations of technology
    (E) causes of frustration throughout the nation

9. According to the author, a belief exists that much of our national dissatisfaction is due to the

    (A) emphasis of science on material goals
    (B) irrelevancy of many of our modern universities
    (C) failure of scientists to solve modern day problems as quickly as they solved problems of the past
    (D) overemphasis on science to the exclusion of other areas of knowledge
    (E) improper use of past discoveries in science and technology

10. It is the feeling of the author that the place of science in solving the problem of pollution will be

    (A) on the same level as social and political influences
    (B) the only thing needed to solve the problem successfully
    (C) as the frontrunner in developing new methods of approaching the problem
    (D) the source of most of the problems
    (E) overshadowed by other areas of knowledge

11. It is suggested that science has been most successful in

    (A) developing material benefits
    (B) solving problems of worldwide concern
    (C) preparing America for a humane future
    (D) preventing further revolution and persecution
    (E) controlling technology as a means of preventing serious problems

12. It is stated that science contributed to all of the following EXCEPT

    (A) a better life
    (B) peace
    (C) health
    (D) help for the poor
    (E) a better environment

13. The author of the article appears to be a

     (A) scientist
     (B) Victorian writer
     (C) university administrator
     (D) rebel
     (E) free thinker

14. The word *eminently* (line 37) means

     (A) prominently
     (B) recently
     (C) viably
     (D) gratuitously
     (E) falsely

15. The author would most likely agree with which of the following sentiments?

     (A) "Beauty is truth."
     (B) "Grow old along with me/The best is yet to be."
     (C) "There is nothing new under the sun."
     (D) "A man's reach is greater than his grasp."
     (E) "The mass of men lead lives of quiet desperation."

16. According to the author, the more knowledge we have, the more our society will become

     (A) diversified
     (B) kinder and gentler
     (C) concerned with technological rather than social issues
     (D) materialistic
     (E) goal oriented

17. The basic tone of this passage is

     (A) light
     (B) pessimistic
     (C) ironic
     (D) hostile
     (E) optimistic

Double Passage, Questions 18–40:

Directions: Sir Richard Steele, a seventeenth- and eighteenth-century Irish essayist, collaborated with Joseph Addison to produce the *Tatler* and the *Spectator*. The first selection below, in which Steele examines the English school system's method of discipline, is taken from the *Spectator*. Following this selection is an excerpt from an essay by Henry Fielding, an eighteenth-century writer, in which the author discusses the breeding of English students.

Passage A

Line I am confident that no boy who will not be allured to letters without blows, will ever be brought to any thing with them. A great or good mind must necessarily be the worse for such indignities; and it is a sad change to lose of its virtue for the improvement of its knowledge. No one who has gone through what

(5)   they call a great school, but must remember to have seen children of excellent and ingenuous natures (as has afterwards appeared in their manhood); I say no man has passed through this way of education, but must have seen an ingenuous creature expiring with shame, with pale looks, beseeching sorrow, and silent tears, throw up its honest eyes, and kneel on its tender knees to an

(10)   inexorable blockhead, to be forgiven the false quantity of a word in making a Latin verse: the child is punished, and the next day he commits a like crime, and so a third with the same consequence. I would fain ask any reasonable man whether this lad, in the simplicity of his native innocence, full of shame, and capable of any impression from that grace of soul, was not fitter for any

(15)   purpose in this life, than after that spark of virtue is extinguished in him, though he is able to write twenty verses in an evening?

Seneca says, after his exalted way of talking, *As the immortal gods never learnt any virtue, tho' they are indued with all that is good; so there are some men who have so natural a propensity to what they should follow, that they*

(20)   *learn it almost as soon as they hear it.* Plants and vegetables are cultivated into the production of finer fruit than they would yield without that care; and yet we cannot entertain hopes of producing a tender conscious spirit into acts of virtue, without the same methods as is used to cut timber, or give new shape to a piece of stone.

(25)   It is wholly to this dreadful practice that we may attribute a certain hardness and ferocity which some men, though liberally educated, carry about them in all their behaviour. To be bred like a gentleman, and punished like a malefactor, must, as we see it does, produce that illiberal sauciness which we see sometimes in men of letters.

(30)   The Spartan boy who suffered the fox (which he had stolen and hid under his coat) to eat into his bowels, I dare say had not half the wit or petulance which we learn at great schools among us: but the glorious sense of honour, or rather fear of shame, which he demonstrated in that action, was worth all the learning in the world without it.

(35)   It is methinks a very melancholy consideration, that a little negligence can spoil us, but great industry is necessary to improve us; the most excellent natures are soon depreciated, but evil tempers are long before they are exalted into good habits. To help this by punishments, is the same thing as killing a man to cure him of a distemper: when he comes to suffer punishment

(40)   in that one circumstance, he is brought below the existence of a rational creature, and is in the state of a brute that moves only by the admonition of stripes.

Passage B

Line   Having thus shown, I think very clearly, that good breeding is, and must be, the very bane of the ridiculous, that is to say, of all humorous characters, it

(45)   will perhaps be no difficult task to discover why this character hath been in a singular manner attributed to this nation.

For this I shall assign two reasons only, as these seem to me abundantly satisfactory, and adequate to the purpose.

The first is that method so general in this kingdom of giving no education to

(50)   the youth of both sexes; I say general only, for it is not without some few exceptions.

Much the greater part of our lads of fashion return from school at fifteen or sixteen, very little wiser, and not at all the better, for having been sent thither. Part of these return to the place from whence they came, their fathers' country
(55)   seats; where racing, cock-fighting, hunting, and other rural sports, with smoking, drinking, and party become their pursuit, and form the whole business and amusement of their future lives. The other part escape to town, in the diversions, fashion, follies and vices of which they are immediately initiated. In this academy some finish their studies, while others by their wiser parents
(60)   are sent abroad to add the knowledge of the diversions, fashions, follies, and vices of all Europe, to that of those of their own country.

Hence then we are to derive two great general characters of humour, which are the clown and the coxcomb, and both of these will be almost infinitely diversified according to the different passions and natural dispositions of
(65)   each individual; and according to their different walks in life. Great will be the difference, for instance, whether the country gentleman be a Whig or a Tory; whether he prefers women, drink, or dogs; so will it be whether the town spark be allotted to serve his country as a politician, a courtier, a soldier, a sailor, or possibly a churchman (for by draughts from this academy,
(70)   all these offices are supplied); or lastly, whether his ambition shall be contented with no other appellation than merely that of a beau.

Some of our lads, however, are destined to a further progress in learning; these are not only confined longer to the labours of a school, but are sent thence to the university. Here, if they please, they may read on; and if they
(75)   please, they may (as most of them do) let it alone, and betake themselves as their fancy leads, to the imitation of their elder brothers either in town or country.

18.   In passage A, Steele asserts that

    (A) the Romans advocated the use of rewards and punishment
    (B) the Spartans were lax in matters of child rearing
    (C) corporal punishment is not a good motivation for learning
    (D) men of letters were never severely punished
    (E) Seneca disagreed with the Spartans

19.   The word *entertain* in line 22 has the same meaning as in:

    (A) I will entertain such a motion.
    (B) We are not here to entertain you.
    (C) The mime tried to entertain his audience.
    (D) The school must inform, not entertain.
    (E) We should strive to teach actors how to entertain small groups.

20.   In line 28, Steele uses the word *malefactor* as

    (A) a synonym for gentleman
    (B) the epitome of a liberal
    (C) a synonym for one who is uneducated
    (D) an explanation for the ills of society
    (E) a contrast to gentleman

21. Steele feels that as a result of being punished when young there are many educated men who

    (A) are not men of letters
    (B) have become Latin scholars
    (C) display impudence and disrespect
    (D) chastise their own children
    (E) withdraw from society

22. Seneca compares people with the gods

    (A) to show that both are opposed to extreme measures
    (B) to illustrate how foolish humans can become
    (C) to show how difficult it is to train some people
    (D) to add a note of spirituality to the essay
    (E) to point out that there are some who have an almost inborn leaning to follow the right path

23. Steele feels that Seneca's style is

    (A) clear and precise
    (B) muddied
    (C) lofty
    (D) incomprehensible
    (E) rambling

24. A synonym for *suffered* in line 30 is

    (A) hurt
    (B) yielded
    (C) pained
    (D) allowed
    (E) punished

25. The purpose of the anecdote about the Spartan boy is to show that

    (A) the Spartan way of life was inferior to that of Steele's time
    (B) although the boy endured much, the result was not worth the pain
    (C) the end result was valuable to the lad
    (D) Spartans had no lack of shame or honor
    (E) Spartans and Romans were alike in many ways

26. When Steele writes of curing a patient of distemper (lines 38–42), he is

    (A) paraphrasing Plutarch, who wrote, "The cure is not worth the pain."
    (B) stating that harsh illnesses deserve harsh treatments
    (C) justifying corporal punishment
    (D) explaining the dilemma faced by doctors
    (E) giving a rationale for euthanasia

27. How would Steele react to the proverb "Spare the rod and spoil the child"?

    (A) He would be ambivalent.
    (B) He does not address this issue in his essay.
    (C) He would be opposed to this concept.
    (D) Although he would essentially agree, he would see some of the shortcomings.
    (E) He would be in complete agreement.

28. It may be inferred from passage B that when Fielding says that "good breeding is . . . the very bane of the ridiculous" (lines 43–44), he means that

    (A) good breeding is envied by the ridiculous
    (B) good breeding is avoided by the ridiculous
    (C) the ridiculous will be strengthened by good breeding
    (D) the ridiculous will be destroyed by good breeding
    (E) good breeding and the ridiculous are synonymous

29. Fielding holds that the average English student is

    (A) scholarly
    (B) pleasure-seeking
    (C) morose
    (D) creative
    (E) realistic

30. The essential tone of lines 59–61 is

    (A) satiric
    (B) sanguine
    (C) morose
    (D) angry
    (E) confused

31. It may be inferred from passage B that a *coxcomb* (line 63) is

    (A) a diversified individual
    (B) a somber person
    (C) a conceited dandy
    (D) a passionate individual
    (E) a lad in charge of a crew

32. Fielding condemns

    (A) country life for its inferiority to the lifestyle of the town
    (B) the lack of concern for important matters of "educated" young people
    (C) excessive reliance on outmoded curricula
    (D) young people for not returning to their roots
    (E) universities for being too narrow and self-serving

33. To which of the following statements would Fielding be *least* likely to subscribe?

    (A) "Education has for its object the formation of character."
    (B) "Education is not preparation for life; education is life itself."
    (C) "I regret the trifling narrow contracted education of the females of my own country."
    (D) "Education is the provision for old age."
    (E) "Let early education be a sort of amusement."

34. As used by Fielding in line 69, *draughts* would most likely refer to

    (A) currents of air
    (B) loss in weight of merchandise
    (C) selection of personnel
    (D) early stages of composition
    (E) the pull of a load

35. When Fielding writes of *fancy* in line 76, he means a young man's

    (A) tutelage
    (B) extravagance
    (C) imagination
    (D) upbringing
    (E) diversity

36. It can be inferred after reading passage B that Fielding's general tone is one of

    (A) amusement
    (B) dismay
    (C) hostility
    (D) amazement
    (E) approval

37. Fielding and Steele

    (A) agree that education is not for the masses
    (B) disagree on public education as a social remedy
    (C) both feel that the education of English youth should be addressed and improved
    (D) agree that private education is far better than public education
    (E) both are disturbed by the methods by which teachers are chosen in British schools

38. The topic of corporal punishment

    (A) is addressed by both writers
    (B) is not germane to either writer
    (C) is more opposed by Fielding than by Steele
    (D) is seriously evaluated by Steele and not considered by Fielding
    (E) is treated more lightly by Fielding than by Steele

39. In comparing Fielding's style of writing with that of Steele,

    (A) Fielding is more pessimistic
    (B) Fielding is less concerned with education
    (C) Fielding is less educated
    (D) Fielding is more scholarly
    (E) Fielding is more optimistic

40. It cannot be inferred from comparing the excerpts that

    (A) Fielding and Steele are both concerned with education
    (B) neither writer is completely satisfied with the British system of educating children
    (C) the way an adult behaves often results from the type of education to which he or she was exposed
    (D) classical education is often challenging and necessary for the cultured adult
    (E) education in English schools has shortcomings

Questions 41–59:

Directions: Each of the following sentences contains one or two blank spaces to be filled in by one of the five choices listed below each sentence. Select the word or set of words that *best* fits the meaning of the sentence as a whole.

41. The governor's _____ from fiscal _____ has led our state to bankruptcy.

    (A) adherence—prudence
    (B) aversion—debt
    (C) avoidance—propensity
    (D) retreat—responsibility
    (E) gratitude—management

42. It would be _____ to ask for a promotion this year, since our profits are at an all-time low.

    (A) efficaceous
    (B) propitious
    (C) malignant
    (D) fortuitous
    (E) impolitic

43. His childish behavior was decidedly _____ .

    (A) venerable
    (B) puerile
    (C) sagacious
    (D) malleable
    (E) gratuitous

44. Learning is a _____ pleasure; _____ and instructive, one of the real joys of life.

    (A) genuine—perverse
    (B) pathetic—dramatic
    (C) natural—inborn
    (D) compulsive—disciplined
    (E) infantile—delightful

45. Some readers would rather look into the _____ of the play than to see it _____ .

    (A) characters—concluded
    (B) acts—dramatized
    (C) scenery—enacted
    (D) speeches—read
    (E) text—performed

46. The first five congressmen from our district encompassed a _____ of character types.

    (A) gamut
    (B) proclivity
    (C) value
    (D) compliance
    (E) verity

47. They enjoy the _____ of being part of a _____ movement.

    (A) fear—group
    (B) deprivation—popular
    (C) nemesis—mass
    (D) excitement—political
    (E) scarcity—general

48. Your grandfather _____ the finest element of the aristocratic _____ .

    (A) embodied—ideal
    (B) gathered—rabble
    (C) exhumed—group
    (D) relinquished—mass
    (E) criticized—rustics

49. The angry students were _____ demands for changes in the grading system.

    (A) seeking
    (B) retracting
    (C) genuflecting
    (D) starting
    (E) issuing

50. The point of this _____ is to explore the environment in which she was _____ .

    (A) outcry—placated
    (B) dilemma—gathered
    (C) vignette—raised
    (D) critique—startled
    (E) anecdote—obliterated

51. He lived in a time when the premises on which society is structured were being _____ , sharply _____ and profoundly changed.

    (A) praised—criticized
    (B) lauded—negated
    (C) accepted—cheered
    (D) avoided—eradicated
    (E) analyzed—challenged

52. Late in the summer the seas will be _____ with fish.

    (A) redolent
    (B) ebullient
    (C) mating
    (D) teeming
    (E) swimming

53. Every hour that _____ makes it _____ likely that the missing child will be found.

    (A) passes—more
    (B) arrives—hardly
    (C) evanesces—exceedingly
    (D) goes by—quite
    (E) elapses—less

54. The regulations now in force can _____ from revision.

    (A) benefit
    (B) hurt
    (C) be avoided
    (D) be mismanaged
    (E) be obliterated

55. There is nothing to _____ you for the _____ of growing old.

    (A) hurt—pleasure
    (B) assist—melodrama
    (C) cure—value
    (D) prepare—experience
    (E) enable—dilemma

56. Despite its undisputed, all-powerful _____ , the bear is mild and _____ , seeking only the solitude of its own domain.

    (A) strength—hostile
    (B) jaws—calm
    (C) call—quick
    (D) might—shy
    (E) cubs—shrewd

57. From the long-range point of view, every community, whether already _____ with an air pollution problem or in the period of rapid _____ that almost automatically signals coming problems, needs to plan ahead.

    (A) liquidated—decay
    (B) assisted—change
    (C) destroyed—flux
    (D) troubled—growth
    (E) served—progress

58. Although aphids are small insects, their importance to _____ is far out of proportion to their _____ .

    (A) people—value
    (B) the environment—damage
    (C) mankind—size
    (D) food—number
    (E) gardeners—ability

59. One light meal daily is sufficient for fishes if there are plenty of plants among which they can _____ .

    (A) infiltrate
    (B) browse
    (C) emigrate
    (D) hibernate
    (E) estivate

Questions 60–78:

Directions: Each of the following questions contains a pair of words in capital letters, followed by five pairs of words. Choose the pair that best expresses a relationship similar to the one expressed by the capitalized pair.

60. NAIL: FINGER

    (A) faucet: water
    (B) toe: foot
    (C) scabbard: machete
    (D) mouth: nose
    (E) hammer: hit

61. FIRMAMENT: SKY

    (A) termagant: shrew
    (B) constellation: heaven
    (C) erudite: boorish
    (D) clod: rough
    (E) billowy: cloudy

62. QUERY: RESPONSE

    (A) enter: knock
    (B) itch: scratch
    (C) chew: bite
    (D) resplendent: lackluster
    (E) effete: important

63. ANTE: ANTEBELLUM

    (A) anti: antipathy
    (B) ante: antenna
    (C) ante: anteroom
    (D) anti: antiwar
    (E) anta: antagonist

64. MAXIMUM: MINIMUM

    (A) superlative: excellent
    (B) warm: tepid
    (C) scroll: parchment
    (D) red: white
    (E) apogee: nadir

65. FLOWER: SEED

    (A) pistil: stamen
    (B) rose: petal
    (C) chicken: hen
    (D) bird: egg
    (E) fledgling: adult

66. RABBIT: WARREN

    (A) animal: nest
    (B) pig: pen
    (C) cat: litter
    (D) human: child
    (E) aerie: eagle

67. PRIDE: LION

    (A) school: fish
    (B) animal: hunter
    (C) soldier: brave
    (D) talent: actor
    (E) sky: rainbow

68. ZEUS: JUPITER

    (A) Vulcan: volcano
    (B) Brahma: Hindu
    (C) Olympus: mountain
    (D) Hera: Juno
    (E) Elijah: prophet

69. PSALMS: DAVID

    (A) Exodus: creation
    (B) Genesis: Bible
    (C) Kings: monarchy
    (D) Temple: Jerusalem
    (E) Proverbs: Solomon

70. COBALT: BLUE

    (A) mint: green
    (B) beige: brown
    (C) gray: black
    (D) pink: red
    (E) color: rainbow

71. SHOUT: SPEAK

    (A) bend: break
    (B) yell: whisper
    (C) sing: song
    (D) hurt: crack
    (E) talk: communicate

72. MILK: LIQUID

    (A) coffee: caffeine
    (B) tea: lemon
    (C) meat: solid
    (D) fish: protein
    (E) orange: tangerine

73. LUGUBRIOUS: GLOOMY

    (A) mourning: death
    (B) happy: life
    (C) birth: pregnant
    (D) malignant: destructive
    (E) joyful: florid

74. MENDACIOUS: VERACIOUS

    (A) liar: honest
    (B) thief: steal
    (C) police: jail
    (D) restive: calm
    (E) somnolent: sleepy

75. GARRULOUS: LOQUACIOUS

   (A) taciturn: silent
   (B) talkative: reflection
   (C) worrisome: tedious
   (D) succinct: florid
   (E) capitalist: society

76. DERMATOLOGIST: SKIN

   (A) podiatrist: children
   (B) cardiologist: heart
   (C) hospital: patients
   (D) physician: medicine
   (E) ophthalmologist: optometry

77. CHALLIS: WOOL

   (A) dress: wear
   (B) glove: hand
   (C) stockings: linen
   (D) jacket: suit
   (E) chambray: gingham

78. CYGNET: SWAN

   (A) cat: kitten
   (B) puppy: dog
   (C) duck: goose
   (D) graceful: agile
   (E) bird: canary

Answers

1. E	21. C	41. D	61. A
2. B	22. E	42. E	62. B
3. E	23. C	43. B	63. C
4. E	24. D	44. C	64. E
5. D	25. C	45. E	65. D
6. B	26. A	46. A	66. B
7. C	27. C	47. D	67. A
8. B	28. D	48. A	68. D
9. C	29. B	49. E	69. E
10. C	30. A	50. C	70. A
11. A	31. C	51. E	71. B
12. B	32. B	52. D	72. C
13. A	33. E	53. E	73. D
14. A	34. C	54. A	74. D
15. D	35. C	55. D	75. A
16. B	36. B	56. D	76. B
17. E	37. C	57. D	77. E
18. C	38. D	58. C	78. B
19. A	39. A	59. B	
20. E	40. D	60. B	

Explanatory Answers for Sample Test 1 _____

SAT I: Verbal Reasoning

1. **(E)** The author of this article is reviewing a book on the subject of animal extinction. Answer **(A)** is incorrect. Although the main idea of the book may be to relate the history of animal extinction, this is not the purpose of the article presented to the reader. Choice **(B)** is not a factor in the passage, and choices **(C)** and **(D)**, although mentioned, are not the main idea of the selection.

2. **(B)** The first sentence of the selection states that the smaller the population of an organism, the more difficult it is to study. It is a known fact, although it is not stated in the review, that the number of buffalo in existence today is rather low. Therefore, a study of the buffalo would be the most difficult of the animals listed among the choices.

3. **(E)** Paragraph four discusses the effects of colonization on the rate of extinction of animals. Using the figures given in that section, answer **(E)** —85%— would be the correct choice, as a decline from 180,000 to 12,000 represents that percentage. The 12,000 figure is used because that is the number presented for the colonization by modern (European) man. The 30,000 figure mentioned in the article represents the decline as a result of aboriginal (not modern) man.

4. **(E)** Records indicate a mean life of birds at about 2 million years. This is a mean, or average, so this animal has existed and been faced with extinction for more than 2 million years.

5. **(D)** The final paragraph lists the causes of extinction. Answers **(A)**, **(B)**, **(C)**, and **(E)** are all mentioned as causes and are therefore incorrect.

6. **(B)** *Taxonomic* refers to the classification of organisms in established categories.

7. **(C)** According to the passage, Fisher estimates that serious population declines of between 70 to 80 percent (well over half) can be attributed to man's actions.

8. **(B)** The author's main concern is best expressed in answer **(B)**. Answer choices **(A)**, **(C)**, **(D)**, and **(E)** have little to do with the selection and are wrong responses.

9. **(C)** The third item the author lists in the article regarding meeting our current problems is our dissatisfaction that we are not moving as quickly on present problems as we did on past problems. Answer **(C)** best expresses this point and is the appropriate answer. Choices **(A)**, **(B)**, **(D)**, and **(E)** are not mentioned in the author's discussion of our dissatisfactions.

10. **(C)** Science is a leader in that it promotes the creation of new tools to solve problems. Choice **(A)** is incorrect, as the contributions of science will be on a higher level than social or political influences. Nor is answer **(B)** correct, as science will not be the only thing needed to solve the problems. **(D)** is a ridiculous statement, and choice **(E)** is a false statement.

11. **(A)** Answer **(A)** is supported by the statement "We . . . have encouraged scientific discovery and its application intensively for 200 years to our vast material benefit."

12. **(B)** Answer **(B)**, *peace*, is the only choice not mentioned in the selection as having been benefited by science.

13. **(A)** The author states (line 26) that he is among those who have chosen a career in "science and engineering."

14. **(A)** *Eminently* means "prominently" or "remarkably."

15. **(D)** The author indicates that "it is our rising expectations rather than our failures" that distress us; therefore, our reach goes beyond our grasp.

16. **(B)** Since the author feels that the use of knowledge is related to a "humane future," we can infer that he has a vision of a kinder, gentler society.

17. **(E)** The author believes that people are better off today than those who lived 50 or 100 years ago and that we can use our "stores of wealth and of knowledge . . . to solve new problems." This is a hopeful and optimistic point of view.

18. **(C)** Steele calls corporal punishment a "dreadful practice" and further states that "no boy who will not be allured to letters without blows, will ever be brought to anything with them." Choice **(C)** is completely in keeping with these remarks. Choice **(A)** is not alluded to, and the other choices are in contradiction to Steele's facts.

19. **(A)** When Steele uses *entertain* he means "to consider," as in choice **(A)**. The other choices show different meanings for the word.

20. **(E)** Steele contrasts *malefactor* with *gentleman*, stating that those who are raised as or brought up (bred) like gentlemen are still punished like criminals (malefactors).

21. **(C)** In lines 27–28, Steele asserts that the child who is punished often becomes an adult with "illiberal sauciness" or impudence.

22. **(E)** The quotation from Seneca states that the gods are "indued with all that is good." Just so, there are men who have the same natural propensity to follow the right path.

23. **(C)** Steele describes Seneca's writing as "exalted," or lofty.

24. **(D)** The word *suffered* has many meanings. In line 30, it has the meaning of "permitted" or "allowed," choice **(D)**. The sense is "The Spartan boy who allowed the fox . . . ."

25. **(C)** Steele states that the end result to the lad who endured such dreadful pain was "worth all the learning in the world." In the context of this excerpt from the *Spectator*, choice **(C)** is accurate.

26. **(A)** Both Plutarch and Steele would agree that it is unwise to cure someone of an illness and cause the person to die as a result of the harsh treatment given. Thus, Steele writes that to try to improve a person by punishment is "the same thing as killing a man to cure him of a distemper."

27. **(C)** As Steele says, "no boy who will not be allured to letters with blows, will ever be brought to anything with them." Thus, harsh punishment never succeeds in producing great minds; conversely, no great harm is caused by withholding physical punishment.

28. **(D)** *Bane*, from Old English *Bana* (slayer), suggests death, destruction, or ruin. Good breeding can overcome the ridiculous.

29. **(B)** In lines 54–61, Fielding points out that, for the most part, the average English student is pleasure-seeking, fond of "diversions."

30. **(A)** In a tongue-in-cheek statement, Fielding suggests that some students "finish their studies" by absorbing the follies and vices of the city while others are sent abroad only to bring the follies and vices of all Europe back to England with them. Fielding mocks their parents by satirically labeling them as "wiser" and makes fun of the skills acquired by the young people abroad.

31. **(C)** A *coxcomb* is a "conceited dandy"; in the context of paragraph 5 of passage B, choice **(C)** makes the best sense.

32. **(B)** Fielding clearly deplores the lack of concern for matters of significance of young people who have been educated in the English schools. He points out that some return to their homes and indulge in rural sports of no value, and the remainder "escape to town, in the diversions, fashion, follies and vices of which they are immediately initiated." He feels that education has made them "very little wiser, and not at all the better."

33. **(E)** In this essay, Fielding is down on frivolity in general. With his seriousness of purpose, he surely would take issue with the suggestion that early education serve only for amusement and not for edification.

34. **(C)** In the context of the sentence—all these offices are supplied by draughts from this academy—the meaning of *draughts* clearly is selection of personnel. In its modern American spelling and usage, the same word applies to a *draft* for military service.

35. **(C)** *Fancy* has several meanings. Fielding uses the word, as does Shakespeare ("Tell me, where is fancy bred . . ."), as a synonym for *imagination*.

36. **(B)** Fielding is greatly saddened about the state of education in his country. He clearly deplores the result of a school system that does not prepare a young person to take a position of leadership in his country, but rather equips him only to engage in frivolous and worthless pursuits.

37. **(C)** Both writers appear to be concerned with the education of English youth. Their emphases differ. Steele is upset with the use of corporal punishment as a device to train young people; Fielding's essay is a more basic call for restructuring the education system and its goals.

38. **(D)** Fielding makes no mention of corporal punishment. Steele considers corporal punishment "a dreadful practice" and condemns the "admonition of stripes" (threatening blows with a whip).

39. **(A)** Both Fielding and Steele are educated, scholarly, and concerned with pedagogy. Both express themselves well. Steele's tone is essentially optimistic; he recognizes the innate positive qualities in human beings and feels that they can learn and choose proper paths without corporal punishment. Fielding, on the other hand, makes no constructive suggestions. His tone is deploring and pessimistic.

40. **(D)** There is no reference whatsoever in either essay to the value of classical education, so no inferences can be made with regard to this topic. All other choices are clearly treated in the two essays.

41. **(D)** The only word that fits idiomatically with *from* is *retreat*. This pairing **(D)** is in harmony with the sentence sense that the state is bankrupt because of the governor's actions.

42. **(E)** Since profits are low, it would not be a good time to request a promotion. *Impolitic* is the correct choice, because it means "unwise" or "inexpedient." *Malignant* also expresses a negative concept but it is too strong since it refers to something evil or very harmful. Choices **(A)**, **(B)**, and **(E)** are positive and therefore unsuitable.

43. **(B)** *Puerile* is a synonym for "childish" and therefore the correct response.

44. **(C)** The sentence means to state that learning is *natural* and *inborn*. The words *perverse, pathetic, compulsive,* and *infantile* have negative connotations and are inappropriate.

45. **(E)** Since the sentence contrasts "reading" and "seeing," the difference between the text and the performance makes choice **(E)** correct.

46. **(A)** The correct choice is **(A)**, since the congressmen encompassed a "wide range," or *gamut*, of personalities.

47. **(D)** Since *enjoy* indicates a positive feeling, *fear, deprivation, nemesis,* and *scarcity* are unsuitable, representing, as they do, negative ideas.

48. **(A)** The sentence makes a positive statement, indicating that the grandfather represented the best of the aristocratic elements. *Rabble* and *rustics* are inappropriate with *aristocratic*. *Exhumed* and *relinquished* do not make sense.

49. **(E)** The sentence states that students were not happy with the grading system and desired changes. Therefore, they were "making," or *issuing,* demands.

50. **(C)** A person grows up or is *raised* in an environment. Therefore, *placated, gathered, startled,* and *obliterated* are unsuitable.

51. **(E)** The sentence conveys the idea that there were those who were displeased with the structure of their society and sought to alter this structure. Therefore *praised, lauded,* and *accepted* are not fitting since they have positive connotations. Since the premises were being "changed," they were not being *avoided* or *eradicated*.

52. **(D)** In late summer, the ocean will "be filled" with newly hatched fish. Thus, *teeming* is the correct response.

53. **(E)** As time passes, the likelihood of locating the missing child is reduced. A negative word is needed to modify *likely*. Therefore, *more, exceedingly,* and *quite* are not suitable. The verb *arrives* is not appropriate with the subject *hour*.

54. **(A)** Revision of rules can have either a positive or a negative result. Responses **(C)**, **(D)**, and **(E)** do not convey either meaning. Response **(B)** is not correct since the passive tense, "be hurt," would be required.

55. **(D)** Choices **(A)** and **(C)** contain opposite pairings and are therefore inappropriate. The phrases "assist you for" and "enable you for" are awkward. Therefore, only choice **(D)** is correct.

56. **(D)** The key word in this sentence is *mild*. The completion requires selection of a word that is consonant with *mild*. This requirement rules out choices **(A)** and **(E)**. Choice **(B)** is not a good one because *jaws* are not *undisputed*; *call* in choice **(C)** makes no sense.

57. **(D)** Although the sense of the first part of the sentence requires a negative word, *liquidated* and *destroyed* are too absolute, so choices **(A)** and **(C)** are not suitable. *Assisted* in choice **(B)** and *served* in choice **(E)** are not at all negative. Choice **(D)** best fits the sense of the sentence, especially since rapid growth often leads to sudden pollution.

58. **(C)** The sense of the missing word in the second part of the sentence requires a word to go with the smallness of the insect. The word *size* accomplishes this. Choice **(B)** is tempting but it ignores the reference to size.

59. **(B)** Fish do not *infiltrate*, nor do they *emigrate* or *hibernate*. Further, to suggest that they *estivate*, that they pass the summer in a dormant state or away on vacation, makes no sense at all. Choice **(B)** *browse*, meaning "to feed upon," is perfectly suitable.

60. **(B)** A *nail* is at the end of a *finger*; a *toe* is at the end of a *foot*.

61. **(A)** The relationship between *firmament* and *sky* is that of two synonymous nouns, the first less commonly used than the second. Similarly, *termagant* and *shrew* are synonymous nouns for a quarrelsome or scolding woman.

62. **(B)** A *query* (the asking of a question) precedes a *response* (the answering of a question); an *itch* precedes a *scratch*.

63. **(C)** *Ante* is the prefix in *antebellum* and conveys the meaning "before"; thus *antebellum* means "before the war." Similarly, the prefix *ante* means "before" in the word *anteroom*.

64. **(E)** *Maximum* and *minimum* are antonym nouns. *Apogee*, the highest point, is the opposite of *nadir*, the lowest point.

65. **(D)** Just as a flower has its origin in a *seed*, a *bird* has its origin in an *egg*.

66. **(B)** A *rabbit* lives in a *warren*; a *pig* lives in a *pen*. An *animal* does not live in a *nest*; a *bird* does. An *aerie* is a nest where *eagles* might live, but the order is reversed.

67. **(A)** The relationship expressed is that of a greater number to the singular component. A *pride* is a company or group of *lions*; a *school* is a large group of *fish*.

68. **(D)** *Zeus* is the Greek counterpart of the Roman god *Jupiter*. *Hera* is the Greek goddess identified with the Roman goddess *Juno*.

69. **(E)** The *Psalms* are associated with *David* in the Bible, who is reputed to be the author of many of these lyrical poems; the *Proverbs* are associated with *Solomon,* whose name is mentioned in this section of Biblical wisdom literature.

70. **(A)** *Cobalt* is an adjective describing a shade of *blue*; a color may be described as ''cobalt blue.'' *Mint* is an adjective describing a shade of *green*; a color may be described as ''mint green.'' None of the other combinations may be used together to describe a color.

71. **(B)** To *shout* is much louder than to *speak*; to *yell* is much louder than to *whisper*. The relationship is a matter of intensity or volume.

72. **(C)** The relationship is one of classification. *Milk* may be included under the general heading of *liquid*; *meat* may be included under the general heading of *solid*.

73. **(D)** *Lugubrious* and *gloomy* are synonymous adjectives, both meaning ''mournful''; *malignant* and *destructive* are also synonymous adjectives meaning ''injurious.''

74. **(D)** The relationship concerns adjectives that are antonyms. *Mendacious* (untruthful) is the opposite of *veracious* (truthful); *restive* (restless) is the opposite of *calm*.

75. **(A)** *Garrulous* and *loquacious* are synonymous adjectives, meaning ''talkative.'' *Taciturn* and *silent* are also synonymous adjectives.

76. **(B)** A *dermatologist* is a doctor who specializes in treating problems related to the *skin*; a *cardiologist* is a doctor who treats problems related to the *heart*.

77. **(E)** *Challis* is a fabric that is often woven in *wool*; *chambray* is a fabric that is a variety of *gingham*.

78. **(B)** A *cygnet* is a young *swan*; a *puppy* is a young *dog*. In choice **(A)** the order of young animal to mature animal is reversed.

CHAPTER 9

SAT II: Writing Test

Many colleges require prospective students to take the SAT II: Writing Test. In addition to its value in the admissions process, this test is used to help place the student in an appropriate English class. The test requires the individual to write an essay and to respond to a wide spectrum of multiple-choice questions concerning writing skills.

Format of SAT II: Writing Test

The Writing Test allows 20 minutes for an impromptu writing sample and 40 minutes for 60 multiple-choice questions.

There are three kinds of questions that appear on the writing test: usage (identifying sentence errors), sentence correction (improving sentences), and revision-in-context (improving paragraphs).

The approximate distribution is:

Usage—30 questions
Sentence Correction—18 questions
Revision-in-Context—12 questions

Overview of SAT II: Writing Test Questions

Usage

This section is a test of your knowledge of usage, diction, and idiom. Read the following sentence slowly and carefully:

<u>One of the strongest boys</u> in the <u>class</u>, John, <u>was requested</u> to take the chair
　　　　　　A　　　　　　　　　B　　　　　C

back to the <u>schools auditorium.</u> <u>No error</u>
　　　　　　D　　　　　　　　　E

You will notice that there are four parts of the sentence underlined and labeled **A**, **B**, **C**, and **D**. In addition, following the sentence is the phrase "No error," underlined and labeled **E.** You must decide whether any of the four underlined parts of the sentence contains an error or whether the sentence is acceptable as it stands. If it is acceptable, choose **E.** If one of the underlined parts is not acceptable, choose the letter under the underlined word or phrase that contains an error. In this question you would choose **D,** since an apostrophe is needed in *school's auditorium* to indicate that *school* is in the possessive case.

Sentence Correction

This section tests the ability to recognize the most effective way to express a thought and to reject unacceptable usage in grammar, word choice, sentence structure, or punctuation. A sentence is given, and part or all of the sentence is underlined. Following the sentence are five ways of phrasing the underlined portion. You must decide which of the five phrasings makes the best possible sentence. Study the following example:

Everyone in the family, <u>except my brother and I, was</u> invited to the wedding.

    (A)   except my brother and I, was
    (B)   except my brother and I, were
    (C)   except my brother and me, was
    (D)   except my brother and me, were
    (E)   except my brother and me was

The first choice, **(A),** is always an exact repetition of the underlined phrase; **(B), (C), (D),** and **(E)** are ways of rephrasing the original. If you feel that the original sentence is perfectly acceptable, choose **(A);** if you feel that one of the other choices is a more acceptable way of expressing the idea, select that answer. Read all five possible choices carefully, paying close attention to usage, idiom, punctuation, and sentence construction. In the sample question the correct answer is **(C).** In a prepositional phrase, the object of the preposition must be in the objective case. The objective case is *me,* not *I;* therefore **(A)** and **(B)** are incorrect. **(D)** is incorrect since the verb must be singular—*was*—to agree with the singular subject *Everyone; were* is plural, so choice **(D)** is incorrect. Choice **(E)** is incorrect since the comma following *me* is missing.

Revision-in-Context

This section presents an essay that might have been an early draft of a student's writing and that contains some sentences that should be reworked and corrected. After you read the essay, you answer a series of questions that may relate to diction, usage, tone, or sentence structure as well as to organization, development, logic, or appropriateness of language. You must choose the response that makes the meaning most clear and precise and that does not violate the rules of standard written English. For example, read the following passage:

(1) Is television an enhancer or a deterrent to education? **(2)** Some educators feel that properly managed, television can open up educational vistas to children and expose them to ideas; others say that television stifles activity and makes children into passive creatures.

(3) Certainly most people will agree that television is here to stay and that parents must accept the fact that their children are going to watch programs and they will have to deal with it. (4) By this, they must learn first of all what kind of programs are available and also the time schedule. (5) Perhaps they will have to preview programs. (6) Then parents must decide which programs will be beneficial for children. (7) Also they will have to decide which programs can overstimulate children. (8) They will decide also which programs are filled with needless violence which will overstimulate children.

Answer the following question:

1. In relation to the entire passage, which of the following best describes the writer's intention in sentence 2?

      (A) to evaluate an opinion set forth in paragraph 2
      (B) to show that there is a difference of opinion regarding the opening sentence
      (C) to restate the opening sentence
      (D) to provide examples
      (E) to summarize contradictory evidence

The correct answer is (C). The first sentence, phrased as a question, presents the two opposing views of television vis-à-vis education. The second sentence rephrases this by using the two camps of educators, the first viewing television as an enhancer and the second viewing television in a negative way. Thus, sentence 2 restates the first sentence.

Answer another question:

2. Which of the following is the best revision of the underlined portion of sentence 3 below?

Certainly most people will agree that television is here to stay and that parents must accept the fact that their children are going to watch programs and they will have to deal with it.

      (A) will have to deal with their children's watching television programs.
      (B) will as a result be forced to accept their children as they watch television.
      (C) must accept and deal with their children if they watch television.
      (D) must accept this, children will watch television and this must be handled.
      (E) will have to deal with their children since they will watch television.

The correct answer is (A). The portion underlined is awkward and wordy, and the last word, the pronoun *it*, has a weak antecedent, one that is not clear. Choice (A) corrects this weakness, whereas choices (B), (C), and (E) change the meaning of the sentence, and choice (D), with its comma-splice error, is grammatically incorrect.

Answer one more question:

3. Which of the following is the best way to combine sentences 4, 5, and 6?

(A) Parents will have to learn time schedules, programs, and how to evaluate television.

(B) The availability of programs as well as the time schedule will help parents to evaluate programs beneficial to children.

(C) Subject matter of programs, time scheduling, and even actual previewing are factors that can help parents decide on the suitability of television for children.

(D) In order to decide on what programs are beneficial for their children, parents will have to develop criteria.

(E) It is up to parents to evaluate programs for their children.

The correct answer is (C). Choice (B) omits the idea that parents will have to preview programs; choice (A) is poor since the original does not indicate that parents must learn how to evaluate programs and the phrase "to learn . . . programs" is awkward; choice (D) changes the original meaning of the sentences being combined; and choice (E) omits much of the sense of the original.

SAT II Mini-Test

The Mini-Test that follows is designed to help you discover your strengths and weaknesses in areas of grammar, usage, diction, sentence construction, and punctuation. It is modeled after the SAT II: Writing Test, but it contains fewer questions in each of the categories. Following the test are an answer key and an explanation of the answers. Use this material to guide your study in those areas in which you need the most practice. After you have reviewed relevant areas in the Guide to Good Writing, you will be prepared to take the full-length practice test that follows the Mini-Test.

Usage

Directions: Some of the sentences below contain an error in grammar, usage, word choice, or idiom. Other sentences are correct. Parts of each sentence are underlined and lettered. The error, if there is one, is contained in one of the underlined parts of the sentence. Assume that all other parts of the sentence are correct and cannot be changed. For each sentence, select the one underlined part that must be changed to make the sentence correct and mark its letter on your answer sheet. If there is no error in a sentence, mark answer space **E**. No sentence contains more than one error.

1. We <u>were traveling</u> <u>Southwest</u> on the <u>highway</u> when we <u>noticed</u> the accident.
   A   B   C   D
<u>No error.</u>
   E

2. Mrs. James <u>would of come</u> to the <u>celebration</u> if she <u>had received</u> an invitation
                  A   B   C
<u>from them.</u> <u>No error</u>
   D   E

3. They <u>hadn't had hardly</u> any time to <u>consider the</u> matter when the <u>chairperson</u>
              A   B   C
<u>called the meeting to order.</u> <u>No error</u>
              D   E

4. The soup tastes <u>most peculiarly</u>; it <u>may be</u> <u>because</u> we have not added
                        A   B   C   D
enough salt. <u>No error</u>
                 E

Sentence Correction

Directions: The sentences below may contain problems in grammar, usage, word choice, sentence construction, or punctuation. Part or all of each sentence is underlined. Following each sentence you will find five ways of expressing the underlined part. Answer choice (A) always repeats the original underlined section. The other four answer choices are all different. You are to select the lettered answer that produces the most effective sentence. If you think the original sentence is best, choose (A) as your answer. If one of the other choices makes a better sentence, mark the answer sheet for the letter of that choice. Do not choose an answer that changes the meaning of the original sentence.

5. It's eleven o'clock, it's time to begin the examination.

      (A) o'clock, it's
      (B) o'clock, its
      (C) o'clock; it's
      (D) o'clock; its
      (E) o'clock it's

6. Being that there had been an accident, the bus was delayed for fifteen minutes.

      (A) Being that there
      (B) Being that their
      (C) Owing that there
      (D) Since their
      (E) Since there

7. He will refer the matter to Mr. Jones and me for resolution of the claim.

      (A) Mr. Jones and me
      (B) Mr. Jones and myself
      (C) Mr. Jones and I
      (D) Me and Mr. Jones
      (E) Myself and Mr. Jones

8. Every student is responsible for completing their own assignment by Friday.

      (A) completing their own
      (B) completing his own
      (C) the completion of their own
      (D) having completed their own
      (E) completing there own

Revision-in-Context

Directions: Questions 9–12 concern an essay that might have been an early draft of a student's writing and that contains some sentences that should be reworked and corrected. After reading the essay, answer the questions that follow it. The questions may relate to diction, usage, tone, or sentence structure as well as to organization, development, logic, or appropriateness of language. Choose the response that makes the meaning most clear and precise and that does not violate the rules of standard written English.

(1) Everybody is talking about gun control. (2) Some people say that according to the Bill of Rights, every person is allowed to carry a gun. (3) Others say that if you allow guns to be placed in the hands of every citizen, the crime rate will go up.

(4) I think that each person should be thoroughly investigated before they are allowed to own a gun. **(5)** I know that the rifle associations and all the hunting groups would not agree, but I do. **(6)** Just think what would happen if each family had a gun. **(7)** Children and teenagers would begin to experiment with these weapons. **(8)** At first it would be fun. **(9)** But then they would put these guns to use, to commit armed robberies, petty thievery, murdering and killing. **(10)** We would soon turn all our major cities into a replica of Dodge City and there would be chaos and lawlessness.

(11) If people have a legitimate need to own a gun, then they should get a permit. **(12)** This would allow the authorities time to investigate the background of the person who wants to own a gun. **(13)** Don't put guns in the hands of potential criminals, but screen each person carefully. **(14)** Perhaps this way we will lessen the number of crimes that plague our cities and also do away with many accidental shootings.

9. Which of the following choices is the best way to combine sentences 2 and 3?

   (A) There are some people who say that every person is entitled because of the Bill of Rights to possess a gun, others say that the crime rate will go up if guns are placed in the hands of every citizen.

   (B) There are those who claim that the Bill of Rights stipulates that every person is entitled to bear firearms; others maintain that the crime rate will rise if guns are placed in the hands of every citizen.

   (C) Allowing guns in the hands of every citizen, contrary to the Bill of Rights which states that every person should be allowed to bear arms, will cause the crime rate to rise.

   (D) Some people say that the Bill of Rights gives each person the ability to bear arms, others say that the crime rate will go up if this happens.

   (E) There are some who say that the crime rate will be affected by allowing us to bear arms, while others claim that the Bill of Rights addresses this issue.

10. Which is the best revision of the underlined portion of sentence 4 below?

    I think that each person should be thoroughly investigated <u>before they are allowed to own a gun.</u>

    (A) prior to their owning a gun.
    (B) before a gun is issued to them.
    (C) before receiving permission to own a gun.
    (D) prior to the receipt of permission for them to own a gun.
    (E) before they may possess a gun.

11. Which of the following is the best revision of the underlined portion of sentence 9 below?

    But then they would put these guns to use, <u>to commit armed robberies, petty thievery, murdering and killing.</u>

    (A) to commit armed robbery, petty theft, and murdering.
    (B) committing armed robberies, petty thieving, and for murdering.

(C) to commit robbery, thievery, murder, and killing.

(D) for robbing, thieving, and murder.

(E) to commit armed robbery, petty theft, and murder.

12. In the context of the sentences preceding and following sentence 13, which of the following is the best revision of sentence 13?

(A) Don't allow potential criminals to own guns, but let each person be screened carefully.

(B) Guns should not be placed in the hands of potential criminals, each person being carefully screened.

(C) Instead of putting guns in the hands of potential criminals, screen each person carefully.

(D) Guns should not be put in the hands of potential criminals; rather, each prospective buyer should be screened carefully.

(E) Guns should not be placed in the hands of a potential criminal; but they should be carefully screened.

Answers

SAT II Mini-Test

Usage	1.	B
	2.	A
	3.	A
	4.	B
Sentence Correction	5.	C
	6.	E
	7.	A
	8.	B
Revision-in-Context	9.	B
	10.	C
	11.	E
	12.	D

Explanatory Answers for SAT II Mini-Test

Usage

1. **(B)** A capital letter is not required to indicate direction.

2. **(A)** The correct form of the verb is *would have come* (informal: would've come).

3. **(A)** Double negatives are incorrect. The correct form is *had had hardly*.

4. **(B)** After the verb *tastes*, a verb referring to one of the senses, the adjective *(peculiar)*, not the adverb *(peculiarly)*, is used.

Sentence Correction

5. **(C)** It is incorrect to separate two independent clauses with a comma. A semicolon can be used to correct the comma-splice error.

6. **(E)** In formal usage, the phrase *Being that* should not be used. It is preferable to use *since*. Choice **(D)** is incorrect since *there* is misspelled.

7. **(A)** The sentence is correct.

8. **(B)** Since *Every student* is singular, the pronoun with which it agrees must also be singular.

Revision-in-Context

9. **(B)** Choices **(A)** and **(D)** contain comma-splice errors. Choice **(C)** is a confused statement. Choice **(E)** gives incorrect information. The two distinct thoughts in this sentence are best separated by a semicolon, as in **(B)**.

10. **(C)** The antecedent of *they*, a plural pronoun, appears to be *each person*, a singular subject of the clause. Only choice **(C)** correctly deals with this error.

11. **(E)** The error is twofold. The catalog of crimes is not parallel, and *murdering* and *killing* are repetitive. Only choice **(E)** corrects both errors.

12. **(D)** Sentence 13 is cast as a direct command; this is inappropriate to the general tone of the essay. Choice **(A)** repeats this error. Choice **(E)** offers an unclear antecedent; to whom does *they* refer? Both **(B)** and **(C)** make a suggestion that is unfeasible—that *each person* be screened. **(B)**, in addition, is awkward. In the context of the essay, the suggestion in **(D)** that prospective purchasers be screened makes sense, and **(D)** is well written.

CHAPTER 10

Writing the SAT II Essay

The first 20 minutes of your test will be devoted to planning and writing an essay on a single assigned topic. The remaining 40 minutes of your test will consist of answering the multiple-choice questions just described in Chapter 9.

The essay assignment is preceded by a quotation or statement that is intended to stimulate your thoughts on the subject. Only one topic is offered and you must fulfill the requirements of the assignment in your essay. Each essay is evaluated by experienced high school and college English teachers. Each reader assigns a rating to the essay based upon your overall competence to write a college-level composition. The prime objective of your essay is to demonstrate to the reader that you can develop a thesis, support it with appropriate facts or illustrations, and come to a conclusion in a clear, well-written, well-organized composition.

Guidelines for Essay Writers ———————————

Aim for:

1. Originality of approach
2. Clarity of organization
3. Freshness of expression
4. Logical development
5. Variety of sentence patterns

Avoid:

1. Technical errors in sentence structure, spelling, grammar, and usage
2. Poor paragraphing
3. Unnecessary repetition of material
4. Substandard level of English—illiteracies, mixed metaphors, trite expressions, overuse of colloquialisms
5. Stylistic problems such as oversimplification, incoherent writing, wordiness

Sample Essay Tests

This section contains three essay topics, similar to the topics assigned on the actual test. For each question, write your own answer before looking at the sample responses provided. The sample essay answers have been annotated to indicate errors and analyzed for content and style to help you evaluate your own essay response.

Sample Essay Test A

Directions: You have twenty minutes in which to plan and write the essay assigned below. Make certain that you do not stray from the topic, that you give specific details as supporting evidence, and that you organize your ideas logically. Remember to proofread carefully to be certain that you have expressed your ideas in standard written English.

Essay Topic

Will Rogers often stated, "All I know is what I read in the papers." He realized that the media did not always give a clear and accurate picture of events. We see the world through the eyes of reporters who are prejudiced and whose views are biased. We would be better off with stricter government control over the press; at least then we might be protected from distortions and personal bias.

Agree or disagree with this statement, drawing upon your personal experiences, your observations of others, or your reading.

Sample Response 1

An educated person should be able to read several newspapers and then weigh all factors before making up his or her own mind on any issue. Certainly news reporters are biased and prejudiced and very often they can slant the news so that the facts fit in with their own opinions, but a concerned reader should be able to recognize where the truth is, especially in a country where there are many newspapers and magazines.

In Communist countries and in the Arab world the newspapers are controlled by the government and all the reporters must follow the party line. Then the people never get to see both sides of the issue only the side that the leaders want them to see. This is certainly much worse. At least in our country if we disagree with a reporter we can write to the paper and express our viewpoint and if we are very upset, we can stop buying the paper and switch to reading another newspaper.

I remember that once in my social studies class we learned that the Hearst papers stirred up the people so much that they influenced our country into going to war. They slanted the news to such an extent by exaggerating details and distorting facts that a war-spirit took over the country. This is a danger that we must always be aware of but if we are careful readers and educated men and women we can prevent this from happening.

A free press is important. Our Bill of Rights protects the newspapers and the people. We must do our best to keep the press free and also responsible for telling the truth fairly and honestly.

Sample Response 2

I agree our newspapers do tell us what to think but I think that could be good. After all sometimes when its time to elect people we don't really know who anyone is or his background or what they believe. Then the newspapers tell us things and even give us advise on who to support this could be helpful. I know that some people could say that the reporter are prejudice but everyone is and at least they say what they believe and after they have study a lot about each candate and the one who are running in the election. I dont want the government to interfer with the newspaper and controll what is written and said on tv or the radio because then we will be in a dictator state and thats not good for nobody. Maybe you dont agree with what I said but thats my opion.

Analysis of Sample Response 1

The writer presents his ideas in four well-constructed paragraphs. The essay is logical, coherent, and relevant. The writer uses illustrations from his studies to support his concept that stricter government control over the press is not consistent with the democratic idea. Sentence structure is well handled with a good balance between simple and complex sentences. The ideas and vocabulary are mature and the tone is strong.

Analysis of Sample Response 2

There are many serious weaknesses in this single paragraph response. The essay should be divided into distinct paragraphs of introduction, development, and conclusion. The response is meager and immature.

There are numerous errors in technical English. Sentence structure is weak. For example, the third sentence contains a run-on and the fourth sentence contains an especially confusing fragment. In several sentences, a comma should be added to separate and clarify ideas. The writer needs to review the rules on the use of the apostrophe for contractions. Finally, a multitude of spelling errors and careless errors in diction make the essay difficult to comprehend.

Sample Essay Test B

Essay Topic

According to Dr. Abraham Heschel, "Old age is not a defeat, but a victory." And yet it is extremely difficult for many people to meet the expenses brought on by long-term illnesses. The elderly, especially, are often at a loss when it comes to providing for health care for themselves or for family members. For this reason, the Federal Government should provide additional insurance to assist people during periods of long-term catastrophic illness.

Are these statements justified? Using your observations, reading, and study, explain and justify your answer.

Sample Response 1

We are all living longer thanks to medical knowledge and perhaps we should be grateful for this. But I am not at all sure this is true. Sometimes I feel that living longer presents many problems.

For example, I know that my friends grandmother is now in a nursing home where she is suffering a slow death. Each week the family pays huge amounts of money to keep her in the home. Soon all of her savings will be gone and her husband will be reduced to living on welfare if he survives. This is only one case but there are many others.

The goverment should step in and assist. People who have worked all of their lives and have paid taxes should expect some help in their final years of live. Help in the way of additional money would be of great emotional and economic value. We provide social security it is true but this is not enough to cover unusual medical expenses. We cannot desert these victims of old age when they are ill. We must help.

I urge the goverment to help provide funds to cover home care and to relieve our ill seniors of the worry and dispair that comes from catastrophic illness. We know that the physical pain they bear is great. Lets at least take away some of the economic hurt.

Sample Response 2

The Federal government should definitely provide enough insurance coverage so that families or individuals faced with the problem of long-term catatrophic illness will be able to meet the rising cost of health care. Without government assistance, many people today are unable to provide proper care for seriously sick relatives, and as the population of older people increases, the problem will only get worse.

Right now my cousins are face with a problem that is a good illustration of the need for a better health care program. Their mother has been ill for nearly a year, suffering from heart disease and diabetes. First she was in the hospital, then in a nursing home. Medicare covered a lot of her expenses at first, but not all. Later, the family had to pay from their own savings, and when their funds got low, they took her out of the hospital. Besides, she was not really so happy there, and they missed her too.

At home my cousins have a nurse, which is very expensive. They both work so they need someone to look after mother. But again they are hurting for money and are getting worry about what to do. If they had government coverage, they could keep her at home and take good care of her for as long as it takes.

In conclusion, my observation of this very sad situation proves that the Federal Government should help people who have long term illnesses.

Analysis of Sample Response 1

This is a well-organized four paragraph response. The student provides a good introduction which presents the topic and a strong conclusion to summarize the position taken. In addition, in the second paragraph an example is offered to illustrate the problem. The vocabulary and sentence structure are good, as is the somewhat emotional tone. The few spelling errors (goverment, live, dispair) and the omissions of apostrophes (friends grandmother, lets) could be corrected through careful revision. The closing sentence, although effective, might be better phrased by avoiding the address to the reader and maintaining a third person approach. A possible revision could be:

"The Federal Government should at least take away some of the economic hurt."

Analysis of Sample Response 2

This is an interesting and well-written essay. It begins with a strong statement of the author's thesis and employs a two-paragraph personal example to support its view. The writer demonstrates an understanding of the question and an ability to organize a coherent and logical response.

Although the essay is developed in some depth, it would appear that the conclusion is somewhat skimpy. Perhaps the writer might have budgeted the allotted time more effectively to provide for an additional sentence in the final paragraph. In addition, the concluding sentence of paragraph 2 might have been deleted and more careful proofreading might have eliminated the few errors.

Sample Essay Test C

Essay Topic

"Criminals are not born; they are made." Recently there has been an outcry against the government's cutting programs designed to help those on a poverty level. There are many who feel that without public assistance the underprivileged will turn to crime, and this will create a great drain on the taxpayer.

React to this comment, utilizing your own experiences, your reading, and your observations of others.

Sample Response 1

Its true that people should be responsible for themselves and not depend on government agencies for a handout. If we remember a hundred years ago no one helped you if you were poor or without money and yet our country managed.

I remember a film I once saw. It was about a group of kids who grew up in Hell's kitchen. A slum in New York City. Not all of them turned out to be bad. Although some did become theives and robbers and one even became a murder. But many also grew up to be priests and lawyers and doctors and even cops. They made it by developing character and fighting to better themselves.

So I feel it's really up to each person. If the city or the government gives you money it might make you lazy and not willing to fight harder to overcome bad conditions. Everyone must make his own way in life.

Analysis of Sample Response 1

The writer has a sense of organization and development. The use of a film to illustrate his point is valid and the tone, although informal, is consistent. However, more careful proofreading is necessary to eliminate spelling errors (for example: Its-It's; theives-thieves; murder-murderer). In addition, it is preferable to substitute a noun like "people" for the pronoun "you" when the writer is not really referring to the reader. (Paragraph 1—"If we remember, a hundred years ago, no one helped people who were poor, and yet our country managed." Paragraph 3—"If this government gives a person money, he might become lazy and unwilling to fight harder to overcome bad conditions.") Moreover, there are two fragments in the second paragraph which require correction—("A slum in New York City" should be connected to the preceding sentence; the fragment beginning with "Although" should be joined with either the sentence that precedes it or with the sentence that follows it.)

Sample Response 2

Government assistance very often robs the individual of his initiative and his desire to achieve. As a result, many people feel it is a waste of the taxpayer's money to provide handouts for those who are on the poverty level.

I agree that there is a lot of waste and that a good deal of funds designed to help the poor never reach the right person. What we need are programs to provide jobs and to train people to earn a living. Of course, giving out free cheese sounds good. But that only happens once a year or so, and then the poor people are right back to where they started, on the bread line or in the soup kitchens.

I say let's spend our money to wipe out illiteracy, to provide better inexpensive housing, to offer jobs to the needy. Then I feel that fewer will turn to crime because they will have better outlets for their energy.

Analysis of Sample Response 2

This essay indicates that the writer is capable of performing on a college level. The comments are intelligent and technical aspects (spelling, grammar, punctuation) are sound.

There are two ways by which the essay might be improved. An additional paragraph would be helpful as a transition to clarify the writer's viewpoint, to state clearly that the writer believes that there is a need for a better direction for government assistance. Also, in the concluding paragraph, rather than write, "Let's spend our money . . . ," it would be preferable to state, "money should be spent . . . " or "the government should spend money . . . "

Hints for Writing a Successful Essay —————————————————

Do:

1. Take a minute or two (but no more) to read the question, to underline important phrases, and to consider the implications of the statement or quotation.

2. Plan on writing a three- or four-paragraph essay containing an introduction, a development, and a conclusion.

3. Use supporting details to back up your ideas.

4. Keep your writing clear and relevant.

5. Spend the full 20 minutes on the essay. If possible, use the last minute or two to proofread your work and correct mistakes.

Do not:

1. Attempt to produce a sophisticated outline.

2. Plan on rewriting the entire essay.

3. Write so quickly that your handwriting becomes illegible.

4. Write notes or incomplete sentences hoping the examiner will understand what you have *not* written.

5. Spend more than 20 minutes on the essay. When time is called, go on to the multiple-choice questions.

Guidelines for Taking the Sample Test —————————————————

1. Do not guess wildly, since there is a penalty for choosing the wrong answer. If, however, you can make an ''educated guess'' by narrowing your possible choices, you should do so.

2. Do not spend too much time on any one question. You have a better chance of scoring high if you go back and answer the more difficult questions only after you have answered all the questions you know.

3. Do not choose answers that contain colloquial phrases, slang expressions, or informal usage. Remember, this is a test of your command of standard written English.

4. After taking the test, check your answers with the answers and explanations that follow. Analyze your errors and consult the appropriate sections of the Guide to Good Writing to eliminate weaknesses.

Answer Sheet for Sample Test 2: SAT II

Essay Section

Use this space for your essay response.

_____

_____

_____

_____

_____

_____

_____

_____

_____

_____

_____

_____

_____

_____

_____

_____

_____

_____

_____

_____

_____

Multiple-Choice Section

1. Ⓐ Ⓑ Ⓒ Ⓓ Ⓔ	21. Ⓐ Ⓑ Ⓒ Ⓓ Ⓔ	41. Ⓐ Ⓑ Ⓒ Ⓓ Ⓔ
2. Ⓐ Ⓑ Ⓒ Ⓓ Ⓔ	22. Ⓐ Ⓑ Ⓒ Ⓓ Ⓔ	42. Ⓐ Ⓑ Ⓒ Ⓓ Ⓔ
3. Ⓐ Ⓑ Ⓒ Ⓓ Ⓔ	23. Ⓐ Ⓑ Ⓒ Ⓓ Ⓔ	43. Ⓐ Ⓑ Ⓒ Ⓓ Ⓔ
4. Ⓐ Ⓑ Ⓒ Ⓓ Ⓔ	24. Ⓐ Ⓑ Ⓒ Ⓓ Ⓔ	44. Ⓐ Ⓑ Ⓒ Ⓓ Ⓔ
5. Ⓐ Ⓑ Ⓒ Ⓓ Ⓔ	25. Ⓐ Ⓑ Ⓒ Ⓓ Ⓔ	45. Ⓐ Ⓑ Ⓒ Ⓓ Ⓔ
6. Ⓐ Ⓑ Ⓒ Ⓓ Ⓔ	26. Ⓐ Ⓑ Ⓒ Ⓓ Ⓔ	46. Ⓐ Ⓑ Ⓒ Ⓓ Ⓔ
7. Ⓐ Ⓑ Ⓒ Ⓓ Ⓔ	27. Ⓐ Ⓑ Ⓒ Ⓓ Ⓔ	47. Ⓐ Ⓑ Ⓒ Ⓓ Ⓔ
8. Ⓐ Ⓑ Ⓒ Ⓓ Ⓔ	28. Ⓐ Ⓑ Ⓒ Ⓓ Ⓔ	48. Ⓐ Ⓑ Ⓒ Ⓓ Ⓔ
9. Ⓐ Ⓑ Ⓒ Ⓓ Ⓔ	29. Ⓐ Ⓑ Ⓒ Ⓓ Ⓔ	49. Ⓐ Ⓑ Ⓒ Ⓓ Ⓔ
10. Ⓐ Ⓑ Ⓒ Ⓓ Ⓔ	30. Ⓐ Ⓑ Ⓒ Ⓓ Ⓔ	50. Ⓐ Ⓑ Ⓒ Ⓓ Ⓔ
11. Ⓐ Ⓑ Ⓒ Ⓓ Ⓔ	31. Ⓐ Ⓑ Ⓒ Ⓓ Ⓔ	51. Ⓐ Ⓑ Ⓒ Ⓓ Ⓔ
12. Ⓐ Ⓑ Ⓒ Ⓓ Ⓔ	32. Ⓐ Ⓑ Ⓒ Ⓓ Ⓔ	52. Ⓐ Ⓑ Ⓒ Ⓓ Ⓔ
13. Ⓐ Ⓑ Ⓒ Ⓓ Ⓔ	33. Ⓐ Ⓑ Ⓒ Ⓓ Ⓔ	53. Ⓐ Ⓑ Ⓒ Ⓓ Ⓔ
14. Ⓐ Ⓑ Ⓒ Ⓓ Ⓔ	34. Ⓐ Ⓑ Ⓒ Ⓓ Ⓔ	54. Ⓐ Ⓑ Ⓒ Ⓓ Ⓔ
15. Ⓐ Ⓑ Ⓒ Ⓓ Ⓔ	35. Ⓐ Ⓑ Ⓒ Ⓓ Ⓔ	55. Ⓐ Ⓑ Ⓒ Ⓓ Ⓔ
16. Ⓐ Ⓑ Ⓒ Ⓓ Ⓔ	36. Ⓐ Ⓑ Ⓒ Ⓓ Ⓔ	56. Ⓐ Ⓑ Ⓒ Ⓓ Ⓔ
17. Ⓐ Ⓑ Ⓒ Ⓓ Ⓔ	37. Ⓐ Ⓑ Ⓒ Ⓓ Ⓔ	57. Ⓐ Ⓑ Ⓒ Ⓓ Ⓔ
18. Ⓐ Ⓑ Ⓒ Ⓓ Ⓔ	38. Ⓐ Ⓑ Ⓒ Ⓓ Ⓔ	58. Ⓐ Ⓑ Ⓒ Ⓓ Ⓔ
19. Ⓐ Ⓑ Ⓒ Ⓓ Ⓔ	39. Ⓐ Ⓑ Ⓒ Ⓓ Ⓔ	59. Ⓐ Ⓑ Ⓒ Ⓓ Ⓔ
20. Ⓐ Ⓑ Ⓒ Ⓓ Ⓔ	40. Ⓐ Ⓑ Ⓒ Ⓓ Ⓔ	60. Ⓐ Ⓑ Ⓒ Ⓓ Ⓔ

(Answers appear on page 203)

CHAPTER 11

Sample Test 2:
SAT II: Writing Test

Essay Section

Time: 20 minutes

Directions: You have 20 minutes in which to plan and write the essay assigned below. Make certain that you do not stray from the topic, that you give specific details as supporting evidence, and that you organize your ideas logically. Remember to proofread carefully to be certain that you have expressed your ideas in standard written English.

Topic: Years ago, many people believed in the idea "My country, right or wrong." But now we are told that patriotism is a thing of the past. Today's generation no longer enjoys displaying the American flag, marching in parades, singing songs or praising our country.

Agree or disagree with this statement, drawing upon your personal experiences, your observations of others, or your reading.

Multiple-Choice Section

Time: 40 minutes

Directions: Some of the sentences below contain an error in grammar, usage, word choice, or idiom. Other sentences are correct. Parts of each sentence are underlined and lettered. The error, if there is one, is contained in one of the underlined parts of the sentence. Assume that all other parts of the sentence are correct and cannot be changed. For each sentence, select the one underlined part that must be changed to make the sentence correct and mark its letter on your answer sheet. If there is no error in a sentence, mark answer space **E**. No sentence contains more than one error.

1. I think we should find out if either his parents or Jim are going to be at the celebration. No error
   A   B   C   D   E

2. The writer pointed out that many people live out their life "in quiet desperation." No error
   A   B   C   D   E

3. Although Juan appears to be more agile than I, he is not so good an athlete. No error
   A   B   C   D   E

4. She was pleased by the crowds applause when she achieved a perfect score in the second event of the evening. No error
   A   B   C   D   E

5. I would of been happy to babysit for my brother if my parents had given me notice a few days in advance. No error
   A   B   C   D   E

6. At the museum, the guide convinced us that the paintings of Van Gogh were more detailed and developed than Cézanne. No error
   A   B   C   D   E

193

7. My sister is two years older than Sarah—Sarah is a year ahead of her in
   　　　　　　　　A　　　B　　C　　　　　D
   school. No error
   　　　　　E

8. When I asked my cousin what she thought of the Christmas tree in Rockefeller
   　　　　　A　　　　　　　　　　　　　　　　　　　　　　　　　　　　　　　B
   Center, she replied, "It's beautiful!" No error
   　　　　　　C　　　　　　　　D　　　　　E

9. The policeman claims that you drunk too much liquor before you drove home
   　　　　　　　　A　　　　　　B　　C　　　　　　　　　　　　　　D
   last night. No error
   　　　　　E

10. I would much rather be outside playing football then inside studying for the
    　　　　　A　　　　　　　　　　　　　　　B
    math test, but I know I will never pass the course unless I learn the material
    　　　　　C　　　　　　　　　　　　　　　　　D
    thoroughly. No error
    　　　　　　E

11. When the instructor's pen ran out of ink, I let him borrow mines so he could
    　　　　　A　　　　　　　　　　　　　　　B　　　　　C　　　　　D
    finish grading the essays. No error
    　　　　　　　　　　　　　E

12. This evening when I went outside to feed my cat, the animal was nowheres
    　　　　　　A　　B　　　　　　　　　　　　　　　　　　　C　　　D
    to be found. No error
    　　　　　　E

13. Last month, Maria asked her mother if it would be all right if she attended
    　　　　　A
    summer school instead of working again as a nurse's aide in the hospital?
    　　　　　　B　　　　　　　　　　　　　C　　　　　D
    No error
    E

14. Mr. Jones, a veritable martinet, was both aggravated and dismayed when
    　　　　　　A　　　　　　　　　B　　　C
    he read the report of the incident. No error
    　　　　　　　　　　D　　　　　E

15. The most exciting part of the novel was when Matilda rejected Count Vladimir
    　　　　A　　　　　　　　　B　　　　　　　　　　　　　C
    and accepted the proposal of the peasant, Hugo. No error
    　　　　　　　　　　　　　D　　　　　E

16. It was a ominous sign and one which struck fear in our hearts. No error
    　　A　B　　　　　　　　　　　C　　　D　　　　　　　E

17. We accumulated so many books over the past years that we now realize that
    　　A　　　　　　　　　　　　　　　　　　　　　　　　B
    we shall have to donate a large number to various organizations. No error
    　　C　　　　　　　　　　D　　　　　　　　　　　　　　　E

18. We were constantly arguing with John and her concerning their support of
    　　　　A　　　　　　B　　　　　C
    our government's policies. No error
    　　D　　　　　　　E

19. I can hardly believe that you drank all the coffee and didn't leave none for
    　　　A　　　　　　　　B　　　　　　　　　　C
    the other workers. No error
    　　　　　D　　　　　E

20. Today's problems are different than those we faced when we were younger;
    　　A　　　　　　　　　B　　　　　C
    they appear to be less involved. No error
    　　　　　D　　　　　　E

Directions: The sentences below may contain problems in grammar, usage, word choice, sentence construction, or punctuation. Part or all of each sentence is underlined. Following each sentence you will find five ways of expressing the underlined part. Answer choice (**A**) always repeats the original underlined section. The other four answer choices are all different. You are to select the lettered answer that produces the most effective sentence. If you think the original sentence is best, choose (**A**) as your answer. If one of the other choices makes a better sentence, mark your answer sheet for the letter of that choice. Do not choose an answer that changes the meaning of the original sentence.

21. He <u>couldn't scarcely but hold</u> back his tears when he heard the violin concerto.

    (A) couldn't scarcely but hold
    (B) could not hardly but hold
    (C) can scarcely hold
    (D) could scarcely hold
    (E) couldn't hardly hold

22. It is possible that the reason that he felt <u>so badly was that</u> he had done very poorly on the test.

    (A) so badly was that
    (B) so badly is that
    (C) so bad was because
    (D) so bad was when
    (E) so bad was that

23. <u>Mr. Brandeis who is a most caring counselor,</u> forgot to attend the conference.

    (A) Mr. Brandeis who is a most caring counselor,
    (B) Mr. Brandeis who is a most caring counselor
    (C) Mr. Brandeis, who is a most caring counselor,
    (D) Mr. Brandeis, who is a most careful counselor
    (E) Mr. Brandeis, being a most caring counselor,

24. The third act <u>is set in the time of</u> the fall of the Holy Roman Empire.

    (A) is set in the time of
    (B) is when there is
    (C) is during the
    (D) was when there is
    (E) occurs during the decline of

25. I <u>have taken his name off of</u> the list of English-speaking dentists in Rome.

    (A) have taken his name off of
    (B) took his name off of
    (C) have taken his name off
    (D) have taken his name off from
    (E) removed his name off

26. <u>The womens outer garments were</u> placed in the cloak rooms.

    (A) The womens outer garments were
    (B) The womens' outer garments was
    (C) The women's outer garments were
    (D) The womans' outer garment was
    (E) The woman's outer garments was

27. When writing a theme, you must be certain that <u>you use</u> standard English.

    (A) you use
    (B) one uses
    (C) there is used
    (D) of the use of
    (E) when you use

28. The doctor's address is 4120 East Broadway New York New York.

    (A) 4120 East Broadway New York New York.
    (B) 4120 East, Broadway New York, New York.
    (C) 4120 East Broadway, New York, New York.
    (D) 4120, East Broadway, New York, New York.
    (E) 4120 East Broadway New York, New York.

29. They <u>arrived</u> on time and were able to witness the entire graduation ceremony.

    (A) arrived
    (B) have arrived
    (C) were arriving
    (D) did arrive
    (E) arrive

30. One reviewer called the play, <u>Broadway's Musical Sensation!</u>

    (A) Broadway's Musical Sensation!
    (B) "Broadway's Musical Sensation!"
    (C) "Broadways Musical Sensation!"
    (D) "Broadway's Musical" Sensation!
    (E) Broadway's "Musical" Sensation!

31. He was <u>more upset than we</u> by the boy's behavior.

    (A) more upset than we
    (B) more aggravated than us
    (C) more annoyed then us
    (D) more aggravated than we
    (E) more upset than us

32. Playing ball, swimming in the pool, and <u>a diet without starchy foods help</u> keep his weight down.

    (A) a diet without starchy foods help
    (B) avoiding starchy foods help
    (C) dieting without starchy foods helps
    (D) avoiding starchy foods helps
    (E) a diet without starchy foods helps

33. The intention of the candidate <u>is to serve</u> all the people.

    (A) is to serve
    (B) are to serve
    (C) are serving
    (D) are the service of
    (E) is in the service of

34. Give the book <u>to whomever asks</u> for it.

    (A) to whomever asks
    (B) to whomsoever asks
    (C) to whoever asks
    (D) to whom asks
    (E) to anyone whom asks

35. She <u>had been laying</u> on the beach for well over an hour when we arrived.

    (A) had been laying
    (B) had been lying
    (C) had been lieing
    (D) is lying
    (E) has lain

36. Each person is entitled to <u>their rights</u> in this community.

    (A) their rights
    (B) their right
    (C) one's rights
    (D) his rights
    (E) their own rights

37. <u>It's too difficult a question to answer to.</u>

    (A) It's too difficult a question to answer to.
    (B) Its too difficult a question to answer.
    (C) It's too difficult a question to answer.
    (D) It's to difficult a question to answer to.
    (E) Its' too difficult a question to answer.

38. He <u>has hardly any papers</u> left to grade.

    (A) has hardly any papers
    (B) has scarcely no papers
    (C) hasn't hardly any papers
    (D) hasn't scarcely any papers
    (E) has hardly no papers

Directions: Questions 39–44 concern an essay that might have been an early draft of a student's writing and that contains some sentences that should be reworked and corrected. After reading the essay, answer the questions that follow it. The questions may relate to diction, usage, tone, or sentence structure as well as to organization, development, logic, or appropriateness of language. Choose the response that makes the meaning most clear and precise and that does not violate the rules of standard written English.

(1) Today, more than ever, people are developing a concern for their environment. **(2)** A century ago, we took clear streams for granted. **(3)** We were not concerned about the air we breathe. **(4)** We did not give a second thought to the forests or woodlands. **(5)** But now all that has changed.

(6) Population growth has been a definite factor in this area. **(7)** People have encroached on the farmlands, and cities have sprung up where once it was open spaces. **(8)** As a result, forests have been destroyed. **(9)** The smoke from factories has polluted the air. **(10)** More and more garbage is produced, and the streets are covered with litter.

(11) This is but one example. **(12)** There are many others. **(13)** You should stop and think before you destroy nature. **(14)** Perhaps men and women can find more ecologically sound ways in which to help our environment be maintained. **(15)** If the environment is destroyed, then even though people may not suffer directly, certainly their children.

39. Which of the following is the best way to combine sentences 2, 3, and 4?

  (A) A century ago we did not care about the environment with its streams and water.
  (B) A century ago, we were not interested in preserving forests, streams, and air.
  (C) A century ago, clear streams, clean air, and the preservation of forests and woodlands were not our concern.
  (D) A century ago, we were not aware of clean air, or forests, or streams.
  (E) Clean air, streams, and forests were not part of our environment a century ago.

40. Which of the following is the best revision of the underlined portion of sentence 7?

People have encroached on the farmlands, and cities have sprung up where once it was open spaces.

  (A) where once it was open space on the land.
  (B) on what used to be once open spaces.
  (C) where once there was open spaces there.
  (D) where once there were open spaces.
  (E) when once there were open spaces.

41. In context of the sentences preceding and following sentence 13, which of the following is the best revision of sentence 13?

  (A) Stop and think before you destroy nature.
  (B) Stop, think before nature is destroyed.
  (C) You must stop destroying nature.
  (D) Nature will be destroyed if you do not stop and think.
  (E) People must stop and think before they destroy nature.

42. Which of the following is the best revision of the underlined portion of sentence 14 below?

Perhaps men and women can find more ecologically sound ways in which to help our environment be maintained.

  (A) in which our environment be maintained.
  (B) in which our environment can be helped to be maintained.
  (C) to help maintain our environment.
  (D) in which help maintain our environment.
  (E) in which help in the maintenance of our environment.

43. Which of the following is the best revision of the underlined portion of sentence 15 below?

If the environment is destroyed, then even though people may not suffer directly, certainly their children.

  (A) certainly their children are.
  (B) certainly our children may not.
  (C) certainly their children do.
  (D) their children certainly can.
  (E) certainly their children will.

44. The writer's main intent in the second paragraph is to

(A) expand upon the thesis developed in the first paragraph
(B) offer a simple definition of *pollution*
(C) propose a solution to the problem posed in the initial paragraph
(D) provide a summarizing transition from paragraph 1
(E) provide contradictory examples following sentence 5

Directions: Questions 45–50 concern an essay that might have been an early draft of a student's writing and that contains some sentences that should be reworked and corrected. After reading the essay, answer the questions that follow it. The questions may relate to diction, usage, tone, or sentence structure as well as to organization, development, logic, or appropriateness of language. Choose the response that makes the meaning most clear and precise and that does not violate the rules of standard written English.

(1) There are many people who feel that if young people commit crimes, they should be treated as adults. (2) These young people are called youthful offenders. (3) The people say that it is the crime that must be considered, not the person who committed it.

(4) Putting a young person in prison will not necessarily rehabilitate them. (5) They will come in contact with all sorts of hardened criminals. (6) In addition, they will be exposed to drugs, alcohol, and excessive violence. (7) But there are people who feel strongly that these young offenders should be removed from the mainstream of society. (8) Here they prey on the elderly and the weak. (9) They are a menace to law-abiding citizens. (10) Society, along with the entire judicial system, is confronted with a very serious problem. (11) Should we be concerned with the lawbreaker and try to rehabilitate him or with society as a whole?

(12) I know that there is no easy solution to this dilemma. (13) You have to evaluate both sides of the coin. (14) Young offenders cannot be turned loose to prey on others. (15) But they must be helped to become part of the mainstream of society and take their places as law-abiding, valuable citizens.

45. The writer's purpose in the first paragraph appears to be to

(A) show two divergent points of view
(B) indicate that there are no easy solutions to a difficult problem
(C) convince the reader to accept one point of view
(D) introduce the problem by presenting one point of view
(E) highlight a current problem by offering an apt example

46. Which of the following is the best way to combine sentences 1 and 2?

(A) Many feel that youthful offenders, young people who commit crimes, should be treated as adults.
(B) Young people commit crimes; they are called youthful offenders and should be treated as adults.
(C) Young people who commit crimes are called youthful offenders, many feel that they should be treated as adults.
(D) Treating young people as adults is one way of handling a difficult situation.
(E) Treating young people who commit crimes, that is youthful offenders, as adults.

47. Which of the following is the best revision of the underlined portion of sentence 4 below?

Putting a young person in prison will not necessarily rehabilitate them.

(A) Putting a youthful offender in prison
(B) Imprisoning a young person
(C) Putting them in prison
(D) Putting youthful offenders in prison
(E) Having put young people in prison

48. In relation to the passage as a whole, which of the following best describes the writer's intention in the second paragraph?

(A) To propose possible solutions to the problem
(B) To show that there are two different viewpoints
(C) To summarize the opposing position
(D) To illustrate the fallacious reasoning of one position
(E) To provide an evaluation

49. Which of the following is the best way to combine sentences 7, 8, and 9?

(A) But there are those who feel strongly that youthful offenders should be removed from mainstream society where they prey on the elderly, weak, and law-abiding.
(B) There are some people who wish to protect the elderly and weak from the people who prey on them and who become youthful offenders.
(C) Youthful offenders menace the law-abiding citizens by preying on the weak and elderly.
(D) Should we remove the young hoodlums from mainstream society and protect the law-abiding as a result?
(E) By protecting those who would prey on the elderly and weak, we menace the law-abiding as well.

50. In the context of the sentence preceding and the sentences following sentence 13, which of the following is the best revision of sentence 13?

(A) Be sure to look at both sides of the coin.
(B) You have to weigh both sides of the coin.
(C) Both sides of the coin must be evaluated.
(D) They should judge both sides of the coin.
(E) Keep both sides of the coin in mind when making your evaluation.

Directions: Some of the sentences below contain an error in grammar, usage, word choice, or idiom. Other sentences are correct. Parts of each sentence are underlined and lettered. The error, if there is one, is contained in one of the underlined parts of the sentence. Assume that all other parts of the sentence are correct and cannot be changed. For each sentence, select the one underlined part that must be changed to make the sentence correct and mark its letter on your answer sheet. If there is no error in a sentence, mark answer space **E**. No sentence contains more than one error.

51. One <u>must</u> be careful about <u>one's</u> attire if <u>you expect</u> to be treated <u>as a</u>
         A   B   C   D
    <u>professional.</u> <u>No error</u>
                      E

52. You are <u>liable to</u> <u>be chosen</u> to be the next <u>chairperson</u> of our department
             A   B   C
    <u>since</u> you possess the necessary skills. <u>No error</u>
     D   E

53. We are not pleased with <u>him</u> being <u>chosen</u> as our new <u>president</u>, but we
                        A   B   C
    know that we have to become <u>reconciled</u> to the decision made by our peers.
                                D
    <u>No error</u>
      E

54. <u>Irregardless</u> of the situation and the problems you <u>doubtless</u> face, <u>you</u> must
       A   B   C
    complete all the <u>term's</u> work by Christmas. <u>No error</u>
              D   E

55. He <u>reported back</u> to the <u>professor</u> and asked for <u>additional</u> time <u>to complete</u>
          A   B   C   D
    the research. <u>No error</u>
             E

56. John has demonstrated <u>his</u> ability to score <u>higher</u> <u>then</u> any <u>other</u> boy on the
                       A   B   C   D
    basketball team. <u>No error</u>
                E

57. There are a <u>number of</u> reasons <u>for her</u> refusal <u>to participate</u> in the function.
       A   B   C   D
    <u>No error</u>
      E

58. Since there <u>not</u> coming to the <u>celebration</u>, we <u>will have</u> <u>additional</u> space for
           A   B   C   D
    your guests. <u>No error</u>
             E

59. It was <u>neither</u> my decision <u>or</u> my intention <u>to distribute</u> the material at the
          A   B   C
    staff's meeting. <u>No error</u>
      D   E

60. A nation must be concerned about <u>their</u> citizens, even <u>those who</u> are living
                            A   B   C
    in countries that are <u>politically unstable</u>. <u>No error</u>
                   D   E

Sample Essay Responses

Essay Test A

Sample Response

No one wants to be patriots any more. Its a waste of time and it doesn't mean anything.

I know that when we had the Vietnam war, everybody said your crazy to go to fight and made fun of the soldeirs who went off to get killed. My uncle told me that everybody he knew didn't want to get drafted and thought of all kinds of excuse like they were conscience objections and didn't beleive in killing and things like that.

So I think that maybe today is still a carryover from the 60's. People still not wanting to believe in theyre country. Not like during the World War Two when everyone was together and were patriotic.

Annotated Sample Response

No one wants to be *a* patriot*s* any more. It's a waste of time and it doesn't mean anything.

I know that ~~when we had~~ *during* the Vietnam war, ~~everybody said your crazy~~ *many people said that young men were foolish* to go to fight and made fun of the ~~soldeirs~~ *soldiers* who went off to get killed. My uncle told me that ~~everybody~~ *no one* he knew ~~didn't want~~ *wanted* to ~~get~~ *be* drafted and thought of all kinds of ~~excuse like they were conscience objections~~ *excuses, such as that they were conscientious objectors* *people* and didn't ~~beleive~~ *believe* in killing.~~and things like that.~~

~~So~~ I think that ~~maybe~~ *perhaps* today *there* is still a carryover from the *19*60's. *Many* People still *do* not wanting to believe in ~~theyre~~ *their* country, ~~Not like~~ *unlike* during ~~the~~ World War ~~Two~~ *II* when everyone was ~~together~~ *unified* and ~~were~~ patriotic.

Analysis

Although the writer shows awareness of the topic and even offers an illustration to support his view, the essay is barely developed and contains many spelling and sentence structure errors. As the annotated copy demonstrates, the opening sentence contains an error in agreement, while the second sentence begins with an incorrect homonym. In paragraph 2, in addition to homonym and spelling errors, there is a lack of clarity of expression. The lack of clarity continues in the opening sentence of the third paragraph and the concluding ideas are not expressed in complete sentences.

Essay Test B

Sample Response

We are still patriotic. Holidays like July 4th and Veterans' Day are still very special. I know that my entire family gets together for a big meal or a picnic and we really count our blessings and are greatful that we live in a fine country like America.

My parents were born in Europe and they tell me that they didn't have the freedom that we have here. They worried about being taken prisoner. And were forced to serve in the army and fight and even get kill. So they appreciate living in the United States and even if sometimes we take things for granted deep down we love our country and are patriotic.

I think that everyone should learn about what it is like to live in a country where there is no freedom. And no liberty to be able to worship where you want and to be able to vote and to have free speech. Then we would all be even more patriotic here in our country, the United States of America.

Analysis

This writer is sincere and consistent, has a sense of organization, and knows how to write an introduction and suitable conclusion. In addition, the illustration in the developmental paragraph is drawn from the writer's own background and is both interesting and appropriate. Unfortunately, the errors in spelling (*greatful*), the omission of final letters (*kill*), and the fragments (paragraph two, sentence three; paragraph three, sentence two) detract from the value of the presentation.

Essay Test C

Sample Response

Patriotism has many faces. I think that I am still patriotic even though I do things in a different way than my parents and grandparents did.

Maybe I don't march in parades and wave a flag. But I still get a wonderful feeling when I see the Statue of Liberty. Maybe I don't sing patriotic songs but I still am proud that I live in a country that allows me to have free speech and the freedom to worship if that's what I believe. Maybe I don't repeat patriotic sayings that my parents memorized but I still am thrilled that in my country I can disagree with the government and not be thrown into jail.

I am patriotic and I show it when I vote, when I study about my country and when I do all I can to make my country better so that my children will continue to be patriotic in their way.

Analysis

This essay is well thought out, clear, and well written. The writer possesses a fine style and is creative in language and approach. The point of view is consistent, and each paragraph is logical and connected to the central idea. The repetition of the word "maybe" as an initial word in the second paragraph provides a neat balance, as do the several specific illustrations. In sum, the essay clearly indicates that the writer is capable of doing college-level writing.

Multiple-Choice Answers

1. D	21. D	41. E
2. C	22. E	42. C
3. E	23. C	43. E
4. B	24. A	44. A
5. A	25. C	45. D
6. D	26. C	46. A
7. D	27. A	47. D
8. E	28. C	48. B
9. B	29. A	49. A
10. B	30. B	50. C
11. C	31. A	51. C
12. D	32. B	52. A
13. D	33. A	53. A
14. C	34. C	54. A
15. B	35. B	55. A
16. B	36. D	56. C
17. E	37. C	57. E
18. E	38. A	58. A
19. C	39. C	59. B
20. B	40. D	60. A

Explanatory Answers for Sample Test 2 _____

_____ **SAT II: Writing Test**

1. **(D)** In an *either . . . or* construction, the verb agrees with the subject closest to it. In this case, since *Jim* is singular, the correct verb is *is*.
2. **(C)** Since *their* is plural referring to many people, the correct word must also be plural: *lives*.
3. **(E)** The sentence is correct.
4. **(B)** The possessive *crowd's* is necessary to indicate the "applause of the crowd."
5. **(A)** The correct verb form is *would have been*.
6. **(D)** Since the paintings of Van Gogh are being compared with the *paintings of Cézanne* (not with Cézanne), the correct wording should be "than those of" (or "than the paintings of") Cézanne.
7. **(D)** A semicolon or period (or comma and conjunction) is required, since no abrupt change of thought is indicated.
8. **(E)** The sentence is correct.
9. **(B)** The correct word is *drank*.
10. **(B)** The correct word is *than*.
11. **(C)** The correct word is *mine*.
12. **(D)** The standard form is *nowhere*.
13. **(D)** In an indirect question, a question mark is not required.
14. **(C)** The correct word is *annoyed* (or *irritated*).
15. **(B)** The correct phrase is *occurred when*.
16. **(B)** The correct word is *an*.
17. **(E)** The sentence is correct.
18. **(E)** The sentence is correct.
19. **(C)** The correct phrase is *didn't leave any* since the double negative must be eliminated.
20. **(B)** The correct phrase is *different from*.
21. **(D)** The underlined portion contains a double negative. The correct wording is *could scarcely hold*.
22. **(E)** After a verb referring to the senses, the adjective *(bad)*, not the adverb *(badly)*, is preferred. *Reason* should be followed by *that*, not by *because*; therefore, choice **(C)** is incorrect.
23. **(C)** In the middle of a sentence, a nonrestrictive clause is set off by two commas.
24. **(A)** The sentence is correct.
25. **(C)** *Off of* is not used in formal English. The correct preposition is *off*.
26. **(C)** The correct possessive form of *women* is *women's*. The plural *garments* takes the plural verb *were*, so **(E)** is incorrect.
27. **(A)** The sentence is correct.
28. **(C)** Commas are used to separate street, city, state in an address.
29. **(A)** The sentence is correct.
30. **(B)** Quotation marks are needed to indicate all the exact words of the reviewer.
31. **(A)** The sentence is correct.
32. **(B)** The participle *avoiding* is required in order to maintain parallel structure. The compound subject requires the plural verb form, *(help)*.
33. **(A)** The sentence is correct.
34. **(C)** The subjective form *whoever* is required, since it is the subject of *asks*.
35. **(B)** The correct form is *lying*.
36. **(D)** The pronoun *his* is required to agree with the singular *each person*.

37. (C) The final word, *to*, is redundant. Choices **(B)** and **(E)** are incorrect because the contraction should be spelled *It's*.

38. (A) The sentence is correct.

39. (C) Choice **(E)** makes a false statement. Choices **(A)**, **(B)**, and **(D)** overstate the case. The point of the author is simply that the environment was taken for granted a century ago, not that we were unaware of it or that we didn't care at all. Choice **(C)** makes the clear point that a century ago we were simply unconcerned about the environment because we did not identify a problem.

40. (D) The *it* of the underlined portion is vague and makes no clear reference. All choices except **(D)** are equally poorly written.

41. (E) The sudden shift to second-person address ("you") changes the tone awkwardly.

42. (C) Simplicity of statement helps to assure clarity. The preposition *in* of the original and the other choices contributes to the awkward quality of the statements.

43. (E) A verb is needed to complete the idea. Since the author appears to wish to communicate the thought that suffering is inevitable if the environment is destroyed, the verb *will* creates the best completion.

44. (A) The second paragraph develops logically from the first. All other choices are wrong: there is no definition; no solution is offered; there is no summary; and there are no contradictory examples.

45. (D) The first paragraph serves only to introduce the problem of juveniles who commit crimes. The writer presents only one viewpoint in this paragraph, that there are those who feel that youthful offenders who commit adult crimes should be treated as adults.

46. (A) Choice **(B)** implies that the statement is fact rather than opinion. Choice **(C)** contains a comma-splice error. Choice **(D)** omits a crucial part of the material. Choice **(E)** is a sentence fragment.

47. (D) The portion of the sentence that is not underlined must not change; therefore, the plural pronoun *them* requires a plural antecedent in the first part of the sentence. Choices **(A)** and **(B)** maintain the singular. Choice **(C)** offers another pronoun, which does not clarify the antecedent of the second pronoun. Choice **(E)** is awkward.

48. (B) The writer uses the second paragraph to point out the two opposing points of view. Sentences 4, 5, and 6 express one view; sentences 7, 8, and 9 offer the other view. Sentence 11 combines both views.

49. (A) Only choice **(A)** contains all the pertinent details offered by the writer in the three sentences without becoming awkward or convoluted.

50. (C) This question illustrates an error commonly committed by students, that of shifting voice midstream. Choices **(A)**, **(B)**, and **(E)** are all written in the second person as imperatives. Choice **(D)** is not a good one because the antecedent of *they* is unclear.

51. (C) For consistency, the words *one expects* should replace *you expect*.

52. (A) The correct word is *likely*.

53. (A) The participle *being* should be preceded by the possessive *his*.

54. (A) The correct word is *regardless*.

55. (A) Since *reported* means "to carry back" (this is the value of the prefix *re*), the word *back* is redundant and should be omitted.

56. (C) In a comparison, *than* is used.

57. (E) The sentence is correct.

58. (A) The contraction of *they are* is *they're*.

59. (B) The correct phrase is *neither . . . nor*.

60. (A) The singular pronoun *its* is required to agree with the singular antecedent *nation*.

CHAPTER 12

American College Testing Program (ACT)

Once confined to the Midwest, the ACT is gaining nationwide acceptance as a means of assessing a student's ability to do college-level work. This four-part college entrance test is designed to measure skills in English, Mathematics, Reading, and Science Reasoning.

The ACT English Test is a 45-minute test consisting of 75 questions testing knowledge of Usage and Mechanics (punctuation, grammar, and sentence structure) and Rhetorical Skills (strategy, organization, and style). The test questions concern a series of prose passages with portions underlined or otherwise indicated. For each question, four choices are offered. The test taker must decide which choice is most appropriate in the context of the passage.

The questions on the English Test are divided among the content areas approximately as follows:

> Usage/Mechanics—53%
> Rhetorical Skills—47%

ACT Mini-Test

The Mini-Test that follows is designed to help you to discover your strengths and weaknesses in the area of English Usage. It is modeled after the ACT English Test, but it contains fewer questions. Following the test are an answer key and an explanation of the answers. Use this material to guide your study in those areas in which you need the most practice. After you have reviewed relevant areas in the Guide to Good Writing, you will be prepared to take the full-length practice test that follows the Mini-Test.

Directions: In the passage that follows, certain words are underlined and numbered. In the right-hand column you will find alternative ways of expressing each numbered portion. You are to decide which alternative best expresses the idea, makes the statement appropriate for standard written English, or is worded most consistently with the style and tone of the passage. If you think the original version is correct, choose NO CHANGE, options **A** or **F**. Some questions are identified by a number in a box. These questions do not refer to an underlined portion but to a section of the passage or to the passage as a whole. For each boxed question, select the alternative you consider best. Read the passage through quickly before answering the questions that accompany it. In most cases you cannot choose the correct answer without reading ahead to see what comes next.

Sir William Gilbert and Sir Arthur

<u>Sullivan entertainment</u> celebrities of the
1

Victorian Age, are credited with

bringing new life to the English theater

<u>of Queen Victoria's day</u>. Together
2

Gilbert and Sullivan created a series of

<u>brilliant, comic</u> operettas, including
3

Trial by Jury, H.M.S. Pinafore, and *The*

Pirates of Penzance. 4

1. **A.** NO CHANGE
   B. Sullivan—entertainment
   C. Sullivan, entertainment
   D. Sullivan who were entertainment

2. **F.** NO CHANGE
   G. when Queen Victoria reigned
   H. during the reign of Queen Victoria
   J. OMIT the underlined portion

3. **A.** NO CHANGE
   B. brilliant comic
   C. brilliant, comical
   D. brilliant comic-like

4. Suppose at this point the writer wanted to add more information about the works of Gilbert and Sullivan. Which of the following additions would be most relevant to the passage as a whole?
   F. A description of the influence Gilbert and Sullivan's work had on English theater
   G. A list of other plays produced during the Victorian Age
   H. A brief summary of the plots of *Trial by Jury, H.M.S. Pinafore,* and *The Pirates of Penzance*
   J. A bibliography of books about Gilbert and Sullivan

Answers

Mini-Test: ACT

1. C
2. J
3. B
4. F

Explanatory Answers for ACT Mini-Test

1. **(C)** is correct because the phrase *entertainment celebrities of the Victorian Age* is an appositive which is not essential to the sentence and should, therefore, be set off by commas.
2. **(J)** is correct because all other choices unnecessarily repeat *Victorian Age,* which has already been expressed.
3. **(B)** is correct because *brilliant* modifies *comic operettas* and so no punctuation is needed. *Comic* is a better choice than *comic-like* in alternative (D).
4. **(F)** is the best choice because it follows from the topic of the paragraph: Gilbert and Sullivan brought new life to the English theater.

Answer Sheet for Sample Test 3 —————

ACT English Test

1. Ⓐ Ⓑ Ⓒ Ⓓ	26. Ⓕ Ⓖ Ⓗ Ⓙ	51. Ⓐ Ⓑ Ⓒ Ⓓ
2. Ⓕ Ⓖ Ⓗ Ⓙ	27. Ⓐ Ⓑ Ⓒ Ⓓ	52. Ⓕ Ⓖ Ⓗ Ⓙ
3. Ⓐ Ⓑ Ⓒ Ⓓ	28. Ⓕ Ⓖ Ⓗ Ⓙ	53. Ⓐ Ⓑ Ⓒ Ⓓ
4. Ⓕ Ⓖ Ⓗ Ⓙ	29. Ⓐ Ⓑ Ⓒ Ⓓ	54. Ⓕ Ⓖ Ⓗ Ⓙ
5. Ⓐ Ⓑ Ⓒ Ⓓ	30. Ⓕ Ⓖ Ⓗ Ⓙ	55. Ⓐ Ⓑ Ⓒ Ⓓ
6. Ⓕ Ⓖ Ⓗ Ⓙ	31. Ⓐ Ⓑ Ⓒ Ⓓ	56. Ⓕ Ⓖ Ⓗ Ⓙ
7. Ⓐ Ⓑ Ⓒ Ⓓ	32. Ⓕ Ⓖ Ⓗ Ⓙ	57. Ⓐ Ⓑ Ⓒ Ⓓ
8. Ⓕ Ⓖ Ⓗ Ⓙ	33. Ⓐ Ⓑ Ⓒ Ⓓ	58. Ⓕ Ⓖ Ⓗ Ⓙ
9. Ⓐ Ⓑ Ⓒ Ⓓ	34. Ⓕ Ⓖ Ⓗ Ⓙ	59. Ⓐ Ⓑ Ⓒ Ⓓ
10. Ⓕ Ⓖ Ⓗ Ⓙ	35. Ⓐ Ⓑ Ⓒ Ⓓ	60. Ⓕ Ⓖ Ⓗ Ⓙ
11. Ⓐ Ⓑ Ⓒ Ⓓ	36. Ⓕ Ⓖ Ⓗ Ⓙ	61. Ⓐ Ⓑ Ⓒ Ⓓ
12. Ⓕ Ⓖ Ⓗ Ⓙ	37. Ⓐ Ⓑ Ⓒ Ⓓ	62. Ⓕ Ⓖ Ⓗ Ⓙ
13. Ⓐ Ⓑ Ⓒ Ⓓ	38. Ⓕ Ⓖ Ⓗ Ⓙ	63. Ⓐ Ⓑ Ⓒ Ⓓ
14. Ⓕ Ⓖ Ⓗ Ⓙ	39. Ⓐ Ⓑ Ⓒ Ⓓ	64. Ⓕ Ⓖ Ⓗ Ⓙ
15. Ⓐ Ⓑ Ⓒ Ⓓ	40. Ⓕ Ⓖ Ⓗ Ⓙ	65. Ⓐ Ⓑ Ⓒ Ⓓ
16. Ⓕ Ⓖ Ⓗ Ⓙ	41. Ⓐ Ⓑ Ⓒ Ⓓ	66. Ⓕ Ⓖ Ⓗ Ⓙ
17. Ⓐ Ⓑ Ⓒ Ⓓ	42. Ⓕ Ⓖ Ⓗ Ⓙ	67. Ⓐ Ⓑ Ⓒ Ⓓ
18. Ⓕ Ⓖ Ⓗ Ⓙ	43. Ⓐ Ⓑ Ⓒ Ⓓ	68. Ⓕ Ⓖ Ⓗ Ⓙ
19. Ⓐ Ⓑ Ⓒ Ⓓ	44. Ⓕ Ⓖ Ⓗ Ⓙ	69. Ⓐ Ⓑ Ⓒ Ⓓ
20. Ⓕ Ⓖ Ⓗ Ⓙ	45. Ⓐ Ⓑ Ⓒ Ⓓ	70. Ⓕ Ⓖ Ⓗ Ⓙ
21. Ⓐ Ⓑ Ⓒ Ⓓ	46. Ⓕ Ⓖ Ⓗ Ⓙ	71. Ⓐ Ⓑ Ⓒ Ⓓ
22. Ⓕ Ⓖ Ⓗ Ⓙ	47. Ⓐ Ⓑ Ⓒ Ⓓ	72. Ⓕ Ⓖ Ⓗ Ⓙ
23. Ⓐ Ⓑ Ⓒ Ⓓ	48. Ⓕ Ⓖ Ⓗ Ⓙ	73. Ⓐ Ⓑ Ⓒ Ⓓ
24. Ⓕ Ⓖ Ⓗ Ⓙ	49. Ⓐ Ⓑ Ⓒ Ⓓ	74. Ⓕ Ⓖ Ⓗ Ⓙ
25. Ⓐ Ⓑ Ⓒ Ⓓ	50. Ⓕ Ⓖ Ⓗ Ⓙ	75. Ⓐ Ⓑ Ⓒ Ⓓ

(Answers are on page 222)

CHAPTER 13

Sample Test 3:
ACT English Test

45 Minutes—75 Questions

DIRECTIONS: In the passages that follow, certain words are underlined and numbered. In the right-hand column you will find alternative ways of expressing each numbered portion. You are to decide which alternative best expresses the idea, makes the statement appropriate for standard written English, or is worded most consistently with the style and tone of the passage. If you think the original version is correct, choose NO CHANGE, options A or F. Some questions are identified by a number or numbers in a box. These questions do not refer to an underlined portion but to a section of the passage or to the passage as a whole. For each boxed question, select the alternative you consider best. Read each passage through quickly before answering the questions that accompany it. In most cases you cannot choose the correct answer without reading ahead to see what comes next.

Passage I

In 1784, Ben Franklin jokingly suggested that

time be moved <u>ahead of time</u> so that the days

1

would have <u>more usable sunlight.</u> ☐3

2

Almost 120 years later the British picked up on the

idea; <u>the bill being</u> rejected by the House of

4
Commons in 1908. However, in response to the

1. **A.** NO CHANGE
   B. to be ahead
   C. a little ahead
   D. forward

2. **F.** NO CHANGE
   G. more sunlight
   H. more hours of sun
   J. more used sunlight

3. Is the reference to Ben Franklin appropriate here?

   A. No, because it has nothing to do with the topic.
   B. No, because Franklin died long before the introduction of Daylight Saving Time.
   C. Yes, because it provides an appropriate anecdote to introduce the essay.
   D. Yes, because Franklin is the only person mentioned in the essay.

4. **F.** NO CHANGE
   G. idea, but the bill was
   H. idea; therefore the bill was
   J. idea: the bill being

need to conserve fuel during World War II, clocks

were <u>changed</u> in Australia, Great Britain, Ger-
  5

many, and the United States. <u>Over here</u> in the
                                  6

United States, time conservation was in effect

from February 1942 until September 1945, as part

of our all-out war effort <u>which also included ra-
                                          7

tioning food and other vital resources.</u>
                7

Once the war was over, confusion set in as in-

dividual states set their own policies <u>as regards to</u>
                                              8

Daylight Saving Time. Some states changed their

<u>clocks, some states did not.</u> In an effort to maintain
        9

some order, Congress passed the Uniform Time

Act in 1966. Twenty years later, in 1986, Congress

passed a mandatory bill moving the start of Day-

light Saving Time to the first Sunday in April

instead of the last. <u>Expecting</u> not only to boost
                          10

sales of sports and leisure <u>goods, and also</u> to
                                    11

reduce the number of traffic accidents during rush

hours. <u>Being that some people lived in rural areas,</u>
                              12

<u>they</u>
12

5. **A.** NO CHANGE
   B. had been changed
   C. were changing
   D. would have to be changed

6. **F.** NO CHANGE
   G. Back here
   H. Around here
   J. Here

7. **A.** NO CHANGE
   B. that also included rationing food and other vital resources
   C. along with rationing food and other resources
   D. OMIT the underlined portion.

8. **F.** NO CHANGE
   G. regarding
   H. in regards to
   J. to

9. **A.** NO CHANGE
   B. clocks; some not
   C. clocks, others not
   D. clocks; others did not

10. **F.** NO CHANGE
    G. Expected
    H. This was expected
    J. In expectation

11. **A.** NO CHANGE
    B. goods, but also
    C. goods and
    D. goods and so

12. **F.** NO CHANGE
    G. Those who lived in rural areas
    H. Those whom lived in rural areas
    J. People living in rural areas, they

voiced opposition to this change. [13] The Daylight

Saving Time Coalition has spent a great deal of

time and effort on these problems.

What would old Ben think of all this? [15]
14

Passage II

The Stone Age was characterized <u>for using</u>
16

stone as the material from which tools and weap-

ons were made. <u>Previously they used wood or</u>
17

<u>bone and later metals.</u> During this period inhabi-
17

tants of early England <u>create</u>
18

13. Suppose at this point the writer wanted to add more information on the opposition. Which of the following additions would be most relevant to the passage as a whole?

   A. A list of people opposed to the change
   B. A description of the rural areas opposed to the change
   C. A list of benefits of the change to rural residents
   D. Examples of difficulties resulting from the change

14. F. NO CHANGE
   G. What would Ben Franklin think of all this.
   H. What would old Ben say to this!
   J. OMIT the underlined portion.

15. This essay would be most helpful to someone wanting information about

   A. conservation methods employed during World War II
   B. the effect of daylight saving time in Australia, Great Britain, Germany, and the U.S.
   C. the history of daylight saving time
   D. Ben Franklin's contribution to daylight saving time

16. F. NO CHANGE
   G. to use
   H. by the use of
   J. of using

17. A. NO CHANGE
   B. Before there was wood or bone, and later metals.
   C. Previously using wood or bone, and later metals.
   D. OMIT

18. F. NO CHANGE
   G. had been creating
   H. were creating
   J. created

Stonehenge, a circular arrangement of huge stand-
19
ing stones on Salisbury Plain. The 16 outer stones

remaining have an average height of over 13 feet

and an average weight of 26 tons. [20]

Stonehenge over the years has remained both a
21
mystery and a controversy. Its creation was a long

and difficult process, it probably spanned 2000
22
years from conception to completion. The mystery

is how had the people ever carted the stones from
23
Wales to the Salisbury Plain. The wheel, as a

means of transportation, had not yet been in-

vented. Theories suggest that thousands of men

used round logs and rolled the stones along the
24
logs, rushing the back logs forward. [25]

19. **A.** NO CHANGE
    B. Stonehenge, being a
    C. Stonehenge a
    D. Stonehenge; a

20. Is the writer's use of figures appropriate at this point in the passage?

    F. No, because they interrupt the flow of the narrative.
    G. No, because they are too vague to be useful.
    H. Yes, because they are the only figures used in the passage.
    J. Yes, because they contribute to understanding the size of the monument.

21. **A.** NO CHANGE
    B. over the years,
    C. —over the years
    D. , over the years,

22. **F.** NO CHANGE
    G. probably it spanned
    H. probably spanning
    J. it is likely to have spanned

23. **A.** NO CHANGE
    B. how the stones were carried
    C. how the people were transported
    D. how the stones arrived

24. **F.** NO CHANGE
    G. had to roll
    H. to roll
    J. rolling

25. Suppose at this point the writer wished to provide a conclusion for the paragraph. Which of the following additions would be most appropriate to the passage as a whole?

    A. Do you realize how hard that must have been?
    B. Can you image how tough that must have been?
    C. The task must have been a daunting one.
    D. Talk about a difficult task!

The controversy over Stonehenge <u>is concerned</u>
26

<u>about</u> its purpose.
26

Two theories exist <u>today. The</u> sun-worship theory
27

and the sepulchral theory. Some researchers feel

that Stonehenge was oriented to the movements of

the sun and <u>moon a</u> marvel for the time period.
28

Others say it was a sacred burial ground.

<u>Stonehenge was erected</u> in the prehistoric period,
29

this debate may never be resolved. There is,

however, no debate about the fact that such an

<u>important, old antiquity</u> must be protected and
30

preserved for all to see.   31

26. F. NO CHANGE
    G. concerns
    H. concern
    J. is in concern over

27. A. NO CHANGE
    B. today, these are
    C. today; the
    D. today: the

28. F. NO CHANGE
    G. moon—a
    H. moon; a
    J. moon. A

29. A. NO CHANGE
    B. Stonehenge being erected
    C. Having been erected
    D. Since Stonehenge was erected

30. F. NO CHANGE
    G. important antiquity
    H. important old antiquity
    J. ancient antiquity

31. The writer would probably favor all of the
    following EXCEPT

    A. forbidding tourists to remove bits of
        rock as souvenirs
    B. forbidding unsupervised digging at the
        site
    C. discouraging tourists from visiting the
        site
    D. encouraging continued study of the
        mystery of Stonehenge

Passage III

Alice was beginning to get very tired of sitting

by her sister on the bank with nothing to <u>do: once</u>
32

or twice she had peeped into the book her sister

was reading, but it had no pictures or conversation

32. F. NO CHANGE
    G. do; once
    H. do, once
    J. do. Once

in it, "and what is the use of a
33

book thought Alice,
34

without pictures or conversations?"
35

So she was considering, in her own mind,
36
whether the pleasure of making a daisy chain

would be worth the trouble of getting up and

picking the daisies, when suddenly a White Rabbit
37
with pink eyes ran close by her. There was nothing

remarkable in that. Nor did Alice think of it to be
38

so very unusual to hear the rabbit
38

say to himself "Oh dear! Oh dear! I shall be
39

too late!" 41
40

33. A. NO CHANGE
    B. it. "And
    C. it, "And
    D. it: "And

34. F. NO CHANGE
    G. book? thought Alice,
    H. book"? thought Alice,
    J. book," thought Alice,

35. A. NO CHANGE
    B. "without
    C. "Without
    D. Without

36. F. NO CHANGE
    G. thinking
    H. wondering
    J. considering

37. A. NO CHANGE
    B. daisies—when
    C. daisies; when
    D. daisies. When

38. F. NO CHANGE
    G. for the unusualness of it
    H. of it to be so unusual
    J. it so unusual

39. A. NO CHANGE
    B. himself, "Oh dear!"
    C. himself, "Oh dear!
    D. himself, oh dear!

40. F. NO CHANGE
    G. to late!"
    H. so late!"
    J. too late"!

41. Why does the author describe Alice's reactions at this point?

    A. To explain unusual animal behavior
    B. To explore the importance of time
    C. To prepare the reader for events to come
    D. To show how Alice feels about pets and wildlife

But when the rabbit actually took a watch out of <u>its</u>
42

waistcoat pocket,

<u>looks</u> at it and then hurried
43

<u>on Alice</u> started to her
44

<u>feet; for it</u> flashed across her mind that she had
45

<u>never before seen</u> a rabbit with either a waistcoat
46

pocket or a watch to take out of <u>it, and, burning</u>
47

with curiosity, she ran across the field after him

and was just in time to see him pop down a large

rabbit hole <u>under</u> a hedge.
48

   Alice followed, giving no consideration to <u>how</u>
49

<u>she might not ever come up.</u> The rabbit hole went
49

straight on like a tunnel for some way, then dipped

down so suddenly that Alice had not a moment to

42. **F.** NO CHANGE
    G. it's
    H. its'
    J. his

43. **A.** NO CHANGE
    B. to look
    C. was looking
    D. looked

44. **F.** NO CHANGE
    G. on, Alice
    H. on. Alice
    J. on: Alice

45. **A.** NO CHANGE
    B. feet for it
    C. feet, for it
    D. feet. For it

46. **F.** NO CHANGE
    G. never seen before
    H. never seen
    J. never ever seen

47. **A.** NO CHANGE
    B. it; and, burning
    C. it. And burning
    D. it. Burning

48. **F.** NO CHANGE
    G. by
    H. at
    J. around

49. **A.** NO CHANGE
    B. the possibility that there might be no way up
    C. not coming up
    D. how she might get back up

think of stopping herself before she found herself

in a fall down what
50

50. **F.**   NO CHANGE
     G.   making a fall
     H.   falling
     J.   to be falling

ought to be
51

51. **A.**   NO CHANGE
     B.   should be
     C.   ought to have been
     D.   appeared to be

a very, deep well.
52

52. **F.**   NO CHANGE
     G.   very deep
     H.   real deep
     J.   really deep

Questions 53 and 54 refer to the passage as a whole.

53. Is the use of quotation marks appropriate in this passage?

    A.   Yes, they indicate conversation between two or more speakers.
    B.   Yes, because the material enclosed is direct speech or thought.
    C.   No, because a rabbit cannot speak.
    D.   No, because thoughts are not spoken.

54. The tone of this passage may best be described as

    F.   persuasive
    G.   emotional
    H.   matter-of-fact
    J.   whimsical

Passage IV

The paragraphs in the essay that follows may not be in the most logical order. Each paragraph is numbered in parentheses and item 75 will ask you to choose the sequence of paragraph numbers that is in the most logical order.

(1)

For an employer, the most difficult aspect of the

hiring process is the lining up by suitable candi-
                           55
dates for a specific
55

55. **A.**   NO CHANGE
     B.   by suitability
     C.   of suitable candidates
     D.   suitable candidates

job, doing this is indispensable to good
56

56. **F.**   NO CHANGE
     G.   job; so that
     H.   job, but
     J.   job, except

selection. 57 It is better to seek and select than

57. The writer has organized this discussion around which two aspects of the job process?

    A.   its cost and desirability
    B.   its indispensability and cost
    C.   its time and necessity
    D.   its difficulty and necessity

waiting for applications. You can find new em-
   58

ployees through want ads in local newspapers or

placement bureaus of high schools, business

schools, and colleges. 59 Of course, these are

only some of the sources of

58. F.   NO CHANGE
    G.   awaiting
    H.   waiting on
    J.   to wait for

59. Which of the following examples could be used in this sentence to further illustrate the author's point?

    A.   employment agencies
    B.   word of mouth
    C.   friends
    D.   former employees

employees, there are many
   60

60. F.   NO CHANGE
    G.   employees; their
    H.   employees; there
    J.   employees. Their

effective ways to find personnel.
   61

(2)

61. A.   NO CHANGE
    B.   another affective
    C.   other effective
    D.   other affective

    Careful choice of personnel is essential to pro-

tect the reputation of any small business. To select

the right employee, you should have planned in
                           62

advance what you want the applicant to do, and
   62

62. F.   NO CHANGE
    G.   have planned ahead
    H.   plan in advance
    J.   have made a plan in advance

then look for one to fill
          63

63. A.   NO CHANGE
    B.   for filling
    C.   who fill
    D.   who filled

your particular needs. 64

(3)

Often one of the major mistakes in choosing an

employee is to hire an

individual; without a clear knowledge beforehand
        65

of exactly what his or her duties will be.

Although it is true that in a small business you will
        66

need flexible employees who can shift from task to

task and who may be called upon to perform unex-
                            67

pected and unforeseen tasks. Nevertheless, you
     67

should plan your hiring to assure an organization

capable of performing every essential function.

Write down the job descriptions. For example, you

should answer these kind of questions before
               68

hiring; if you are running a retail store, will a sales-
  69

person also do stockkeeping or bookkeeping? In a

restaurant, will a waitress also perform some of the

duties of a hostess?

64. Suppose at this point the writer wanted to add more information about hiring applicants. Which of the following additions would be most suitable for inclusion here?

F. It's important to hire people who are enthusiastic about their work.

G. People without prior job experience are the best employees because they are more open to new ideas.

H. It's often helpful to make a list of questions to ask the applicants.

J. The process of hiring is often very difficult and time consuming.

65. A. NO CHANGE
    B. an individual; without
    C. an individual. Without
    D. an individual without

66. F. NO CHANGE
    G. It being true that
    H. It is true that
    J. While it is true that

67. A. NO CHANGE
    B. unexpecting
    C. unexpected
    D. OMIT

68. F. NO CHANGE
    G. such kind of questions
    H. such kinds of question
    J. such questions as these

69. A. NO CHANGE
    B. hiring; "If
    C. hiring: "If
    D. hiring: If

(4)

By securing applications, you must screen them.
70

70. **F.** NO CHANGE
G. Once you have secured
H. Once you had secured
J. By obtaining

Application forms, filled out by the prospective
71
employees will help. Some applicants may be
eliminated right away by studying the forms. For
each of the others, the application will serve as a
basis for the interview. Each interview is for being
72
conducted in private. Put the applicant at ease by
describing your business in general and the job in
particular. But once you have done this, encourage
the applicant to talk. Do not make the mistake of
doing all or most of the talking. ⬚73

71. **A.** NO CHANGE
B. forms—filled out
C. forms; filled in
D. forms filled in

72. **F.** NO CHANGE
G. Each interview should be
H. Each interview being
J. All interviews needs to be

73. Which of the following sentences best summarizes this paragraph?

A. As we have shown, selecting the right person for the job is a very difficult and tedious job.
B. Although as the supervisor you undoubtedly have important things to contribute to the conversation.
C. Selecting the right person is extremely important and you must learn everything you can about the applicant that is pertinent to the job.
D. You may want to call other employees in at this point to offer their opinions as well.

> Questions 74 and 75 refer to the passage as a whole.

74. This passage was most likely written for which of the following groups?

F. managers of large companies
G. people looking for jobs
H. owners of small businesses
J. people thinking of returning to the job market after an absence

75. Choose the sequence of numbers that will make the passage's structure most logical.

A. NO CHANGE
B. 2, 1, 4, 3
C. 3, 1, 2, 4
D. 2, 3, 1, 4

Answers

Sample Test 3: ACT English Test

1. D	16. H	31. C	46. F	61. C
2. F	17. D	32. J	47. D	62. H
3. C	18. J	33. B	48. F	63. A
4. G	19. A	34. J	49. D	64. H
5. A	20. J	35. B	50. H	65. D
6. J	21. D	36. H	51. D	66. H
7. D	22. H	37. A	52. G	67. C
8. G	23. B	38. J	53. B	68. J
9. D	24. F	39. C	54. J	69. D
10. H	25. C	40. F	55. C	70. G
11. B	26. G	41. C	56. H	71. D
12. G	27. D	42. J	57. D	72. G
13. D	28. G	43. D	58. J	73. C
14. F	29. D	44. G	59. A	74. H
15. C	30. G	45. C	60. H	75. D

Explanatory Answers for Sample Test 3

1. **(D)** *Forward* is the best choice because it eliminates the redundancy of the original sentence.
2. **(F)** The original version is best because it is the most precise statement of the reason for moving clocks ahead.
3. **(C)** The reference to Franklin is an effective attention-getting device to entice the reader.
4. **(G)** This is the only choice that shows the contrast between the clauses (picking up the idea and then rejecting it).
5. **(A)** The past tense is correct to indicate an action that occurred at a particular time in the past.
6. **(J)** The single word *here* is best.
7. **(D)** The information about rationing is irrelevant to the topic of the passage, which is daylight saving time.
8. **(G)** Choices **(F)** and **(H)** are not standard usage. The best word in this context is *regarding*.
9. **(D)** Only **(D)** uses the semicolon correctly to link two related independent clauses.
10. **(H)** This is the only choice that provides the subject and verb needed to make a complete sentence.
11. **(B)** *Not only* is correctly paired with *but also*.
12. **(G)** The original contains the substandard expression *being that*. **(H)** uses *whom* incorrectly and **(J)** includes an unnecessary *they*.
13. **(D)** The only meaningful addition would be an indication of the reasons why people from rural areas opposed the earlier start of daylight saving time; for example, that they would be forced to perform early morning chores in the dark.

14. **(F)** A question ends with a question mark. The final question provides a good conclusion to the essay by referring to the opening sentence. Removing it would weaken the passage.

15. **(C)** The focus of the essay is on the origin and development of daylight saving time.

16. **(H)** The correct idiom is *characterized by*.

17. **(D)** The additional information provided is irrelevant to the passage as a whole and interrupts the flow of the paragraph.

18. **(J)** The past tense is correct for this action, which occurred in the Stone Age.

19. **(A)** A comma is needed to set off the nonrestrictive appositive (*a circular arrangement of huge standing stones on Salisbury Plain*) from the word it explains (*Stonehenge*).

20. **(J)** The figures give the reader an understanding of the size and scope of the undertaking.

21. **(D)** The phrase *over the years* should be set off by commas.

22. **(H)** Changing the second clause to a phrase eliminates the comma splice.

23. **(B)** This choice is more economical and more effective than the original.

24. **(F)** The past tense *rolled* is necessary to parallel the past tense *used*.

25. **(C)** This choice is most appropriate to the tone of the passage as a whole.

26. **(G)** The sentence requires a singular verb in the present tense.

27. **(D)** The original version contains a sentence fragment. A colon is correct between an introductory statement and an explanation that follows.

28. **(G)** A dash correctly indicates an amplification. *A marvel for the time period* is not an independent clause and so cannot be separated from the main clause by either a period or a semicolon.

29. **(D)** Making the first clause subordinate to the second clause solves the comma splice error without introducing a dangling modifier.

30. **(G)** Antiquity does not need to be modified by either *ancient* or *old*.

31. **(C)** The author states that Stonehenge "must be protected and preserved for all to see." Thus, he would *not* want to discourage tourists.

32. **(J)** Because the sentences are long enough on their own, separating them with a period is the best choice.

33. **(B)** Alice is beginning a sentence with the word *And*. The previous sentence must therefore end with a period and the new one begin with a capital letter and quotation marks.

34. **(J)** This is the correct punctuation for a broken quote.

35. **(B)** To continue the quotation, use quotation marks and a lowercase letter.

36. **(H)** Alice was wondering rather than thinking or considering. Selecting the precise word creates the most vivid and accurate writing.

37. **(A)** When a subordinate clause ends a sentence, a preceding comma is optional. In this sentence, because of the surprise element, a comma is effective.

38. **(J)** is the best choice because it is the most concise. The other choices are all wordy.

39. **(C)** A direct quotation in the middle of a sentence must be preceded by a comma. Since the quote continues, do not close the quotation marks.

40. **(F)** *Too*, meaning *more than desired*, is required by the sentence. Since the exclamation is part of the quotation, the exclamation point goes inside the quotation marks.

41. **(C)** The author carefully describes Alice's reactions to the talking rabbit to prepare the reader for the events to follow. That Alice is not surprised at the rabbit's speech paves the way for even more fantastic events to come.

42. **(J)** The rabbit has already been referred to as *he*.
43. **(D)** The three verbs in this series should all be in the same tense. Thus, match *took, looked,* and *hurried*.
44. **(G)** The introductory adverbial clause should be set off by a comma for clarity.
45. **(C)** When a coordinating conjunction separates two independent clauses, it should be preceded by a comma, not a semicolon.
46. **(F)** The original version is best.
47. **(D)** Although correct, the original sentence is very long. For a better style, eliminate *and* and begin a new sentence.
48. **(F)** Holes are *under* hedges, not *by* them, *at* them, or *around* them.
49. **(D)** has the best style because it is the most direct and easily understood.
50. **(H)** The other choices use three words to say what **(H)** says in only one word.
51. **(D)** is the best choice because it implies a realization. The other choices infer a definite observation which is illogical.
52. **(G)** No punctuation is necessary between an adjective and its modifying adverb.
53. **(B)** Quotation marks enclose the thoughts or words of a particular speaker.
54. **(J)** The imaginative tale may best be described as whimsical, meaning *fanciful*.
55. **(C)** *Lining up* should be followed by *of* rather than *by*.
56. **(H)** Correct the run-on sentence by placing the conjunction *but* after *job*.
57. **(D)** The writer has organized the material around the difficulty (*the most difficult aspect*) and necessity (*indispensable to good selection*).
58. **(J)** Only choice **(J)** provides an infinitive (*to wait*) to parallel the previous infinitives (*to seek* and *select*).
59. **(A)** Only **(A)** is both a legitimate way to find an employee and an answer that suits the context of the sentence.
60. **(H)** Use a semicolon to correct the original comma splice. Use the adverb *there* rather than the possessive pronoun *their* to suit the context.
61. **(C)** The correct idiom in this context is *other*. Further, *effective*, meaning *producing the desired effect*, is the appropriate adjective.
62. **(H)** Avoid shifting tenses within a paragraph.
63. **(A)** The infinitive *to fill* is the best choice.
64. **(H)** Since the paragraph specifies that ''you should plan in advance what you want the applicant to do,'' the best answer for this context is **(H)** because it expands upon the idea of planning ahead by making a list of questions.
65. **(D)** No punctuation is needed here.
66. **(H)** Only choice **(H)** provides the subject and verb needed to make the sentence complete.
67. **(C)** *Unexpected* and *unforeseen* mean the same thing. One of them is sufficient to make the point.
68. **(J)** Only **(J)** correctly matches the plural *questions* to the plural *these*. All the other choices have errors in agreement.
69. **(D)** Use a colon to separate an introductory statement from an example when the example forms a complete sentence, as is the case here.
70. **(G)** *By securing* and *By obtaining* do not make sense in this sentence. The helping verb *have* must be used because the rest of the sentence is in the present tense.
71. **(D)** There is no reason for any punctuation here.
72. **(G)** is the most grammatically correct and logical choice.
73. **(C)** Only **(C)** correctly ties together the selection process discussed.

74. **(H)** The phrase *to protect the reputation of any small business* in paragraph 2 reveals that this article is primarily aimed at those concerned with small businesses.

75. **(D)** This is the most logical order for this essay. Paragraph 2 gives the essay's topic and lists the two steps an employer should follow. Paragraph 3 goes into detail about the first steps. Paragraph 1 discusses where to look for applicants, and paragraph 4 explains what an employer should do once she or he has applicants for a job.

CHAPTER 14

Writing Assessment Test
(WAT)

Many colleges throughout the country employ writing tests similar to the one developed by the City University of New York in order to evaluate the student's ability to communicate thoughts effectively and to facilitate placement in the appropriate level English course. The student is required to produce a writing sample in the time allotted, fifty minutes. It is important to bear in mind, therefore, that this time must be carefully apportioned since in less than an hour the following must be accomplished:

1. The student will have to read the question carefully and describe what is meant by the short statement given.
2. The student will probably be asked to take a stand, that is, either to agree or disagree with the position taken in the statement. Remember that there is no correct position. The essay will not be judged on whether it is for or against the comment made. The writer must decide, therefore, which position he feels it would be easier for him to handle in this brief session.
3. A brief outline might be prepared or several jottings made listing the ideas the writer wishes to communicate.
4. The response could well be organized in three paragraphs: a short introduction, a development, and a brief conclusion to tie all the material together.
5. Finally, the student must leave time to proofread; at least five to ten minutes is usually advisable.

The writing samples are evaluated according to the following criteria.

Reasons for Superior Rating

1. Good central focus
2. Well-organized response
3. Clarity of ideas
4. Logical structure of material
5. Supportive material excellent
6. Correct grammar, punctuation, and spelling
7. Vocabulary well suited to context
8. Sentence structure complex and well handled
9. Good use of transitions within and between paragraphs
10. Language and development clear, avoiding oversimplifications and distortions

Reasons for Poor Rating

1. Constant use of informal language
2. Needless repetition of ideas
3. Random presentation of materials
4. Limited vocabulary

5. Misuse of words
6. Confused syntax
7. Lack of clarity
8. Frequent errors in grammar, punctuation, and spelling
9. General incoherence
10. Poor organization

Note: Length of essay is not mentioned as a factor in evaluating; however, if the composition is so brief that any reasonable judgment of the student's ability cannot be determined, then the essay will be rated poorly.

Students are required to support their assertions with explanations or illustrations. Supportive material can come from personal experiences, from readings, or from observations of others.

This chapter presents two sample essay questions. Each of these includes several sample responses. Think about how you would evaluate each response. Which is the best? Which is the weakest? Why? How could each essay be compared?

After each essay question and its sample responses, evaluations of the responses are presented.

Analysis of Sample Essay Questions _____

_____ Sample Essay Question A

Essay Topic

It is better to have schools emphasize practical subjects that prepare young people for jobs than to waste time with the liberal arts. Young people need to be economically independent and a knowledge of art, music, literature, and history offers no help in this area.

Do you agree or disagree with this statement? Support your opinions through your personal experience, readings, or observations of others.

Sample Response 1

All of us, it is true, must prepare ourselves for economic independence and so the school system must assist us to enter the world of work. But to offer students courses which are only vocationally oriented would be very sad.

For example, last summer I worked as a file clerk in a large office. At lunch time when I socialized with my fellow workers, they discussed films, books, and plays that they had seen. I kept wishing that I had taken courses in school that would have helped me to contribute to the conversation. I felt isolated and ill at ease. No one wanted to listen to me discuss my job filing letters.

Very often, many corporations offer a good deal of on-the-job training. Schools should help students become well-rounded individuals, creative adults who can contribute to society and who can make a difference. Courses such as art, history, music, and literature may well prove to be the answer to this need.

Sample Response 2

It is true that the schools must prepare you for life and that means it is work too that we must be prepare for but isnt their more to life then work?

I have a friend who is working at a good job at least he makes a lot of money but whats the use he doesn't no nothing when it comes to talking about anything accept his job. Except for some tv maybe but he never reads a book and he dosent even read the newspapers unless its the sport page. He's got a reputation that he's just a ingrant person. Is that good. Shouldnt the schools better be teaching us more then just a job.

Sample Response 3

I sort of agree with this statement but not all the way. I feel that more important then anything is becoming financially secure and independent and that means getting a job. And being prepare to enter the world of work.

Even in my own family I see how tough it was when my father was out of a job and unemploy for over a year. He is a bright and intelligent man and a good father. He reads and can talk about history or literature. But that didn't put bread on the table.

Perhaps if he had subjects in school that would prepare him for a job today he would be working and more secured. At least that what I think and believe.

Sample Response 4

This is hard question to answer but I will do my best and try. I think the schools should teach all sort of subjects to students then the students would get good jobs and be employ for a long time and be able to rise families without worry.

I think english is important for you you have to write and read even when you work or else you will be fire then you will be out of a job.

The Government should help everyone to get a job this will cut down the crime rate. People rob and steal when they need money and this hurts everyone. So I say lets make jobs for everyone and we will have a better world to live in.

Evaluation of Sample Response 1

The essay is well thought out and clearly organized. The three-paragraph development shows a good introduction and a fine summarizing conclusion. The second paragraph gives a brief but to-the-point valid illustration. Sentence structure is mature, as is the vocabulary and transitions. The writer shows a definite mastery of the basic essay.

Evaluation of Sample Response 2

Although the writer responds to the question with a definite opinion and a valid illustration, the many errors in technical English cannot be overlooked. Frequent misspellings (*ingrant* for *ignorant*, *no* for *know*, and *their* for *there*), the omission of the apostrophe (*shouldn't*), the omission of the "d" ending (*prepare*), as well as poor end-stop punctuation and the double negative indicate that the writer needs additional work in English fundamentals.

Evaluation of Sample Response 3

Careful proofreading and revision might have been of considerable help in improving the essay. For example, the last sentence in the first paragraph is a fragment and should be joined to the preceding one. In the last sentence of the third paragraph the word *is* is omitted after *that*. In the first paragraph the final "d" is omitted in *prepared*, and *bright and intelligent* is redundant. The writer could tighten the essay by reworking both the first and last sentences. This could add considerable strength to the response.

Still, there is a definite three-paragraph development and an overall sincere tone. The illustration offered is valid and follows the general thesis.

Evaluation of Sample Response 4

Although the writer appears to be aware of the need to organize his views and presents some ideas on the issue, the essay has many substantial weaknesses. The second sentence in the first paragraph is a run-on and should be punctuated before *then*. The first sentence in the second paragraph is a run-on as well and needs to be broken down into two sentences. There is faulty capitalization. (*English* is written with a lowercase "e" and *government* with a capital "G.") Verb endings are weak. (The final "ed" ending is omitted in *employ* and *fire*.) *Rob and steal* is repetitious.

In addition, the thinking is immature and confused and the tone not consistent as the writer changes from second to third to first person. The entire first sentence is hardly necessary, and the final sentence is trite and weak.

Sample Essay Question B

Essay Topic

Too many young people drink and then drive. This often results in tragedy for them and for others. Therefore, the drinking age should be raised to twenty-one throughout the United States.

Give your opinion of the above comment, utilizing your own experiences, your observations of others, and your reading.

Sample Response 1

Life is very precious and too many young people are careless about following rules and regulations. They go to bars and drink and when they become intoxicated they go driving and then they have accidents and this results in death for themselves and others.

We must teach people not to drink and drive; the two do not mix. Every life you save might be your own. Even at parties if you drink you should not drive. Its better to take a subway or a bus or ask a friend to drive you home. Why take chances? Its better to be safe than sorry.

Maybe raising the drinking age won't solve the problem completely. But at least, its a step in the right direction. At least it will make our young people aware that we are all concerned about the problem. Remember life is precious and cannot be replaced.

Sample Response 2

Each day we pick up a newspaper and read about the death of someone who was killed in an automobile accident. To often this death involves a teenager who went on a joyride after he was drinking a few beers. If the young person was refused the beers maybe things would be diffrent.

Young people need to grow up and learn that the price they pay for driving and drinking is to high. Young people often act immaturely and make fast decisions. They want to be part of the crowd and if their peers are drinking they join in and then they drink. Their judgment is affected and so could their vision. As a result accidents occur. Young people indeed need to grow up and drunken drivers may not make this possible.

Evaluation of Sample Response 1

The writer presents a definite and valid response and has organized his ideas into three paragraphs. He is consistent in his thinking. However, there are many trite remarks that sizably detract from the apparent sincerity of the writing. *It's better to be safe than sorry* is a cliché. The second sentence in paragraph two and the final sentence of the essay are also trite. As a result, the writing lacks originality.

The writer should also be made aware of the use of the apostrophe in the contraction *it's* and of the use of commas to eliminate run-on sentences and to separate subordinate clauses.

Evaluation of Sample Response 2

Although there are problems with faulty spelling (*To* for *Too*, *diffrent* for *different*) and a confused sentence in the last paragraph (starting with *Their judgment*), the overall writing pattern is mature and sincere. The writer reveals a point of view and shows consistency in his thinking. A stronger developmental paragraph and a clear concluding one would enhance the response.